THE END of MOLASSES CLASSES

RON CLARK

ALSO BY RON CLARK

The Essential 55

The Excellent 11

THE END of MOLASSES CLASSES

GETTING OUR KIDS UNSTUCK

101 EXTRAORDINARY SOLUTIONS

FOR PARENTS AND TEACHERS

RON CLARK

A Touchstone Book

Published by Simon & Schuster

New York   London   Toronto   Sydney   New Delhi

Touchstone
A Division of Simon & Schuster, Inc.
1230 Avenue of the Americas
New York, NY 10020

Certain names have been changed.

First Touchstone hardcover edition July 2011

TOUCHSTONE and colophon are registered trademarks of Simon & Schuster, Inc.

For information about special discounts for bulk purchases,
please contact Simon & Schuster Special Sales at 1-866-506-1949
or business@simonandschuster.com.

The Simon & Schuster Speakers Bureau can bring authors to your live event.
For more information or to book an event contact the Simon & Schuster Speakers Bureau
at 1-866-248-3049 or visit our website at www.simonspeakers.com.

Designed by Ruth Lee-Mui

Manufactured in the United States of America

1 3 5 7 9 10 8 6 4 2

Library of Congress Cataloging-in-Publication Data

Clark, Ron.
The end of molasses classes : getting our kids unstuck :
101 extraordinary solutions for parents and teachers / Ron Clark.
    p.   cm.—(A Touchstone book)
1. Effective teaching.   2. Home and school.   3. Conduct of life.   I. Title.
LB1025.3.C533   2011
371.19'2—dc22   2011011986

ISBN 978-1-4516-3972-8
ISBN 978-1-4516-3973-5 (ebook)

For Kenneth

It is my greatest wish for all of my students to grow into the individual you have become.

Preface

For those who have poured molasses, you know it comes out slowly, dragging itself from the lip of the jar, hesitating in air as it seems to stretch itself to the biscuit, resisting every step of the way. It's some kinda slow, and it's easy to see where my grandma Maude got one of her favorite sayings, "You are moving as slow as molasses."

As a kid in the South, I learned to use molasses as a descriptive word for anything that was slow, and as I traveled to all fifty states to learn about education in our country, I found myself drawing back to this word from my childhood. I witnessed teachers with no energy, students who were struggling to prop up their heads, and classrooms that were just checked out and uninterested. I thought to myself, over and over, "These are molasses classes."

It broke my heart.

In the midst of the molasses, I would also find pockets of classrooms that contained passionate teachers and students who were on fire and thriving. I was furious that every child couldn't have that type of experience, and I wanted to do something, to make a change. I just don't have the patience to try to rebuild the education system in America by going through politics and up against the bureaucracy of the system. For me, the best way to initiate change in the way we educate our children was by starting a revolution from the ground up. I decided the most effective way to ignite the revolution would be to build a school unlike any other in the world. A school full of passion, creativity, and rigor. A school where parents and teachers would work together and support one another in the education of all children. It would be a school that would find new and innovative ways to reach our children in the school and in the home, and the overall mission would be to then share what was learned with others. It would be a school that would hopefully start a change, one person at a time.

Now, years later, that dream is a reality. The Ron Clark Academy in Atlanta, Georgia, has started from that ground-up revolution, and over ten thousand educators from around the world have visited our school to learn about the unexpected ways the teachers and parents of RCA have helped our children achieve great success. The professional development experiences we offer are unique, because we allow educators to sit in our classrooms to watch me and the rest of our exemplary staff in action as we educate our students. As a teacher in North Carolina and New York, I never left my classroom to see what other teachers were doing, and unfortunately that is the norm in our country. Teachers graduate college, enter their classrooms, and stay there thirty years. They rarely venture out to learn from others, and often they don't have access to an exceptional teacher to learn from. Our school offers that experience. We give teachers something to strive for, and we show them what excellence in a classroom looks like. We are by no means perfect, and we make mistakes, but the visitors are then able to see how we handle typical classroom challenges, how we motivate students to apply their best effort, and how we inspire every child to achieve successs. That type of experience is valuable for any educator looking to improve and develop as a professional.

Visiting educators often comment that they wish every teacher and parent could learn about the techniques we are using at RCA. There is nothing like visiting in person, but for everyone else, we have created this book, listing 101 of the most effective strategies we have used to help our children succeed. This book serves as guidance for parents who want more for their children, teachers who need strategies for helping students achieve success, and communities that hope to uplift every child and improve the education of our next generation.

Contents

Part II: The Role of the Parent in the Success of the Child 115

Introduction

I never expected to be a teacher. I grew up in a small town in eastern North Carolina and only dreamed of escaping dirt roads and finding adventure. While attending East Carolina University, I worked fifty hours a week at Dunkin' Donuts and managed to save a whopping $600. After graduation, I used that money to buy a one-way ticket to London, England. My parents weren't too happy as neither had graduated college and they felt that I was throwing away my chance at a career, but I followed my heart and set off to have the adventure that had always been the focus of my dreams.

After six months of dressing as a cowboy and performing my duties as a singing waiter at the Texas Embassy Cantina in the heart of London, I threw everything I had with me into a backpack and set off to explore Europe. Many countries later I was much wiser and had a greater appreciation for the various nations, cultures, religions, and people who were different from me. My trip, however, was cut short by a bad case of food poisoning that I obtained after eating a rat in Romania. Long story!

I flew home to North Carolina and spent two nights in the hospital recuperating. My mother fussed and said, "Ron, you have got to get a job and stop all of these crazy adventures." I told her that I intended to save up more money and purchase a ticket to China, but she then informed me that a fifth-grade teacher at a local school had passed away in the middle of the school year. She said the students were devastated and that if I didn't go teach them they would have substitute teachers for the rest of the year.

I thought about those children and how sad they must have been, and I looked at my mom and without hesitation I said, "I'm going to China."

Mom quickly put me in my place, as mothers so often do, by telling me that if I didn't at least speak with the principal she would never support anything I did for the rest of my life.

Moms.

When I visited with the principal at S. W. Snowden Elementary she let me know that the class was extremely challenging and that she was thrilled that I was interested in the position. She said, "You're just the man for the job."

"No I'm not," I replied.

She looked shocked and quickly asked, "Then why are you here?"

"My mama made me come," was the only reply I could give.

She said that she'd at least like for me to meet the students. We walked down the hall and a student was standing in a trash can in the middle of the hall because of some rule he had broken. I looked in the classroom at the students that I was meant to teach, and the students were throwing paper everywhere. The substitute teacher was floundering and her wig was off to one side. It was a crisis.

A little boy looked up at me and said, "Is you going to be our new teacher?"

My eyes widened and I found myself saying, "I guess so."

Throughout my entire life I have tried to live with no regrets. When I get a feeling in my heart, I go for it, because I am all too aware of how short life can be. I don't want to be old and look back upon my life and wish I had done things differently. If I feel something in my heart, I'm going to make it happen, and that day, when that child asked if I was going to be his teacher, the feeling in my heart had never been stronger.

The next day I walked into that class and instantly fell in love with teaching. It struck me then as it still does every day, that the opportunity we have as teachers and parents to work with young people, to inspire them to believe in themselves, and to take them to a level of true greatness is a miracle. I knew I had found my life's calling, and I threw my entire spirit and soul into my classroom with wild abandon.

After teaching in North Carolina for five years with increasing success, I saw a TV show about schools in Harlem that had violence, overcrowded classrooms, and low test scores. Again, a feeling in my heart led me to move over the summer to New York City, where I began teaching in East Harlem. The enormous challenges and successes I faced were later profiled in the film *The Ron Clark Story*, starring Matthew Perry. I was named the American Teacher of the Year, and had the honor in 2001 of appearing on *The Oprah Winfrey Show*. I recall that during a commercial break she kicked off her shoes and leaned over and said to me, "You've got to write a book about all of the things that you do to inspire children." Now, we all know that when Ms. Winfrey tells you to write a book, you write a book!

Soon after, I sat down to write *The Essential 55*, a handbook for the fifty-five expectations I have for my students in terms of respect, manners, and academic success. When the book was ranked only 140,000th on Amazon.com, I sent Ms. Winfrey a copy. I was thrilled tremendously when she profiled the book on her show, holding it close to her bosom and proclaiming, "America, I want you to go out right now and buy this book."

One hour after the show aired, *The Essential 55* was ranked number two in the nation, right behind *Harry Potter*!

I knew instantly that the funds from the book would go toward fulfilling a dream I had held close for years: a dream of building a school like none other. It would be a school full of innovation, staffed by passionate teachers with a desire to educate children in ways that had never been attempted before. My initial thought was to build the school in Harlem, but I was determined to have Kim Bearden, the American Middle Schools Teacher of the Year, join me as cofounder. And since her family was in Georgia, she said she'd come on board only if the school were in Atlanta.

Her brilliance was worth moving the school to any location, and I used my book royalties to purchase an abandoned hundred-year-old factory in Atlanta. Drug dealers and prostitutes surrounded the factory, but I saw great potential in the midst of the mess and knew it was the place for our school.

I took the members of our board of trustees out to see the warehouse. I had really hyped it up, but as soon as they stepped out of the vehicle, they immediately said, "Ron, get back in the car." It wasn't easy convincing them that this was the right location for RCA, but eventually they agreed.

Ron Clark Academy then and now.

Nineteen break-ins later, it looked as if everyone was right about the location being a bad idea. (People on drugs are crazy . . . and industrious.)

But, instead of giving up on the warehouse, I decided to reach out to the community and encourage them to embrace the mission of RCA. I visited every home in the neighborhood, went to the churches, attended all of the Civic League meetings, introduced myself to the local businesses, and got to know the community. When I approached people's homes in my pinstriped suit and with gelled hair, I was asked more than once, "Are you Mormon?" I explained that I was not a Mormon but that I *was* on a mission. I wanted to build the best school in the world—a school that would be full of innovation, creativity, and the best teachers anywhere. I wanted to create a revolution from the ground up that would eventually affect teachers, parents, and their children everywhere. I explained that it was our intent to invite educators from all over the world to visit RCA to learn from our methods and to take our techniques back with them to implement in their own classrooms.

It worked. The community members saw I was for real and they quickly started to support RCA by attending events, helping to move rubble off the site, and participating in community trash pick-ups. I even called the prostitutes over to help. (Trust me: every time you call them over, the prostitutes will come gladly.) They weren't very willing to help once they realized that I wanted them to help collect trash, but sometimes they would help a little bit and do their part the best they could. Soon everyone else started to do his or her part as well.

When the money from the book eventually ran out, we had to turn to the community to help complete RCA. Step by step, a little here and a little there, small businesses and donors agreed to make their own contributions—to install a door here, a window there, and to add their parts in building our school. With time and patience, every piece eventually came together, and the factory was turned into a two-story building, with two colorful and unique hallways that contain the world's most creative classrooms on either side. RCA is truly a school that the community built, and it has now turned into the heart of the revolution I once envisioned.

When students first arrive at RCA, many of them are, academically speaking, below grade level. Generally, a third of our students have never had success academically, a third are performing at average levels, and a third are already doing quite well in school. Also, in every class, we make a point to accept a portion of students with discipline problems, a portion with struggles in the home, and also a portion that has two dedicated parents and a wonderful support system. We make it a point to have a wide range of students so that we can show our visiting teachers how our methods work with all types of children. The one thing they have in common is that most of their families, about 85 percent, would qualify for free or reduced lunch in the public school system. Within the other 15 percent, we usually have a few students whose family pays for their entire tuition and several who pay a large portion of the amount. We can often count on those students to bring a different perspective to our classroom discussions.

With all things considered, as our first group of students entered our school, their test scores, as a whole, were below the national average in every academic area, they lacked confidence and motivation, and they had rarely traveled outside of the state of Georgia.

Years later on their eighth-grade graduation night from RCA, they received close to a million dollars in scholarships and were honored for achieving double-digit gains in every academic area, with most scoring above the 90th percentile. The students looked back that night on their accomplishments at RCA; they had visited six of the seven continents, garnered worldwide attention for their knowledge of politics and current events, and helped to build a school that now serves as a model for institutions around the world.

As you can imagine, it was a powerful and emotional night, and I wanted to make it as perfect and surprising for them as possible. I decided to ask Ms. Oprah Winfrey if she would attend and provide advice for the students as they entered high school. Her staff informed me that it would be impossible, which is what I expected, so I didn't give it another thought. But then, one night at 2:00 a.m., just two weeks before the graduation, I decided to give it one final shot. I emailed Ms. Winfrey directly, asking her to consider attending the ceremony. I told her that her staff had informed me that it was impossible because she had board meetings in New York that day, but that I would be appreciative if she would consider it. At 2:04 a.m., I received her email response: "What time is graduation?"

Well, I ran around the house in my underwear a few times jumping back and forth over the ottoman, and then I responded, providing all of the details. At 2:59 a.m., she wrote that it was unlikely she could attend, but that she would send a member of her security team to the graduation to be there just in case she could make it. She said it would be a last-minute decision.

I told no one, of course, and ten minutes before graduation began, I saw the security team member. He told me that he felt certain she wouldn't make it, but in case she showed up, he would have someone in the audio booth turn on a red light in the back of the auditorium. He said if I saw the light, it meant she was backstage and that I should go ahead and introduce her.

This photograph from the Ron Clark Academy's first graduation hangs above the doors as you leave our school. It stands as a reminder of that amazing night and of the profound affect that all of us have had on the lives of our students.

Graduation started at seven that evening. At 7:07, the red light was on. Do *what*? Was it a mistake? It couldn't be true. My heartbeat started to overtake me. I was cool on the outside but freaking out on the inside. One thousand guests watched as one of RCA's graduating eighth graders made a moving speech about the impact our school had on her. As the student sat down, I took the stage and said the following: "Kids, as you know, Ms. Oprah Winfrey has supported our school from the very beginning. In fact, she is the reason we even have this school, and she wanted me to deliver a special message to you. She wanted you to know that in life she wants you to always dream big. She wants you never to give up and to hold true to who you are as an individual. She wants you always to strive for greatness. And, she also wanted me to tell you one more thing. And that is, that she wanted to be able to tell you all of those things—in person. Please join me in welcoming to the stage Ms. Oprah Winfrey!"

And I saw no one. I remained on the stage alone as I watched women in the audience pulling at their hair, falling over chairs, running up and down the aisles, and in that moment I thought, *What if that red light was a mistake?*

Then suddenly I heard, "RRRRR . . . CCCCC . . . AAAAA!" Ms. Winfrey walked out, and the crowd truly went bonkers. She hugged me and announced, "Ron, your speech was so convincing, you even had me wondering if I was here."

Priceless.

In her speech, she told the students that their future is so bright it burns her eyes. She also applauded the parents of our students for having the wisdom to place their children in "the best school in the United States of America."

After her speech, she took a seat with our graduates and watched the entire two-hour ceremony. It was filled with tears, shouts of joy, and performances and speeches by RCA's students that brought the house down. It was the perfect ending to three magical years of taking students to a place that no one ever envisioned they would reach.

It was the best night of my life.

Over the past three years, the Ron Clark Academy has welcomed more than ten thousand educators from around the world (from forty-five states and thirty-three countries) to be trained on the "RCA way." They have spent time in our classrooms watching our stellar team of award-winning teachers in action. They have participated in our work-shops, and they have all been "slide certified"! At the heart of RCA is a huge, two-story, electric-blue tube slide; it's how you get from the second floor of RCA to the first, and it is quite a doozy of a ride! When visitors get to the bottom, they are given a sticker saying they have been "slide certified," and teachers come from all over the world to obtain the sticker as proof that they have been inside the school that is revolutionizing education. The slide screams our mission: "Be different. Be bold. Don't do things the same way they have always been done. Instead of taking stairs like everyone else, *slide*! Go for it and live with no fear!"

By reading this book you are joining us in our journey to explore and discover the best ways we all can love, educate, and uplift our children. We realize that not every method at RCA is right for everyone, and we encourage you to find the techniques that speak to you.

One of RCA's 10,000 visiting educators becomes "slide certified."

This book is simply our humble attempt to share the magic, the success, the heartbreaks, the mistakes, and the triumphs that are the Ron Clark Academy. We firmly feel that within the right environment every child can be successful, and we hope these 101 principles we have put into action at RCA will help to guide you in your attempts to inspire, uplift, and educate the child you love.

Each year approximately three thousand educators spend time at RCA to learn about our methods, strategies, and techniques for uplifting children.

RCA's visiting educators are encouraged to take a morning jump on our two-story bungee trampoline. It's a great "rush" to start the day!

PART I

RCA's Core Principles and Values

I work with a faculty of dynamic and award-winning teachers who are the best in our profession. Over the years, we have built a list of principles, ideals, and values that we use to run our school and sum up who we are as a family. These "core principles" are at the heart of how we, as educators, parents, and mentors, obtain success from the children we love.

Teach children to believe in themselves and don't destroy the dream.

As adults, it's our job to inspire students to dream big and then to show them that we believe their dream is possible. I love when my students tell me that they want to be president of the United States, because I already envision one of them one day being just that. That is how I ask my staff at RCA to look at our classes; I want them to realize that they are spending their time preparing someone to be the leader of the free world. I tell them that we can't be sure which of them will hold the position, so we best prepare all of them.

Of course, I realize that the odds of any student becoming president are small, but that isn't important. What is important is that we see that there is potential in our children. Once we see potential in them, they will begin to see it in themselves. If you walk in your classroom and "see" a class of children with discipline problems and learning disabilities, you are sure going to have your hands full. If you "see" a class full of lawyers, business leaders, artists, and presidents, you are well on your way to building a classroom of children who will regard themselves highly and have their own expectation of success.

It makes me cringe when a student says he or she wants to grow up to be a professional athlete. It's such an unlikely goal, but I always tell myself that I don't want to be the person who turned someone away from a dream that could come true. I don't want to squash a possibility, no matter how unlikely it may be. When students tell me that they want to be athletes, I simply remind them that no matter what they do in life, they will enjoy it more if you are educated. I then ask them what they are going to major in at college and take the conversation in that direction.

I recall one student, Sita, I taught in New York City, who was a skinny little scrawny thing like I used to be when I was his age. When I asked him what his goals were, he told me he wanted to go to college on a basketball scholarship. Okay, so this kid looked as if he couldn't lift a five-pound bag of potatoes and his legs were nothing but bone and knee. That's it.

I just said, "Buddy, I love that you have a goal, and I believe in you. If it's what you really want, never give up."

Sita assured me that he was a great basketball player, and I made some time to play him after school. Yikes. He shot the ball with so much confidence, but it went over the backboard. It was bad, but I told him to try again and to focus. His face was so full of confidence. I told him that goals are only good if you're willing to work for them, and he said, "Yes, sir," and went back to throwing the ball over the fence.

I kept up with Sita, and years later he called to let me know that he was trying out for his high school's basketball team. He was so excited and asked if I'd go to one of his games to watch him play. I promised him that I would be there no matter what and that I was so proud of him. I asked him to call me with the game schedule as soon as he received it. When he didn't call me the next week, I gave him a call. Sita talked so softly on the phone I could barely hear him. I was able, however, to make out the words "I didn't make it, Mr. Clark."

It just about killed me. I told him not to worry and that even Michael Jordan didn't make his basketball team his first year of high school. I reminded him not to give up and to continue to work hard. I told him that he found basketball fun, and since basketball brought him so much joy, that practice would be a pleasure. He agreed and promised to work hard.

Two years later, Sita called to tell me that he had joined a basketball club where he was able to play in games each week. He said it wasn't the school team but that he at least got to play. He invited me to come watch, and I told him I couldn't wait. When I arrived, I realized that the game would be played on a small court at the end of a recreation center. There were no bleachers, and I was the only person there to watch the game. When I walked in, however, Sita was overjoyed. He just looked shocked, like he couldn't believe I was there. He said, "You really came,

Mr. Clark." I was also shocked to see him; he was tall enough to hunt geese with a rake and he had filled out . . . a little. I sat to the side of the court, anxious to watch the game.

Sita was so excited. He was trying so hard that he had five fouls in five minutes and fouled out in the first quarter. He walked over to me and said, "I am sorry, Mr. Clark. I was trying so hard."

I said, "Sita, you keep at it, buddy. I enjoyed those five minutes, and I will remember how hard you were trying out there. Those five minutes taught me a lot about the effort we all need to put into everything we do."

I stayed in touch with Sita and saw him a couple of times a year. We never, ever discussed basketball again—until I received a call from him late one night. Sita let me know that since graduating high school, he had been taking classes at a community college. I knew that much, but he then told me that he had also been playing in community basketball leagues, trying his best to get better. He was twenty-two years old and still holding on to his hope of getting a basketball scholarship. He said, "Mr. Clark, remember when you told me that you believed in me and told me never to give up?"

I said, "Of course, buddy."

He said, "Everyone else told me I was crazy. But because you believed in me, that was enough for me. And, Mr. Clark, I didn't give up, and I want you to know that I just signed the paperwork accepting a full basketball scholarship to play in college this fall."

I felt a lump in my throat.

He asked, "Mr. Clark, will you come watch me play?"

I just said, "Of course, buddy. I will be there to see you play." And then after a few seconds, I asked, "Buddy, have they seen you play?"

Luckily, they had, and Sita's abilities had improved dramatically. He was going to college on a basketball scholarship, a goal he achieved because he would not deny his dream.

Imagine if every child refused to deny a dream. Doctor. Veterinarian. Archeologist. Lawyer. Philanthropist.

Imagine if they never gave up. More important, imagine if we always believed in them and let them know we had faith in them. Imagine what would happen if we saw the great potential in them, and, therefore, they saw it in themselves.

I am incredibly proud to see the great success of my former students from New York and North Carolina. I have gone to dozens of their college graduations, and I have often taken my current students with me to show them true role models. When I visit colleges with my current students to introduce them to university life, my former students are almost always the tour guides.

The most important thing I see in my former students, however, is that they all seem to have chosen majors and professions that will allow them to make a difference in the lives of others. I remember Rubina telling me, "Mr. Clark, you have done so much for me, and I can't wait until I am in a position where I can do the same for others."

Alize Beal was in my first class, the "lower-level" fifth-grade class, in Harlem. After traveling to South Africa with our class, she told me that she was inspired to uplift others, not only in our country but also around the world. She told me she wanted to be in international politics. It seemed such a long shot, but I told her she would be wonderful and that we need people like her in charge of important decisions.

When she was in high school, she called to say that the trip to Africa was still very much in her mind and that she wanted to take her current classmates there but that no teachers would sponsor the trip. I told her, "Do it yourself! Find a way to lead the group. You can do it!"

A month later, I got a flyer in the mail from her school letting me know that a group of their students was going to Africa to deliver mosquito nets. The letter said they were currently doing a fund-raiser and were asking for support. In the top right-hand corner of the flyer, it said, "Trip Advisor: Alize Beal."

I said, "Oh, wow. You go, Alize! Get it!"

A few months later, she led the group to Africa and changed their lives forever.

When I took my RCA students to Washington, DC, Alize conducted the tour of her college, Howard University, for us. Her degree is in international relations; she is there on a full scholarship, and she is determined to have an impact on the world.

I recently saw her Facebook page, and there she is standing with Vice President Biden, smiling from ear to ear. I called her immediately and found out that she was doing an internship at the White House. That girl is going places, and there are countless other stories of students I have taught in the past. The potential is there; it is our responsibility to see it, to encourage it, and to let our children know that, without a doubt, we believe in their dreams.

2

Not every child deserves a cookie.

Last year one of our new fifth graders was really struggling. He entered RCA below grade level in every subject and he was failing several courses. When I met with his mom she defended her son by saying, "Well, he made all A's at his other school." When I told her that was shocking, she explained that he had done so well because he had a really great teacher. Urgh!

There is a misconception in our country that teachers whose students make good grades are providing them with a good education. Parents, administrators, and the general community shouldn't assume good grades equal high academic mastery. In fact, in many cases those teachers could be giving good grades to avoid conflict with the parents and administration. It's easier to fly under the radar and give high grades than to give a student what he or she truly deserves and face the scrutiny of the administration and the wrath of an angry parent.

I have attended numerous awards ceremonies where practically every child in the class received an honor roll certificate. Parents always cheer, take pictures, and look so proud. I just sit there and think, *Ignorance is bliss. Are these kids really being challenged, or are they only achieving mediocre standards set forth by a mediocre teacher in an educational system that is struggling to challenge even our average students?* Yet, all of the parents look so proud and content.

The worst part about it, however, is that I am afraid most parents would rather their child get a good education where they received straight A's and praise than an *outstanding* education where they struggled and received C's.

At the beginning of every year, I give my fifth graders an assignment. They have to read a book and present a project on one of its characters—specifically, they have to figure out a way to cleverly show such details as what the individual kept in his heart (what he loved the most), saw with his eyes (his view of the world), "stood for" with his feet, and held to strongly in his backbone (his convictions). I encourage the students to "bring it" and to use creativity and innovation to bring the body of the character to life.

Most of the students will bring a trifold where they have drawn a body and labeled the locations. Some will use glitter, and some will be quite colorful. I am sure in most classrooms the projects would receive high grades, mostly A's and B's. I, however, hand out grades of 14, 20, 42, and other failing marks. The parents and students are always upset, and many want an explanation.

I ask them to trust me, and I explain that if I gave those projects A's and B's, then the students wouldn't see a reason to improve their efforts on their next assignment. Some staff members have even said, "Ron, but you know what that child is dealing with in her home, and you know she did that project all by herself." I quickly tell them that society isn't going to make excuses for their home situations, and we can't either. If we make excuses and allowances, it will send the child the message that it's okay to make excuses for his or her performance based on circumstances, too. We just can't do it. We must hold every child accountable for high standards and do all we can to push the child to that level.

I recall giving one fifth-grade student a failing grade on her first project. She cried and cried. She had never made less than an A on her report card, and her mother was devastated, too. I explained that the low grade would be a valuable life lesson, and I gave the young girl, and the rest of the class, tips and strategies for receiving a higher score in the future. I showed them an example of a project that would have scored 70, a project in the 80s, and a project that would have earned an A.

I was pleased to see that her next project came to life with New York City skyscrapers that were sculpted from clay, miniature billboards that contained academic content, and streetlights that actually worked. The project was much, much better, and it received a 70.

As a final project, the students were instructed to create a time line that would contain a minimum of fifty significant dates in the history of a specific area of the world. The same young lady brought in her final assignment wrapped in trash bags. Removing it, I saw a huge, four-foot pyramid, a replica of the Great Pyramid of Giza. The student had made it out of cardboard and apparently had used sandpaper to make it feel like a real pyramid. It was beautiful, but it didn't contain a time line, so I told her the grade would not be passing.

She grinned at me, walked over to the pyramid, touched the top point, and suddenly three sides slowly fell open, revealing the inside. She had carved her outline on the inside, using detailed pictures, graphs, and descriptions of 150 major events. She even had hand-carved Egyptian artifacts and placed them throughout the inside of the pyramid, just as you would find in the tomb of a great pharaoh. She had handmade mummies that she had learned how to make on the Internet. She looked at me and said, "Mr. Clark, I have worked on this for weeks. I wanted it to be good enough. I wanted it to be an A." It was miraculous and spectacular. I looked at her, full of pride, and said with a smile, "Darling, it's an A."

If her initial project hadn't been an F, she never would have walked in with that pyramid. That child is about to graduate RCA, and she is ready to compete with any high school student across the country. She knows what high expectations are, she understands the value of a strong work ethic, and she knows how to achieve excellence. If we continue to dumb down education and to give students A's and B's because they "tried," we are doing them a disservice and failing to prepare them to be successful in the real world. That young lady couldn't walk into an elite high school and compete with a glitter-filled trifold. However, she can walk into any high school with that pyramid and her overall knowledge of how to achieve that type of excellence and stand high above her peers.

I often bake cookies for my students. I tell them it is my great-great-grandma's recipe and that she handed it to me in secret on her deathbed. (Okay, a stretch.) As I pass out the cookies, the kids who are working hard receive one with delight; the students who aren't working as hard do not. Parents will call and say, "Mr. Clark, I heard you gave every child in the class a cookie except my child. Why are you picking on my child?"

Why does every child have to get the cookie? The parents claim that I will hurt the child's self-esteem. Has it really gotten to the point that we are so concerned with our children's self-esteem that we aren't realistic with them about their performance and abilities? If we give "cookies" when they aren't deserved, then we are telling our young people that they don't need to work hard to receive rewards. We are sending a message that the cookie will always come. That is why we have so many young people in their twenties who have no idea what it means to work hard. And that is why they are still looking to their parents to provide support (and to give them the cookie).

I tell my students who don't receive a cookie that I will be baking cookies the following week. I tell them that I will watch them until that time and that if they are trying hard they'll earn their cookie. It is shocking to see how much effort kids, regardless of their age, will display to get a cookie. And when it is earned, it means something. The students will glow with pride, and they will explain how they are going to eat half the cookie then and save the other half for later. Also, it tastes better than any cookie they have ever eaten, and it sends the message that with hard work comes rewards. If parents and teachers are just rewarding our kids without cause, we aren't teaching the value of personal effort.

We all need to teach our young people that not everyone deserves a pat on the back just because we are attempting to make everyone feel good. Giving praise that isn't earned only sets up our students for more failure in the long run.

If you are a teacher who wants to increase expectations but is afraid of the backlash from giving failing grades on assignments that will cause your parents and administration to freak out, there are some steps you can take to protect yourself. When you give an assignment, show your students beforehand what you expect. Show a detailed description of what would earn a failing grade, a passing grade, and an outstanding grade. Share that with your administration as well to make sure it meets their approval, and then make your parents understand the expectations. Letting everyone know what is expected beforehand will leave no opportunity for complaints after the grades have been given.

If you are going to give rewards, such as cookies, let the parents know the classroom behaviors that will earn the reward and the behaviors that will not. When students are struggling, let the parents know specifically the areas that need to be addressed. If the child still does not meet the criteria, you have been clear about your expectations and therefore negative conflicts can be avoided.

3

Define your expectations and then raise the bar; the more you expect, the better the results will be.

I am a firm believer that you get what you expect from people, and the higher you place your expectations, then the better the results. As I have traveled around the world learning about education, I am always blown away at the level of academic expectations other countries have of their students. I believe it's because the other countries want to position themselves to be where the United States currently is in terms of the world's economy, and they have realized that focusing on educating their population is the way to achieve that goal.

When I have traveled through our fifty states, however, I have not seen the same picture. In many cases, I see teachers who are lecturing in monotone voices, students who are falling asleep, and work that is far too easy. The students are learning only out of a textbook, and there is no movement, no life, and no passion.

Where I see other countries teaching to their brightest and really pushing their young people with a high degree of expectations, I see our country teaching to the middle and rewarding mediocrity. We have an education system in the United States that isn't tailored to meet the individual needs of its students. It's a watered-down approach to educating the masses and herding children through a system that is geared toward quantity over quality with a focus on basic standards instead of having an expectation of excellence for all.

When I first started teaching, I told a fourth-grade teacher that I was struggling because there were so many kids of different levels in my classroom; there were gifted, average, low, and a heavy dose of low-low. Without hesitation, she said, "Teach to the middle, because if you make it too hard, the low ones won't know what's going on." I decided to give it a shot and to focus on the average students. After a week or so, I realized that the smarter kids seemed bored and were starting to cause discipline problems. I met with a mother about her son's behavior and she said, "The reason he is in so much trouble is because he is bored. The work is too easy."

I am sure that is a sentiment felt by parents all over the country, but in this case, she was definitely right. I was sacrificing his needs for the students who were at the lower end academically. I asked myself, "Why should we sacrifice the gifted ones to meet the needs of the lower students?" If we, as a society, continue to sink all of our funds and resources into making sure that not one child is left behind, where will our country be twenty years from now? Other countries are pushing their brightest and raising expectations, and we are placing our greatest attentions on making sure the needs of our struggling students are met.

I was really bothered by it all. I wanted to find a way to address the needs of everyone, but it's nearly impossible when you have a class of more than thirty kids with a full range of abilities and discipline problems. I decided to make an attempt to focus the content of my lessons on the high achievers. I would find the brightest child in my classroom and make sure that he was challenged on a daily basis and hold every child in the class accountable for that same level of achievement. I knew, however, that I would be setting the rest of the class up for failure if I didn't find a way to excite them to find the harder learning fun. If you are really going to hold every student accountable for the highest levels of the curriculum, then you have to figure out a way to lift the students up to that level. You can't just set the bar, sit back, and say, "Get there."

For example, the first year at RCA, my fifth- and sixth-grade classes came to me averaging better than 39 percent of the nation in math on the Stanford 10 (an achievement test administered in public and private schools across the country). I realized that most of the class wasn't even on grade level, so I said to myself, "I'm going to teach them eighth-grade algebra."

When I told the staff at RCA what I was going to do, they said, "Ron, come on now. You're setting those kids up for failure."

But I said, "Nope. The more you expect, the more you get. You will see; I will get those kids up to eighth-grade algebra. But even if they don't quite get there, the gains they will make will be enormous."

They still told me it wouldn't work because I was skipping too much content, but I told them I was sticking to my guns and that it would work.

I started that year teaching eighth-grade algebra. I went in there like a tornado, on fire and ready to get the students up to the eighth-grade standard!

And . . . it didn't work.

Yeah, I skipped too much stuff. I had students cry and parents complain, and there was a general lack of positive spirit and excitement in the room. The students were looking at me as if I was speaking in another language.

I could have easily dropped the level of expectation back to their current grade levels, but at RCA we have a philosophy that you should never lower a goal. When you lower a goal in order to make sure students will find success, we call that "hollow success." Yeah, you were successful, but could you have achieved more with greater expectations? We feel that you should always go for the higher goal, realizing that there is always a way to get there. The road may not be comfortable, and you may have to work harder than you expected and be willing to change your methods and techniques, but we feel there is always a way to make it happen.

Keeping that philosophy in mind, I left the goal where it was, eighth-grade algebra, and decided to figure out a way to get the students to love my classroom. I have always said that if they enjoy your classroom, then they will enjoy the content you are teaching. In order to make that happen, I often try to find whatever it is that the students love at the moment, whether it's movies, songs, or athletic teams, and I use those topics in my class to enhance the lesson.

At the time, their favorite song was "Umbrella" by Rihanna.

I changed the lyrics to apply to the Order of Operations, which was essential to know if I was going to teach the students how to handle the long radical equations we were attempting to do.

My version:

When we begin, we begin together

Parentheses first now, please be clever

Exponents come right next in line

Gonna multiply and divide at the same time

Now subtraction and addition

Walk it out in computation

It's the Order of Operations

It's the Order of Operations

Ations—Ations, A, A, plus

When I introduced the song, the students sat straight up in their seats and looked eager and excited for the first time. They thought it was the coolest thing ever, and they were anxious to learn the chorus as well as all of the other verses of the song that dealt with how to handle the algebra problems.

The next day they showed up for class, eager to sing the song and to work on cool movements to go along with it. I saw in their excitement a window of opportunity. I told them that we would gladly sing the song at the end of class if everyone focused and concentrated the entire period. Boy, those were some attentive children! They were ready to go! Every student sat rapt with attention, and as I taught the lesson, I explained what each line of the song meant and how it would help us learn. The students would collectively go "Ohh" and nod their heads in understanding. At the end of class, we sang the song together, and I let them come up with dance moves and hand signals for division, cubing numbers, and other aspects of the song. When class was over, they all moaned and asked if they could stay longer. I told them they had to go but that we'd get another chance the next day.

When they arrived the next day, they didn't walk; they bounced into class. I let them know we'd sing it again at the end of class if they all tried hard during the lesson. No one seemed to mind a bit, and they earned the chance to sing the song again.

The next day the same thing happened, only this time when they sang the song, it wasn't really singing a song, it looked more like a Broadway production. The students were really letting loose and choreographing the coolest moves! It was incredible!

The end of that week was our first educator visitation ever at RCA, and at the end of the math lesson I thought it would be cool to show the visiting educators the song we had learned. I asked the educators to come to the front of the class, the music started, and the kids took over. I still remember standing there and watching the faces of the visitors. The kids looked so sharp, happy, and full of passion for algebra! They were singing their hearts out, and some kids were so excited that they jumped up on the desks, continuing with the dance moves from up above. It was organized, wild, and beautiful.

When they finished the song, the educators erupted into applause. The kids and I kept tossing one another glances that said "Wow, they really liked it."

When one of the teachers asked a student what he loved most about RCA, he answered, "I love algebra class because it's fun and challenging at the same time." That child came to RCA scoring better than only 4 percent of the nation when compared to other fifth graders (in other words, 96 percent of American fifth graders did better than he did), and his favorite class was algebra. Wow.

Throughout that year, I continued to find ways to make that class fun. We used colored chalk to work out algebra problems on the sidewalk, I played the *Mission: Impossible* theme in the background as they tried to work the challenging problems in sixty seconds or less, and I used football stats, food challenges, and more songs to make the class fun. When the students weren't trying their hardest on the board work that started each class, I gave each child a balloon and Magic Marker. They worked the problem on the balloon, and after sixty seconds the students with the correct answers got to sit on their balloons and pop them. I had to use tricks like that a lot, but it kept the energy and excitement for the class high, and the students were always excited to see what would happen next in algebra class.

At the end of the year, we received the end-of-grade scores for the fifth and sixth graders. On the Stanford 10, the fifth and sixth graders scored on the same level that the average tenth grader would have scored on the test. As a class, they had outscored 86 percent of the nation. That is a 47-point increase in the group's percentile score, and those familiar with the Stanford 10 will tell you that is an incredible feat. They will also tell you that in order to have a class's percentile that high, you can't have students scoring in the single digits, and that is the best news about the scores. While the high-performing students almost all scored in the 99th percentile (that means that only 1 percent of all students taking the test did better), the students who came to me with scores ranging around the 3rd, 10th, and 11th percentiles were now scoring in the 65th, 77th, and 80th percentiles. By teaching to the top and not lowering the expectations of the entire class, all of the students benefited. It was an incredible validation for where our goals should be in every classroom, and it set a tone for high standards leading to outstanding results throughout our entire school.

Looking back on my teaching career, I know I owe a great deal of the success of my students to the philosophies of teaching to the top and not lowering expectations. I found that children like a challenge, and that when it is presented in a positive and encouraging way, they are receptive to giving it a shot.

A common question I receive is how do we deal with students at RCA who would benefit more from a small classroom getting geared toward students with learning disabilities. I have found that being surrounded by peers who are paying attention, trying hard, and eagerly trying to solve challenging problems encourages those students to take on many of those behaviors, and we feel that they are better off in the regular classroom setting.

All kids want to feel that they are normal, and when we separate them from their classmates too much, it can be demoralizing. In my experience, the students who remained with my general education classes showed greater progress, and their test scores increased more than those of students who were removed for part of the day. In some cases, however, for students with autism or academic weaknesses that simply can't be met in the regular classroom setting, individual classes are better. I estimate, however, that less than 20 percent of the students being pulled out for special services in our country actually are better off in the long run from being in the small classroom setting. The other 80 percent will perform better in the regular classroom environment.

Regardless of the level of the students, they all benefit from higher expectations. The more we ask of America's children, the more they will achieve, and if we aren't pushing them academically, then we aren't giving them the tools and skills they will need to compete with other students globally who will be more prepared for the jobs of the future.

From Matthew's Mom

I've been simply amazed at how much my child has "risen to the occasion" in his schoolwork and has grown so much academically in such a short time at RCA. It is true: raise the bar and with good, solid teaching, children will reach that level of performance. And if you continue to raise the bar, they will just continue to keep reaching and exceeding the bar. We were told by Mr. Clark and Mrs. Bearden prior to school starting to be prepared for the amount and the caliber of work at RCA. Well, they really were not kidding. During the first few weeks of school, my fifth grader was doing eighth-/ninth-grade math. We had to search math formulas online, and we were using my tenth grader's high school equation calculator just to check our work. I remember thinking, *There is no way my child is going to be able to do this math.* But I kept reminding myself what Mr. Clark and Mrs. Bearden said, "Trust us—the students will be fine. They will eventually get it, just be patient." We kept working with him, supporting him at home, and making sure he studied every night. I even began developing pop tests—mimicking Mr. Clark. Well, needless to say, my child went from making 41s and 60s to 90s and even some 100s! He did get it . . . just as they said he would! The moral of this story: trust the teachers and be supportive of them and your child. Allow them to "push" them and appreciate them for doing so.

—Mrs. Meadows, parent, Class of 2014

From Tessema's Mom

After the first day at RCA, we got home and saw the homework and were quickly awakened from our stupor into a reality of high expectations. We sat around the table that evening wondering, "What in the world! Did you get the eighth-grade homework packet?"

My husband and I looked at the first math problem on the homework sheet, looked at each other, looked at our son, and looked at the problem again. Unbelievable. The problem was as long as the page. My child had no idea where to start, let alone complete it, I thought.

Obviously frustrated with our simplicity, after a few seconds, our child snatched the paper from us, began singing a song, and set straight to work on the problem like it was a breeze. We watched him and wondered, is he really doing this? Okay, okay, he didn't get it right the first try or the second try, but he was not afraid of trying again and again until he got it right. Oh, there were about twenty-five loooong problems. It took about an hour to finish them all. You should have seen two adults and three children peering at one sheet in the middle of the kitchen table and everyone of us trying to work them out. It was great! I wish I had a picture of that.

The best part, however, was watching Tessema learn to master the algebra to the point where he was handling the problems with ease and actually teaching the rest of the family how to do it as well. The standards were raised for us all, and, as a family, we rose together to the challenge.

—Mrs. Haskins, parent, Class of 2014

✳ 4 ✳

Uplift other adults who play a role in the lives of our children.

When you show people that you appreciate their hard work and that you are aware of their efforts, the job they are doing tends to improve. We need to realize that when parents and teachers uplift one another, they are creating the type of environment where children will soar, and the impact can be profound.

The first year at RCA, our parent association, RCAP (Ron Clark Academy Parents), let us know that they wanted to do a teacher appreciation week. That is pretty standard at most schools, and we were all familiar with the concept. Basically, you receive a thank-you card in your mailbox, and on Friday you find a mug with a red bow on your desk. That seems to be standard procedure for teacher appreciation week.

We let the parents know that we would be grateful for anything they'd like to do for our staff, but we had no idea of the amazing week they had planned. We were served homemade breakfasts and lunches the entire week, courtesy of our parents' kitchens. The parents turned one of our rooms into a spa, and parents who were licensed therapists gave manicures and massages throughout the week. Our favorite treats showed up as mini-surprises; every time I turned around I saw a fresh Coca-Cola, Swedish Fish, and chocolates. Yum. The best part of the week, however, was that throughout each day, parents were hugging us and thanking us with heartfelt words for the impact we were having on their children. It was wonderful. We honestly didn't think it could get any better, but then we were asked to clear our schedules for a small event on Friday night. We agreed and were told to arrive at RCA at six.

Upon our arrival, we saw limousines awaiting us in the parking lot. Parents were there to help us step into the cars and going out of their way to treat us like royalty. The limousines took us about ten minutes away to another school that had allowed our parents to use their gymnasium for the night.

When we pulled up, I couldn't believe my eyes. All of the RCA students, their parents, grandparents, friends, and family had formed a red carpet line out in front of the gym. They were cheering on both sides, and they were so loud, it felt as if the limousines were shaking. I've only ever seen something like that on TV when the Beatles or Elvis were arriving, and I couldn't believe that my staff members and I were receiving the same treatment.

As we stepped out of the limousines, the crowd erupted. Confetti flew and students high-fived and hugged us as we made our way down the red carpet. In the gym we found tables, with tablecloths and candles, set up to accommodate hundreds of people. The parents and grandparents had been preparing a feast for days, and food was everywhere: turkey, barbecue, chicken, collards, cake, string beans, and corn bread. Wow! It could not get better, but then, it did.

A program began with each staff member being called up to receive a basket that contained his or her favorite items. Each staff member also received a plaque of appreciation. And then, the best part happened! The curtains pulled back, and I will never forget what I saw: four grandmas and one great-grandma, decked to the nines and lip-syncing "My Guy" by Mary Wells. The crowd jumped to their feet! It was amazing! As soon as they were finished, the entire Avril family (our student, Osei, along with his mother and sisters), took the stage dressed as the Jackson 5 and sang "I Want You Back," complete with dance moves to rival the originals'! I honestly could not contain myself. I literally jumped onto my seat, jumped over the table in front of me, and ran to the stage. (I can be a tad dramatic.) I absolutely had to be as close to them as I could get, to feel that energy, to be in that moment as solidly and as completely as I could. I loved it.

When I turned around, I realized that everyone had joined me. We had stormed the stage, and everyone was dancing, cheering, and smiling. It was incredible, and as I looked around at Ms. Scott, Ms. Mosley, and our entire staff, they were all crying and I figure as happy as you can imagine people being.

At our staff meeting that Tuesday, we talked for more than an hour about how much that night and the entire week had meant to us. We talked about how we had to do even more to help and uplift our students. We all felt an overwhelming sense to continue to earn the respect that had been shown to us. The staff at RCA works long hours, but I saw everyone staying even later and working harder to be more creative and supportive of our students.

I think a lot of people feel the need to wait until something wonderful is done for them before they show appreciation, but what I have witnessed is that if you show appreciation for others for the job they are doing, even if they really haven't gone above and beyond, it can inspire people to work harder to live up to your gratitude.

As teachers, we need to remember to show appreciation to our parents as well. If you know a parent worked hard to help his or her child study for a test, you should send home a note to the parent attached to that test with stickers and a "Bravo" to the parent for a job well done. Let parents know you can tell how hard they have worked to raise their children with manners and respect, and reach out and tell them the good things their children are doing. Have your students write haiku poems and mail them to their parents for Valentine's Day. What you do specifically isn't as important as making sure that you and your staff are reaching out to the parents and showing them that they are respected and their support in the mission to educate their children is appreciated.

Do This:

One of the greatest ways parents and teachers can support one another is by showing mutual respect. Teachers need to realize that children are the center of a parent's world, and we need to have patience when a parent seems a bit overbearing and hypersensitive. We'd like for them to be more levelheaded, but when they take situations overboard we have to realize it's less about us and more about their love for their child.

Parents need to realize that children will, by nature, complain about the teacher at times. A common complaint is that the teacher doesn't like him or that he is being picked on. When that happens, parents should remind the child of all of the things the teacher has done for the class and for him as an individual. We need to work hard to keep our children positive and not feed into their negativity about a situation.

From Noelle's Mom

It was the first semester of sixth grade, and Noelle had a 63 in global studies, which is an F at RCA. Even though she was doing extremely well in all her other classes, she couldn't seem to get a handle on global studies. Mr. Clark fussed her out with every failed pop test and gave her "tough" love every class. Noelle felt he was being too hard on her (even to the point of thinking that he did not like her), but I assured her that he was hard on her because he believed in her. I did not like the direction this whole thing was going in, and I knew I had to act quickly because this was not the attitude for victory; it was the attitude for defeat.

So I asked Noelle these questions:

Do you remember what Mr. Clark said to you at our very first parent-teacher fifth-grade conference? Reply: He said that I was going to be an RCA all-star.

Were you invited to be in Performance Group when it was invitation only by Mr. Clark? Reply: Yes, and he only picked two fifth graders.

When did you receive your RCA jacket? Reply: The first round and I cried.

Has Mr. Clark ever chosen you to spin the wheel? Reply: Yes, three times, maybe four.

Now, Noelle, do you really believe that Mr. Clark does not like you?

Reply: No, I don't believe Mr. Clark likes me, Mom; I believe that he loves me.

And she burst into tears.

I literally thought I was going to die at that moment, but I stood strong and just held my child. Noelle needed to be reminded of all her accomplishments at RCA and not let her global studies grade lower her morale.

After that conversation, she requested for me to do a parent-teacher-student conference with Mr. Clark, and I set it up. He suggested coming to our home, instead of us going to the school. Noelle was very excited, and I had not seen her that happy in weeks. There was a major global studies test coming up, and this would be her final chance to bring her grade up and pass the class.

From the moment Mr. Clark walked through our front door, I knew in my heart that Noelle was going to pass that global studies test, because now this was personal. The fact that Mr. Clark took the time to come to our home, talk to Noelle, go though her notes, give her study tips, quiz her, and eat dinner with her was going above and beyond. Noelle studied day and night for that test, and she made a 94! This pulled her grade up to an 83, and guess who made A/B honor roll. It was truly one of the happiest days of my life as an RCA parent and as Noelle's mother.

Thank you, Mr. Clark, for showing our children tough love when they need it and for rewarding them when they deserve it.

—Mrs. Bailey, parent, Class of 2013

Listen.

Parents, students, and teachers all want to be heard. They want to feel that you truly hear where they are coming from and that their point has been made. One of the best pieces of advice anyone ever gave me was to allow people to vent and to hear them out completely without interrupting. Once they have said all they want to say, then you may begin answering them calmly. Usually I will say, "I really appreciate hearing everything you had to say, and I understand your point of view."

Several times, parents have been upset, and I let them go on and on, and then right before they finish, they'll say, "But, Mr. Clark, that was real nice of you to listen to me like that, and I feel better now that I know you heard what I wanted to say." Trying to cut them off or disputing their comments throughout their rant isn't going to work. Just relax and listen.

One of the biggest mistakes I ever made as a teacher came because I wasn't there to "listen" when I needed to be. I was walking down the hallway of Snowden Elementary School in eastern North Carolina. I had just taken my fifth-grade class to lunch, and I noticed a little boy standing in the hall by himself. Snowden was a small school with only five hundred kids, and everyone knew them all by name. However, I had never seen this child. He looked up at me with huge eyes that were full of too much sorrow for the eyes of a child. I asked him if he was a new student at the school and he said, "Yes, my dad just dropped me off." He looked completely frightened. I took him into the office and helped to get the process on the right track. From that day forward, I mentored Kenneth. I saw something special in him, and I was determined to make that child smile.

I ended up teaching him fifth and sixth grades, and he was one of the most insightful and intelligent children I had ever taught. He seemed to carry the weight of the world on his shoulders, though, and I struggled to find ways to make him laugh and enjoy himself. I recall talking with him and his stepmother in the hall one day. I said, "This young man is extremely gifted, and you should be so proud."

She looked like I must be crazy as she replied, "Kenneth? Naww."

It was horrible.

Over the next two years, I took his class on trips to Washington, DC, and New York City. When Kenneth didn't have all of the funds for the trip, I sat with him day after day at the Piggly Wiggly grocery store selling Krispy Kreme donuts until he had all of his funds.

I sponsored a basketball league Kenneth played in and did all I could to take him and his classmates to the movies, the bowling alley, and basketball games. Kenneth and I bonded a great deal, but I knew he was dealing with major issues in his personal life. I was with him for hours and hours, but I never once asked him about it.

I continued to mentor Kenneth through junior high and high school. I eventually took him on trips with several of my other students all over the country and even to Costa Rica, Japan, and South Africa. Unfortunately, Kenneth was on crutches during the entire trip to South Africa. We visited dozens of orphanages and schools, but he never complained once.

On the last day of the trip, the boys came rushing to get me. They said, "Mr. Clark, come quick! You have got to see Kenneth!" I ran in his room to see that his armpits were bleeding. The crutches had rubbed him raw, but he didn't want to mention the pain for fear of looking like he was complaining or ungrateful. That story alone sums up the character of that very special young man.

When it came time for Kenneth to go to college, I helped him fill out the paperwork and then helped him buy dress clothes and stock his room at UNC-Greensboro. When he graduated with a degree in sociology, I was there in the audience with my students from RCA. I wanted them to see Kenneth's graduation as an example of what you can be, regardless of your circumstances.

After graduation, we hired Kenneth to work at RCA. There couldn't possibly be a better person to exemplify character, dedication, and respect than he. As Kenneth works with RCA's students, I can tell that he loves them like they are his younger brothers and sisters. He spends every free minute at their sporting events on the weekends, tutoring them after school, taking them to the movies, and spending one-on-one time with children who need a positive influence in their lives. The greatest thing about it is that he never tells me or the staff that he was at the games or that he was working with individual students. I will hear about it from a child or a parent, but Kenneth doesn't care if anyone else knows. He just does it because he wants to, and that is a beautiful thing.

Kenneth and I were talking one day about his experiences growing up and how they mirror what some of RCA's students go through. He said to me, "Mr. Clark, you knew I was going through a horrible time growing up and that I had so much to deal with in my home."

I said, "I know, Kenneth, and it used to bother me so much."

And then he asked, "Mr. Clark, why didn't you ask me about it? I would have told you everything. I needed to tell you. I just wanted you to ask me."

I still haven't gotten over it. It's hard for me to even write about it here because I stop to think about it, to analyze why I didn't ask him. It haunts me. I think part of the reason I never brought it up was because I was afraid of embarrassing him, and in some ways I felt it just wasn't my business. Also, deep down I think I realized that if I knew everything I probably wouldn't have been able to sleep at night. It would have been so hard for me to deal with, and it's easier to just turn a blind eye and be ignorant. I made a foolish mistake.

I can't go back and change what happened, but I can make sure that from here on out to be there for my students and not to hesitate to ask them if there is something they need to talk about. I let kids know that they can come to me with issues, and I don't hesitate to ask them about situations because I am afraid it will embarrass them. I think it's embarrassing when people don't ask, yet you know that it's on their minds.

There is actually a positive outcome from Kenneth holding his feelings inside. In addition to working at RCA, he also has a budding career as a recording artist. In his spare time he is known as K-Green, and he writes and performs outstanding songs about the emotions he felt growing up. The songs are therapeutic for Kenneth and for others who have been in similar situations. I am so proud of him, and it was an honor to dedicate this book in his name. If I ever have a son, I would hope that he would turn out to be exactly like the young boy I have been so honored to watch become a man.

Kenneth is now serving as a mentor for young people the way I was for him.

6

Give all that you have to your children even though you will often receive nothing in return.

When I teach children, I put my whole soul into it. I know I have a short time to make an impact that will last a lifetime, and I don't want to waste one second. I envision that the students are really my own children, and I see my job as a teacher as more of a dual teacher-parent role.

Sometimes there are certain kids who cause me to feel more like a father, and I tend to take on more of that responsibility in their lives. One student, Jai, came to RCA with horrible grades at his previous school. We knew there would be challenges, but we accepted him with open arms. Over the next few years I not only taught Jai, but I also tried my best to mentor and guide him every chance I got. It was almost as if I was molding him into a young man and was forever trying to steer him in the right direction. I was there whenever he needed me, and I always made sure that he was selected for special trips and opportunities so that he could be exposed to what the world has to offer. I sat with him at musicals, sporting events, author readings, and Broadway shows. I took him on college tours, museum visits, and an outdoor camping trip. I tutored him one-on-one and monitored his grades closely. I wanted this young man to know that he was loved and to realize the world of potential within him.

In his eighth-grade year, we took Jai and his classmates to Japan. While there, we visited Peace Park in Hiroshima, the site where the first atomic bomb was detonated in Japan during World War II. I had the students gather so that I could take a group picture, but, for some reason, Jai wouldn't smile. I said, "Jai, smile." No response. He just sat there staring at me like I was crazy. I said, in a louder voice, "Jai, *smile*. I am trying to take the picture." He smiled quickly, but as soon as I lifted the camera, his face switched quickly back to the frown.

That was it. I said, "Fine, Jai, if you don't want to smile, then you don't have to, but I am going to need to ask you not be in this picture. Please step to the side." As he did so, he mumbled some nonpleasantries under his breath, and I wasn't about to ignore it. "Excuse me, Jai?" He continued to mumble. I still couldn't make out what he was saying, but his face looked as if he was on the inside of the outhouse when the lightning struck. I could not believe what I was witnessing.

And there I went.

"All right, Jai, I've got you, you want to talk, we'll talk." I turned back to see twenty-nine faces smiling back at me as if they were in a Disney parade. I snapped the picture and went over to Jai with my eyebrow up and fire in my eyes.

"If you have something to say, I'd like you to say it to my face."

And then Jai clenched his fists and screamed right in my face, "I'm just trying to enjoy my vacation, and you are fussing at me for no reason."

You could have hit me with a brick and it wouldn't have hurt as much.

I heard Ms. Scott in the background say, "Ooookay, kids, let's head to the bus."

I know I should have tried to defuse the situation, but I was hurt. How could he yell at me like that after all I had done for him?

My voice rose, "Oh, I'm fussing for no reason? How about this? I asked you a simple request. Please smile, and you can't even do that. Was it not enough that I brought you all the way across the ocean to experience this beautiful culture?"

He started stomping toward the bus, and the rest of the students were way ahead of us. As Jai and I stormed through the park, we were the only ones there, except for a chorus of one hundred Japanese boys who were singing a song, no doubt about the joy of peace. For a park that seemed to be completely empty except for a crazy-looking teacher stomping after an irate student, it was as if the choir were providing the ironic soundtrack to the fight we were having—in Peace Park.

Disrespectful? Check.

Childish? Check.

A crisis? Check.

The arguing continued all the way to the bus. It was a mess. I know in those situations that, as the adult, we're supposed to be calm and rational. We're supposed to be the voice of reason, but I was hurt. I had been traveling for seven days with teenagers, I was exhausted and tired, and it just all fell apart.

Jai was punished for his behavior in Peace Park. I believe he received a couple of detentions, but it bothered me. I just couldn't let it go. Didn't he realize how much I cared for him? Didn't he realize how much I had done for him? How could he be so disrespectful? I kept a little bit of that with me; I just couldn't shake it.

Later that year, I took the eighth graders on a trip to my parents' house in North Carolina. It was nighttime, and students were about to walk through the woods with my mom and dad. I thought it would be hilarious if some of us hid in the woods to scare them. I saw Jai standing there, so I grabbed him and said, "Come on!" We ran with abandon to get to our hiding places in time, jumping over stumps and running through weeds and branches. We could have barreled headfirst into a tree in the darkness, but neither of us cared. Suddenly, we got to a great spot and fell to the cold dirt.

And we waited.

And we waited.

It seemed they would never get there. We killed time by chatting about this and that, and I finally said, "Jai, you know what? I think you are a really neat kid."

Jai responded, "I love you, too, Mr. Clark."

It shocked me so much I didn't know what to say. I just said, "Thanks, Jai," and we turned our efforts to the approaching group that we were about to frighten beyond belief.

For teachers, that type of moment is rare, and I hope parents understand why a moment like that would mean so much to us. We are in a profession where we devote an entire year to loving, uplifting, and educating children, and then they are gone to a new set of teachers the following year. We rarely get the gratification of hearing a sincere and honest word of thanks or appreciation from children. When it happens, it's beautiful, but it doesn't happen often. That moment with Jai happened after years of working with him, and if it weren't for that very moment in time, it may have never happened.

As teachers, we need to remind ourselves constantly that children aren't wired to give us moments like that. Even though such expressions from children are rare, we still need to love them, to uplift them, and to do all we can to make them better individuals, not because we want acknowledgment for it, but because we love them and it's the right thing to do. You can't expect that because you have tutored them every day for three months, given them a ride home, or even taken them to Japan, that your efforts will be appreciated. You have to remind yourself that it's not appreciation you're after; it's results and an impact on the life of a child.

I tell myself, "Even if they don't understand and comprehend the effort I am putting into them now, they will appreciate it later." It's as if I'm wrapping hundreds of presents that will sit under an imaginary Christmas tree. Long after I am no longer around, the students will continue to open those presents as they realize the impact that RCA had on them.

And even when they are disrespectful, hurt your feelings, and say the worst thing imaginable to you, remember down deep your overall purpose, and remind yourself that the children do love you and appreciate you, no matter how hard it may be to believe at the moment.

When Jai heard I was including the story about us in Peace Park in the book, he asked if I would allow him to include his side of the story, and I agreed.

> When I found out Mr. Clark wrote about me in his book I had to text him
> and find out what in the world did he write about. When I found out it
> was about Peace Park I begged him to let me tell my side of the story.

I was in the museum at Peace Park and I was really paying attention. I love the Japanese culture and I was reading about all of the people who died and all of the people who were affected by the bombing even years after the explosions. It was emotional and I was just standing there in a daze, trying not to cry. Well, here comes Mr. Clark. He goes, "Jai, I would appreciate it if you would make some effort to pay attention and read what these displays are about." And then he just walked off.

I just stood there, like geez.

Then we go outside and Mr. Clark is going on and on about wanting a picture. Well I was still taking in the effects of the people who had died and he wanted me to smile. I wasn't about to do it. He kept telling me to smile but I wasn't feeling it, and then he told me to get out of the picture and I said to him (too low for him to hear because I wasn't that crazy) that he is the one that should go back in there and read the displays because apparently he didn't learn anything about what they meant.

Here he comes storming over. I was about to be hit with my own type of atomic bomb, and there was nowhere to hide. That part is a blur and then suddenly I was storming through the park. I still remember it. There was a choir there singing and I had no idea what they were saying and I was just trying to get away from the situation. I wanted Mr. Clark to just leave me alone because I was hurt. He hurt my feelings so bad. That museum and the experience meant so much to me. I was so appreciative and emotional. How could he think I didn't care? I was hurt because I thought Mr. Clark didn't understand that. When you are Mr. Clark's student, the last thing you want is for him to be disappointed in you.

When I got on that bus my heart broke. I was so sad and wanted to fix it and didn't know how. It was like I was halfway around the world and no had clue how to fix the mess and I was just a kid after all. I just avoided him for the rest of the day, but I could tell he was still thinking about it because you can tell when there is something on his mind.

He later came to me to talk about it, and he assumed I was angry in Peace Park because I was in a bad mood and exhausted. I just let him think that and I apologized, but that wasn't it at all. I was mad because I wanted him to be proud of me and to realize I was appreciative. I don't think adults realize that sometimes when kids get in trouble because they look upset that they're really upset because they have disappointed the adult. We are just kids and we don't know how to put it all together and express ourselves the right way. We try and sometimes it comes out all wrong. All I know is that throughout the entire time with Mr. Clark, I never stopped caring about or respecting him. I know my behavior said the opposite, but just because kids act one way doesn't mean there isn't respect within. Sometimes we're just dealing with emotions that we don't know how to control.

—Jai Springs, RCA Class of 2010

I am so glad I told him I would include his story, because otherwise I would have never known what really happened that day. As a teacher I am always learning, and reading this story was a great lesson for me. Sometimes when we think students are letting us down, that may not be the case. Sometimes, it may be the complete opposite.

Get to know your students in nonacademic settings.

The key to getting students to work hard and to show respect is to develop relationships with them. I always make it very clear to the students that I am not their friend but their teacher. Yet, as a teacher, I know that I need to be a mentor, an educator, an advisor, and sometimes even a parent. Above all, you have to show the students that you care, and when you do that, the rest of the process is so much easier.

One particular student whom we accepted at RCA came with a decorated past of behavior problems. We knew that he could present us with serious issues, and I decided to visit his home and talk with his mother and him before making the final decision to accept him as one of our new fifth graders. As he sat there, Daquan never smiled, and he fidgeted most of the time. When I asked him why he had gotten into so much trouble and had been suspended in the past, he just said, "I don't know." Normally, I can get kids to smile and to show a reaction. I was trying to laugh and be upbeat, but this child wasn't budging.

Daquan's mother told me that she tried to explain to his teachers that he fights so much because he had seen a lot of violence in their home. She said he had seen her beaten by her boyfriend in the past and that he was hitting girls at school because that was what he had seen at home. She said that she felt the school should understand that and not punish him so much.

I knew at that moment that if we accepted Daquan at RCA, we were going to have our hands full. I looked over at him, and he looked at me as if he were bored with our conversation. I thanked the mother for her time and walked out the door with no doubt in my mind that Daquan was going to be a student at RCA.

During his first week with us, Daquan got into a lot of trouble. He received several detentions, and I had to redirect him constantly. He showed no sign that he cared in the slightest. Daquan carried himself with much bravado, and there was no cracking that hard exterior.

After weeks of this, his mother mentioned that he was participating in an athletic event that coming weekend, and I told them both that I would be there. I showed up early to make sure that he would see me. When I arrived, I saw his mom and went to sit with her. She pointed out Daquan, who was standing on the sidelines, and he soon looked over and recognized me.

I saw him smile for the first time.

I cheered the entire game, and he walked up to me afterward. He didn't say anything to me; he just stood there, but that big smile was there again. I said, "Great game, Daquan," and he said thank you and walked away.

In addition to the game, I made a point to eat with Daquan at lunch, stand with him at carpool, smile at him every chance I got, and compliment him whenever he was on the right track.

By the end of that week, Daquan received three detentions from other teachers and as he walked out of my class on Friday afternoon he received another one from me for poor behavior. It appeared my efforts that week had made no change. I handed him his detention slip, and he started to walk extremely slowly out of my class, dragging his feet one after the other. He was by far the last to leave, and as I exited the doors with him, he stopped dead in his tracks, dropped his head, and burst into tears.

I said, "What is it, Daquan?"

After a few seconds of sobbing he caught his breath and replied, "I'm just so tired of getting in trouble."

I put my hand on his shoulder and said, "Daquan, you have the power to control how much you get in trouble. You are a talented and brilliant young man, and I see so much potential in you. You don't have to get in trouble if you don't want to. I am disappointed in your behavior because you are better than that. You can truly be someone great if you want to."

It wasn't until a couple of years later that his mother shared something with me. She told me that the week after I attended the game, upon leaving school one afternoon, Daquan was crying when he got into the car. She said she asked him what was wrong and that he replied, "Mr. Clark is disappointed in me." She said it floored her because she had never seen anyone make him cry. She said she knew then how blessed she was to have Daquan in our school.

After that week, Daquan's attitude changed completely. Initially it was only in my class, then slowly but surely the type of behavior I expected from him was being displayed in other areas around the school as well. He started to try hard in class, focus on his work, and be respectful to his teachers and classmates. He started to laugh, to participate, and to smile. A lot.

I hope that every teacher and parent who is dealing with a "Daquan" will see beyond the exterior and find that child's potential. I have worked with a lot of students who were a "crisis on the outside," but once the barriers were broken down I always found compassionate, intelligent, and talented children within. We can't give up on them. We have to believe in their potential.

One of the best ways to build a bond with students and strengthen the relationship is to take them out for a special treat; it can be a sit-down dinner, but pizza and ice cream are also big hits. I ask restaurants all over Atlanta for their help with providing a small group of my students a wonderful dining experience. It is rare that a restaurant will turn me down, and I can almost always count on them to cover the cost of at least a few students. I then take those kids out to eat, and afterward we send student-drawn thank-you cards and photos from our dinner. The next time I ask the restaurants, they always agree and are usually willing to accept even more students, too.

Those experiences provide the best time to get to know one another, to laugh, and to bond as students and teachers. I recall one dinner when we were served elaborate desserts. They were the most beautiful and scrumptious desserts I have seen in my entire life, and we were digging in headfirst! Jayla was sitting to my right, and I noticed that there was a huge cookie placed atop her sundae. Now, I love cookies, and I politely commented, "Jayla, that cookie on your sundae sure does look good."

"Yes, sir," she replied.

I watched her out of the corner of my eye, waiting for the moment when she would eat that cookie. I couldn't stand it. I tried again: "Jayla, you sure are taking a long time to eat that cookie. You are eating all the way around it. Are you sure you want it?"

With a face that was all too innocent, she sweetly replied, "Oh, yes, Mr. Clark. I'm looking forward to eating this delicious cookie."

At that point she was just being cruel. As I finished my own dessert, an apple crêpe that paled in comparison to that cookie, I saw that Jayla had eaten the entire sundae, leaving only the vanilla cookie alone and untouched. That was it. I couldn't take it anymore. I reached over, took the cookie, and popped it into my mouth. Jayla turned toward me, and she and the other girls screamed, "No! Mr. Clark!"

I said, "That's right! I ate that cookie. You took too long tempting me with it!"

The other girls exclaimed, "No, Mr. Clark! She was saving that cookie till the end! She has been licking on it off and on the entire time!"

Okay, yikes. That was so gross, but we laughed and laughed, until I almost snorted that cookie out of my nose. The point is, we bonded. We weren't focused on grades or projects or the causes of the Spanish-American War. We were just being real, having fun, and getting to know one another. Sometimes that's what it takes to set in place the bond necessary for then guiding the students toward academic success.

Do This:

An easy way to create a bond is to have your friends, family, or church members make a homemade lunch for you and six of your students. Have them deliver it to your school and set it up in a conference area. While the other members of the class are in the lunchroom, you can take the six students to the room for their special feast!

Attend your students' athletic games, spelling bees, and events held at their church. Take your family along as well and make it a learning experience for your own children. Even consider having your own kids make posters to congratulate and cheer on your students.

Read whatever comics or novels your students enjoy. It provides a great conversation starter.

And the last one is the easiest: smile at them. If children think you are happy to see them and that you enjoy being around them, they will like you more and they will soon start to smile back.

✶. 8 ✶

Be selfless with your contributions to the team.

The best thing about our staff and our parents is that they are willing to jump in at any time and for any reason to help our children.

I was teaching a unit on Egypt and wanted our hallway at RCA turned into an Egyptian catacomb that the students would have to crawl through instead of just walking down the hall. I got on the phone and called several men—our students' fathers, uncles, and a grandfather—and asked them if they would build a sixty-foot-long catacomb in the school. I told them that I had no money for the tunnel and no idea how to build it. The next night those men showed up, along with three others who heard about the project, and built an amazing catacomb that cut through the middle of our school.

A friend of mine who is also a teacher was visiting from out of town, and she asked, "How in the world do you get the fathers to help like that?"

My response: "We ask."

To those of you who will read this and say, "That wouldn't work for me," or "Yeah, right, our fathers wouldn't do that," I ask you: Have you ever asked the male members of your students' families to do anything? If you haven't, give it a try. You will be surprised how helpful people can be when you let them know you need them and you let them know exactly how they can help.

Our staff at RCA is the most amazing, brilliant, and giving group of individuals with which I have ever worked. No matter what the task—from cleaning the bathrooms, to tutoring on Saturdays, to driving two hours to pick up Roman columns, to staying for play rehearsals, to attending late-night dinners with students—they are always there and willing to stay longer and do more if needed. Our entire staff teaches after-school classes until 5:45 p.m., and no one has ever asked to receive extra pay. They attend all field trips, stay for Midnight School, attend athletic games, help one another transform their rooms for theme days, and always show up with a smile and an eager spirit.

That is what every staff needs to be.

It breaks my heart to hear of teachers who leave at 3:30 p.m. and who don't offer to help one another. It's almost as if they think they are above it. I recall preparing for a big event at RCA for Dell Computers. We were running behind in preparations, and the school wasn't spotless. Let me tell you, we are adamant that it should always be spotless.

I was running around the school making sure that every area was ready, and I walked into the boys' bathroom to find two teachers scrubbing toilets and another dusting the *T. rex* head. Yes, we have a gigantic *Tyrannosaurus rex* head in our boys' bathroom. It hangs directly over a toilet, as if he is about to chomp down on the boy sitting on the toilet, à la *Jurassic Park*.

Anyway, the point is that the teachers were cleaning the bathroom and didn't think twice about it. That is beautiful, and that is why our staff are so content; they know that they all have one another's backs and that they can turn to anyone for help.

During the first year of RCA, I visited a young boy's home and was heartbroken by what I saw. There were splatter stains on the door, black marks all over the carpet, roaches crawling on the couch, and nothing at all hanging on any wall. The TV was on, but there was just snow on the screen, and the only furniture in the home looked old and mildewed. The mother and her son sat there staring at me. Her eyes were so intently focused on mine that it was almost as if she were willing me to look at her so that I wouldn't see the rest of the house.

I left that apartment, sat in my car, and cried. We have many stories like that, but for some reason, that one just got me. That look in her eyes—I can still feel how intense she was.

I decided I had to do something, so I called the mother on Thursday and asked her if she would mind if we painted her apartment and possibly put down some new carpet and add some new furniture and decorations. I told her that a local store had called us and offered the items for free but that we had to pick them up that weekend. I explained that I was hoping she would allow us to use the items for her because, if not, we might miss out on the opportunity.

She said we could definitely do it.

"Great!" I exclaimed. I asked her if she and her son could go away that weekend so that we could make it a surprise for him, and she said they would go to her grandmother's the next day and stay until Sunday. I hung up the phone and began to panic, as I had absolutely no idea where I was going to get paint, carpet, furniture, or any of the other items to go in that apartment.

My first step was to send out a blast email to the RCA team and let them know what I was doing and that I could use their help. Within an hour, staff members had connected me with friends at local stores that did indeed donate the carpet and paint. It was delivered on Friday at four p.m., and there I stood alone in the empty apartment with three huge rolls of carpet, twelve gallons of paint, and a roach on my foot.

I am usually pretty good about handling stress, but I started to freak out. I am not a rugged, put-down-carpet type. I will look at color swatches with you for an hour, but don't ask me to nail something. I just can't help you there.

Just when I was about to lose it, the door opened and there was Mr. Kassa. He said, "What's up, playa playa?" as he walked in and gave me one of his huge bear hugs. I was so happy I could have fallen on the floor and laid right there with the roaches. Behind him came Ms. Mosley and then Ms. Scott. I was overjoyed! I asked them how long they could help, and I will never forget Ms. Mosley saying, "As long as it takes."

Over the next twenty-four hours, we worked like dogs, cleaning closets, rearranging clothes, and putting cabinets and desks together. Ms. Scott went to IKEA and told the manager she just couldn't leave there without furniture for this boy's home, and he gave her an enormous discount. The staff members pitched in to buy every possible thing that the apartment needed, from new dishes and an entertainment center, to a table for the kitchen, paintings for the walls, and a beautiful new comforter for the mother's bed. The final touch was added on Saturday night: a Christmas tree, complete with lights, decorations, and dozens of presents purchased by staff members and wrapped especially for the boy and his mother.

As we put the last ornaments on the tree, I looked around at everyone applying the final touches. I suddenly realized that every single staff member at RCA was in the apartment. I stood there, closed my eyes, and simply gave thanks.

We left that night, so we weren't there when the young boy arrived. I told the mom it was probably best if he never knew that the staff did the makeover; I didn't want him to be uncomfortable or to feel awkward about it.

The mother told me, however, about his reaction. She said they came back from the grandmother's house and she told her son to go ahead and open the door. When he did, she said he jumped back and said, "Oh, crap, we're at the wrong apartment!" She just laughed and told him it was a Christmas miracle and to go on inside. He ran around the house ten times before he stopped screaming and jumping up and down and asking her, "How did this happen?"

She told me that as he ran around the house, she was following him, trying to keep up, and looking just as crazy as he did. She said, "You even scrubbed our bathtub. We thought those black stains were permanent."

The following Monday I was teaching math, and right in the middle of my lesson the boy's hand flew in the air. I called on him, and he said, "Mr. Clark, this weekend I was on one of those *Extreme Makeover* shows."

I said, "Really? You were on TV?"

He said, "Well, I don't think so, but they did come and do the makeover."

I asked, "Well, was it nice?"

And he replied, "It was, Mr. Clark. It was a Christmas miracle."

That miracle happened because I work with people who are selfless, compassionate, and dedicated to our mission of uplifting children. All staffs should approach their jobs with the determination that being a teacher isn't a job; it's a call to serve a higher purpose, to give of ourselves until we can give no more, and to make the happiness and well-being of our children our first priority.

And the more you offer help to others, the more you will find them coming to your aid as well. When you lend a hand, you make the team stronger, and when the team is stronger, the children are the ones who truly benefit.

Make it happen.
Don't give excuses; find solutions!

Everyone knows I have certain pet peeves. For example, if I ask you to contact someone and I check with you a few days later to hear how it went, the last thing I want to hear is, "I sent an email, but I didn't get a response." It drives me absolutely crazy. In my mind, that's an excuse, and if you don't hear from someone, then you email a second time or you pick up the telephone and call him. We are trying to change the world by uplifting children and motivating teachers, and we have a dedication to excellence! Don't tell me someone didn't email you back.

Make it happen.

Those three words are common at RCA, and they can be the most dreaded words RCA staff members will hear. I don't want to hear that Home Depot is out of pots. I don't care that you are having trouble getting parents to volunteer to shelve books. I don't want to hear that Stephen isn't doing his homework in your class. Figure out a solution. Find a way to create success. Make it happen.

If you are taking the time to make an excuse, then you are wasting time that could be spent on finding a solution.

If you need advice or guidance, then by all means come to me, but I want to see that you have attempted your own solutions and have taken every step possible to find success beforehand.

During the election of Barack Obama, our students traveled all over the country and were featured on CNN and various TV shows with their election songs and debate skills. We actually had a large group in New York City performing on *Good Morning America* and another large group in Ohio encouraging people to vote at the same time.

I was in the hotel in New York City on Election Day morning. Right before the students went out to perform, my phone rang. It was CNN. They wanted to know if we were doing anything special at our school that night for the election. They said if we were having a rally, they'd like to broadcast directly from there during part of the election coverage. I said, "Well, actually, we are going to have a huge rally with all of our students and parents. There will be food, ribbons, hundreds of balloons, music, and a grand ol' celebration!"

They said, "Great, plan on us being there at seven p.m. to set up our cameras."

"No problem!" I told them that our plane would land in Atlanta at six that evening and that we would meet them there.

I hung up the phone and instantly called the office manager at RCA.

"Ms. Mosley, we have a problem."

Ms. Mosley is the gatekeeper at RCA. She has been with us from the very beginning. I spoke at a church a couple of years before RCA opened, and she was in the audience. The preacher invited people to come to the front to pray for me and the vision of my school. Ms. Mosley said she found herself being pulled to me. It was as if she wasn't even walking; she was being carried.

People laid hands on me as we prayed, and as soon as it was over, Ms. Mosley kept her hand on my arm. I looked up and saw that she was staring directly at me. The first words she ever said to me were: "I am going to work at your school."

She volunteered for months before finally quitting a job she had held at Bell South for most of her life. She said God called her to RCA to help the children and to help me carry the load the school would bring.

That morning when I called to tell her that we had to throw together a "grand election rally" at RCA, she didn't flinch; she was ready to carry that load as well. She called my assistant, who then called me in a panic. She said, "Ron, what in the world? A rally for hundreds of people?"

I just said in my calmest voice, "Make it happen."

And soon things were happening. Ms. Mosley sent an email blast out to parents and told them she needed them at RCA ASAP. She said, "People, we're about to make magic up in here."

Volunteers were called, and everyone started to reach out to local businesses. Soon, a design for an election T-shirt was emailed to a local printer who produced three hundred "RCA ELECTION NIGHT" T-shirts in less than three hours. Parents all over Atlanta were cooking food, children were blowing up hundreds of balloons, uncles were hanging streamers, and volunteers were placing laptops with voting updates for each state all over the school at "election stations."

That night when we arrived, you would have thought Barack Obama himself was supposed to be there. Good grief—there must have been more than three hundred people, all wearing the awesome election T-shirts. The room was filled with streamers, camera crews, and huge boards displaying the United States where students could make predictions about which states would go red and which ones would go blue. Music was ringing through the halls of RCA, and the energy was contagious.

And, as always, RCA-style "attention to detail" was there. Even the buffet dishes had names: "Barac-oli Casserole," "Palin Punch," "Off-Shore Oil Dip," and "Left Wings" and "Right Wings," to name a few. It was an event worthy of CNN coverage.

The moment they announced that Barack Obama had been elected our forty-fourth president, our students' parents fell to the floor. People were crying and shouting, and Ms. Mosley was crying as she said, "Praise God, praise God." I saw Jai grab another student and hug him, saying, "This is an amazing night. What a miracle."

The joy of that moment was shared all over the world on CNN because a small group of people with a dedication to excellence didn't make excuses or doubt themselves. They found a way to make it happen.

We all need to have that type of dedication and will to "make it happen" when it comes to the education of our children. There is a way for every child to understand every concept. There is a way for each student to perform at the highest levels and there is a way to teach children to be good individuals who care about others. If we spend time complaining that they aren't where we want them to be, then we are wasting time when we could be finding those precious solutions.

> ## Do This:
>
> One of the greatest ways to find a solution is to ask for help. We need to encourage our young people to approach teachers for extra assistance instead of suffering in silence. The majority of teachers will bend over backwards to help if a child asks for it. Also, parents shouldn't hesitate to let teachers know they need advice on how to help their children. Ask for specific ways you can help at home and good teachers will always have great suggestions.

Be excellent!

One of the biggest challenges facing our education system is that we have college professors all over our country sitting behind desks lecturing their education students on how to be dynamic and engaging teachers. The professors are dull, boring, and doing the exact opposite of what they are asking. Most of them haven't been in a classroom in years, if not decades. They not only teach to the test, they focus on what to do and not to do to get that precious tenure position. They aren't truly dedicated to preparing the next great generation of educators, and, therefore, the local teacher training is being shaped by the low bar set by the local public school system.

As Kim and I work with our teachers and our students, we want to make sure that if we are asking them to be innovative and to strive for excellence, we are always requiring the same of ourselves. If you expect something from others, you need to make sure you are demonstrating it yourself as well.

During our preplanning activities, Kim and I had a ton of information to share with our staff members, but we didn't want to just present it in a PowerPoint or go over it with a handout. That is the exact opposite of how we're asking our staff members to teach. Instead, we decided to turn the entire first day of planning into a Japan-themed event. We both dressed in traditional Japanese attire and hung Japanese lanterns all over the room. We placed pillows on the floor, hung a tent over the middle of the room, and turned each part of our presentation into an activity that matched the theme.

We tied *The Essential 55* and the expectations for our staff to the Code of the Samurai. We had the staff members write out wishes for our students and attached them to a wish tree. We served a traditional Japanese tea where we allowed each individual to express his or her goals and expectations for the upcoming year. After our traditional Japanese lunch, we went to my room where Kim and I had set up an activity where we all participated in authentic sumo wrestling! Well, we did our best, and we ended up rolling on the floor laughing more than anything else. And that was the point. We bonded and learned at the same time. It was a wonderful day, and it set the tone for the level of energy and effort we want our staff members to put into every activity that they do with our students.

During the first week of school, we asked all staff members to prepare an hour-long presentation for the students. We wanted them each to introduce themselves to the students, to show pictures of their families, and to tell about their hobbies and interests. We feel it is crucial for the students to see the staff members as people they can relate to. We gave no more instruction than that, and as the presentation started, I decided to stick my head in the door to see how it was going.

Wow.

It completely blew my mind. The room was pitch-black, and the *Mission: Impossible* theme was playing. I saw Mr. Kassa standing at the front of the room with the rest of the staff, who were wearing all black and killer black shades. Mr. Kassa was telling the students that they were about to embark upon a mission, if they chose to accept it, and that it would involve working harder than they ever thought they could. It would require long nights, attention to detail, and pushing themselves beyond their academic limits. He told them that if they did, indeed, accept the mission, that they would not be alone. He then proceeded to introduce them to the support team for their educational mission, the faculty and staff of RCA.

As the staff was introduced, they each described their personal qualities that could help the students' mission and when and how the students should turn to each of them. As each person talked, a vogue-ish picture appeared of him or her on the Activboard, in his or her best James Bond pose. Various pictures of them as children and with their families scrolled as each person talked about who they were and how they could contribute to the mission. The entire presentation was clever, flawless, and impressive. In short, it was excellence.

At RCA with everything we do, we ask ourselves the following questions:

How can we make this better?

How can we use this opportunity to create a special moment?

Have we taken every effort to make sure that we have covered all of our bases?

Are we prepared for any issue that may arise?

And, most important, have we done all we can to make it excellent?

In all we do, we want to make sure we are going above and beyond to work at the highest standards possible. I remember years ago reading an article about actress Betty White. It said that she was a perfectionist who always showed up to the set with every single line memorized. She had committed every word to memory and was on point and ready to go. The article said that because she was so sharp and prepared, everyone with whom she worked learned their lines to the best of their abilities because they didn't want to let her down. They increased their effort because of the example of excellence she set.

We have to remember that the level of performance we show others—especially our children—is what they will learn is acceptable.

I recall a time when many students performed poorly on a challenging science exam for Mr. Townsel. It was six in the evening, and before I went home for the day, I stopped by his room to ask his plan for getting the students up to the high level we expect at RCA. When I got to his room, I saw Mr. Townsel teaching a review session. Every single student in the entire grade was sitting with his or her parent as Mr. Townsel went through the material step by step to ensure that the students, as well as their parents, mastered the information before he moved on. Now, that's excellence.

At RCA we are all committed to excellence in all areas, even our stomachs. I knew I loved Gina Coss the first day she showed up for work. She came in carrying enough homemade Hawaiian biscuits with ham for the entire staff. Bringing food for one another is beautiful, and it adds a sense of warmth and makes the school feel more like a home. That's excellence.

Mr. Bernadin is in charge of technology at RCA, and I call him Superman. He is a ge-

Mr. Bernadin really is Superman!

nius and has a commitment to excellence like I have never seen. He was
driving back from a technology conference on a Friday night. He had
driven ten hours and was almost home. I sent him a text message and let
him know that my computer wasn't working correctly and asked him to
take a look at it on Monday. I went to the school the next day, on Saturday, to do some work and noticed that my computer was working. I later
found out that Mr. Bernadin had gone to the school to fix the computer
before going home. He was at the school until four that morning. He
said, "Mr. Clark, I just couldn't sleep until I knew everything was working properly at the school." That's excellence.

When I told Mr. Dovico the title of this book was going to be
The End of Molasses Classes he asked me if I had lost my mind. I love
the title and felt in my heart it was the name for the book, and even
though it might not resonate with everyone initially, I just had a feeling in my bones it was the right call. Mr. Dovico could tell by the look
on my face that his comment had hurt my feelings, and the next morning when I arrived at school there was a bottle of molasses on my desk
with a note of apology and congratulations on the new book. That's
excellence.

The first school where I taught, in Aurora, North Carolina, was being
torn down. My dad found a way to get in there and get them to let him
take down the door to my classroom. He mailed it to me as my birthday
present with this note:

> I thought you might like to use this door as the desk in your office. It
> will provide you support as you continue to change the lives of children,
> just like you changed the lives of the students who walked through this
> door, year after year.

That's excellence.

In each situation, I never expected those individuals to go that far above
and beyond; they all had such respect for their jobs and for living their
lives at a high standard that they pushed themselves to go a little further,
to be clever, and to strive for excellence in all they do. When you have a

team and people around you who work at that level, anything is possible in terms of happiness and achievement.

Do This:

Some of the things our teachers and parents do are actually easy, but they send a message to our students and have a wonderful impact:

1. Don't gossip. If you are spending your time complaining about people who are gossiping, you're still gossiping. Stop.
2. Show up on time. Whether you are a staff member showing up for work or a parent showing up to pick your child up from school or to attend a meeting with your child's teacher, it is imperative that you are on time. When you aren't on time you send a message that you don't respect the time of others, and it can be perceived as extremely rude and send the wrong message to children. Ms. Mosley shows up at RCA before 7:00 a.m. each morning. She has never been late in her four years at RCA. She said she knows that children learn their behaviors from watching adults, and she is sending a message to them that being on time every day shouldn't be something that is unusual; it is expected.
3. Return forms to the school in a timely manner. We hate having to track down parents for signed permission slips, report cards, and other items. Turn them back in the next day, not only to help the school but also to teach your children about the value of being prompt and on time with assignments.
4. Teachers and parents should stop to pick up even the smallest pieces of trash in their school. Work hard to

(continued)

keep it spotless and show your students, especially the ones who tend to be cluttered and disorganized, the strength of spirit and feeling of success that can be born out of living and working in a clean and organized environment. I am sure most parents don't even think of picking up trash as they walk through the school hallways or parking lot, but if they did the message it would send to others would be powerful.

5. Teachers should correct grammar and triple check emails and letters that they send home to parents. Show that each email you send is worthy of being checked thoroughly. Parents should make sure their emails to teachers are respectful and appreciative.

6. Dress your best—no wrinkles, rips, or sloppy clothing, especially for parents when they go to their child's school. Your child wants you to look sharp when you pick him up from school. He wants to be proud of you and show others that his parent is a professional.

Create moments that will have a lasting impact on children's lives.

You can't put a price on a moment. In life, we view the past in broad strokes, but there are certain events that stick out that we will never forget. There are instances that touch us deeply and that will stay with us forever. In many ways, those moments help us become who we are, understand what we believe in, and shape how we see the world. We realize that at RCA and do all we can to make special moments for our students that they will never forget.

When we headed to New York City for a trip with our fifth graders, we knew we wanted to make it special. We were completely out of funds, but we wanted to add a moment to the trip that the kids would never forget. The problem was that the moment had to be something we could get for free. I asked myself, "What would be the coolest thing that could happen to a child in New York?" and the answer came to me: we would need to find a way to get pictures of our students' faces on the big electronic billboards in Times Square. We just had to! I could just see all the enormous, glittering, smiling faces looking down over all of Times Square. It would be the coolest thing ever! I remember the team saying, "Sure, Ron, that's something we can do for free."

But I said, "We have to find a way! We just have to!"

After contacting Panasonic, the owners of one of the largest screens in Times Square (fifty feet high!), we discovered that the advertising costs are too expensive and that they wouldn't be able to accommodate our request. We didn't give up, however, and we sent a more formal request (including the pictures of our students on a disk) by way of our great friend Jeff Anderson with Audio Enhancement. We were told that because of the expense of the advertising time, it might have to be at 3:00 a.m. We said, "That'd be great! We can wake the kids up. It's no problem! We'd just be so grateful for anything you can do for us!"

That did it. They agreed to help, and they said they could make it happen at 11:30 p.m. and it would last for only about ten minutes. They said that they would use each kid's portrait and rotate them all multiple times. We were thrilled!

That night in New York, we gathered the students in the center of Times Square. I asked all of the students to face me, and so their backs were toward the big fifty-foot-high screen, the largest and most prominent in Times Square.

I stood on a ledge and said, "Kids, as you know, all year long we have

told you that we think your futures are as bright as these lights, and that
your potential is as big as these buildings."

I looked at the clock. It was 11:30.

Nothing.

I continued. "And we think that you are all amazing and wonderful,
and we care about each of you so much."

11:31.

Nothing.

"And, well, you are just great. Yes, you are all just great."

11:32.

Nothing.

Crap.

I figured either the CD of pictures didn't work or they forgot it was
tonight or that something just went wrong somewhere. Argh!

I tried to finish up my speech. "And, I mean, what more can I say,"
and then it happened. The face of Richard Douglas appeared on the
board. It was fifty feet high, towering over Times Square. Each of his
teeth must have been the size of a small child. I felt tears come to my
eyes, and I simply said to the students, "Turn around."

Aleyna Bratton-Stalworth (all fifty feet of her).

The reaction sent shock waves through all of Times Square.

Instantly, they all screamed, "Richard!"

Richard's hands flew to his face and he said, "Oh, my gosh!" Then, Aleyna's face appeared, and she freaked as well!

One by one, the students had their moment to shine, and there was complete pandemonium. The students were taking pictures of the billboard, of one another, and of themselves!

They were screaming so loudly that they drew the attention of the pedestrians in the area as well as some taxi drivers who stopped and turned to see what the commotion was about. As they realized the students were cheering at their pictures, you could see people all around pointing at the screen and then pointing at our students. People started taking pictures of the group and soon they were coming over to congratulate them. It was a wild moment.

That night as we sat in the circle discussing our day, the students could not stop talking about the billboard. They said they felt strong and big and important. They said they felt special. That is how we want our students to feel at RCA, whether we are in the classroom or on a trip. We want them to know how much they are loved and how much potential we see in them.

Another special moment we made for our kids happened on New Year's Eve when Kim invited the seventh- and eighth-grade girls to her home to celebrate together and spend the night at a slumber party. I saw this as a perfect opportunity to spend time with the boys and to make a moment none of them would ever forget. I had fourteen of the boys come to my house to plan a New Year's Eve attack on the girls at Mrs. Bearden's home!

The boys were beyond psyched, and we headed to Walmart to purchase Nerf guns. We drove to Mrs. Bearden's home, parked three blocks away, and surrounded her house with boys hiding behind every bush. I rang the front doorbell and was soon bombarded with girls hugging me and jumping up and down. They said they had no idea I would be there. I told them to all come outside because I had a surprise for them. They all hurried outside to the middle of the yard, and as I slammed the front door, the boys jumped out, dressed all in black, and they let it rip! Nerf arrows flew all over the yard, and the girls ran screaming everywhere! It was complete chaos for ten minutes.

The girls finally ran around to the back of the home and made their way into the back door. The boys followed suit, running after them inside. Soon, however, some of the girls overpowered the boys, taking guns for themselves, and then the battle truly got started! Girls were hiding behind couches, leaping out from closets, diving behind counters, and shooting as well!

Eventually, everyone collapsed from exhaustion, and we just laughed and laughed. Many of the students screamed, "That was the most fun moment of my entire life!"

Do This:

We work hard to make those special moments when the kids know we have gone out of our way to show them just how important they are to us and how amazing they are in our eyes. The events don't have to be in Times Square or on New Year's, however, they can be much more simple and easy to accomplish:

When I was in the fifth grade I won a coloring contest, and my teacher put my photo along with two other winners in the paper. I still have that clip to this day, and it meant just as much to me as seeing my face on a billboard in Times Square. I felt that the contest must have been some kind of important for Mrs. Edwards to spend so much effort to actually get it in the paper. In actuality, most papers are more than willing to publish photos of local students doing well when teachers reach out to them for help.

Other ways to get a similar reaction include posting pictures of students who have done well on a classroom bulletin board. Mrs. Coss contacted a local caricature artist and provided him with pictures of the honor roll students in her room. She let him know their favorites hobbies and he designed a personalized picture for the children that she then placed on her "Top Stars" bulletin board. If you want to take an even bigger step, have the students' parents organize a campaign to have a picture of the school's honor roll students appear on a local billboard.

You can also have a local radio show do a shout-out to outstanding students. If you time it perfectly, you can have the radio playing in the background as your students are working on an assignment. Suddenly, the radio announcers will start calling out the names of students in your class who you wanted to recognize for outstanding accomplishments. Wow! Can you just see the students' faces?

⋆12⋆

Set the tone for a love of learning.

The absolute best way to get a child excited about learning is to display the amount of emotion and passion for learning that you hope to see in the child. Whenever I am talking with my students and they ask me a question I don't know the answer to, I will say, "Oooh, let's look that up!" I act genuinely giddy at the prospect of finding out information that I don't know.

As parents and teachers, that level of interest and curiosity is important to show our children. As a parent, when your child wants to know "Why is the sky blue?" it's time for you to jump to it and pull out all of the research tools you have to get to the answer together with your child.

As a teacher, when your students ask you a question and you are unsure of the answer, please don't lie. Some adults want to look like they always know everything, but that sends the wrong message to children. No one knows everything, and the real lesson we need to teach our children is that the man who can actually find the answers to any question presented to him is the true genius.

It is also crucial that we, as adults, show our children that we are lifelong learners and that we still have a constant thirst for knowledge. As a child growing up, I remember thinking that after college I wouldn't have to learn anything else, and I thought that would be a glorious day when I finally did know everything. We want to make sure our young people don't have that mind-set and that we show them that the joy of learning can be everlasting.

I love taking our students on trips with our science teacher, Mr. Townsel. No matter where we are—museums, temples, events—he always has to make his way to the front. He is absolutely so eager to see what is going on and to learn from his surroundings that he can't stand it. I love it. He sets the perfect example of how we all need to see the world. His eyes glow with excitement and wonder, and he wears a constant smile that stretches from ear to ear.

Because of the travel opportunities we have at RCA, I have been able to watch that "glow" on six of the seven continents with Mr. Townsel, and it has been remarkable. The joy he brings to the trips actually makes the experiences better for all of us. When we were given an opportunity to have one of our staff members journey to Antarctica to learn about the effects of global warming, we knew without a doubt that it had to be Mr. Townsel. I still remember the moment he returned from the excursion. We were all at school when I heard a big explosion of cheers in the lobby. I walked down to see Mr. Townsel, standing in the middle of the lobby, still wearing the outfit he had worn as he stood atop the South Pole. He hadn't changed or shaved throughout the entire journey back home, and he looked rough. I ran down to join everyone in celebration, and as I threw my arms around him he said, "It was beautiful, Mr. Clark. It was just . . . so beautiful," and he burst into tears.

We crowded into his classroom, and he started telling all of us what he had seen and experienced: rough seas, curious penguins, gigantic glaciers, and the eroding of a paradise. He said he had a picture to show us, and as he started to pull it up, he told us that they had encouraged the passengers onboard the ship to take the "icy plunge" into the water, which was basically frozen slush. The kids all shivered and then quickly jumped to attention because they knew Mr. Townsel wouldn't have passed up that opportunity.

As the picture appeared, he said, "I was scared to death, but I had the spirit of every one of you with me, and since I was the only one there, I wanted to do it for all of us. And so I did. I took the plunge. And . . . I took the plunge . . . wearing only my boxers. And . . . I dove headfirst."

I just shook my head and smiled. Of course you did, Mr. Townsel. Of course you did.

Mr. Townsel with our students in Wakayama, Japan.

We all need to remember that we must constantly take the plunge to live our lives with a greater sense of curiosity and to show our children what it means to be a lifelong learner. If they learn that while they are young, that spirit will remain with them for the rest of their lives. And when they are presented with a chance to "plunge," hopefully, they will go for it and in the same classy and daring style as did Mr. Townsel.

✲ 13 ✲

Treat every child as if he or she were your own.

While on a trip with the students in Amsterdam, I realized that one of them was having a birthday. This child, Jalen, had a mother who was struggling with cancer and a father who wasn't present in his life. He had a great deal to cope with, and at 11:30 that night, I realized that the entire day had passed without anyone wishing Jalen a happy birthday. Now all of the students were in bed, and I was exhausted and in bed, too. I had spent eight days with thirty students in England, France, and Amsterdam, and all I wanted to do was pass out and get some rest. It would have been so easy to curl up into that pillow, but I rolled over, got out of bed, threw on my clothes, and made my way down to Jalen and Jule's room.

I knocked on the door a few times before they answered, and when Jalen finally opened the door, I whispered, "Get dressed, fellas. I'm breaking you out of here!"

Without questioning me, Jalen said, "Yes, sir," and after the door closed briefly for about sixty seconds, he and Jule appeared in their doorway, a bit disheveled, but nonetheless dressed and ready to go!

We started sneaking down the hall, and I told them that they had to be extremely silent. I said, "Jalen, we have ten minutes left of your birthday, buddy, and we're going to make the best of it." Seeing the joy on his face is one of my most joyous moments at RCA. To see a child who had experienced so much pain show so much delight was beautiful.

As we walked down the hall, I heard another door open directly behind us. On our trips, we have an extremely strict policy forbidding students to open their hotel doors. I figured it must be a chaperone coming outside, and I told Jalen and Jule to hide! Jalen and I darted into opposite two-foot-wide alcoves in the hallway where the doors to other rooms were, but Jule, moving a bit too slowly, wasn't able to slip to the side in time. Out of panic, he just started running full speed down the hall. The chaperone, one of RCA's teachers, Rhonda Lokey, saw him. Suddenly I heard a sound that appeared to have come from the pit of all darkness:

"JUUUUUUUULLLLLLLEEEEEEEE!"

Then I heard her footsteps approaching, *boom, boom, boom.* Mrs. Lokey was on her way to strangle Jule. As she approached where Jalen and I were hiding, I inhaled deeply and tried my best to plaster my entire body against the wall. Jalen copied my actions, because as soon as he realized that I was scared, he looked like he was about to vomit.

Suddenly, she was right beside me. She halted her steps instantly, jerked her head to the right to see Jalen, and then jerked her head to the left to see me. She instantly slapped me on the arm, screaming, "Mr. Clark, don't you realize I was about to kill that boy!" Mrs. Lokey and I just rolled on the floor laughing!

After Jule caught his breath and after I pulled Jalen off the wall, we composed ourselves and headed outside. We stopped at a little shop about two blocks from the hotel and ordered French fries with mayonnaise and flavored juices. We talked and laughed for about twenty minutes, and then I took the boys back up to bed. Yes, it was after midnight. Yes, I had the boys out at an hour that probably wasn't appropriate. And, yes, that was a night Jalen will never forget.

At the end of their eighth-grade year at RCA, we ask the students to list their top twenty moments at our school. During their time with us, they have had unreal educational experiences, traveled all over the world, been part of a magical family, and been loved and uplifted by their teachers and classmates. Jalen's top moment:

> When Mr. Clark went out of his way to make me feel special in Amsterdam. I didn't even know he knew it was my birthday. He gave me the best moment of my life.

When we got back to Atlanta, Jalen's mother thanked me for making her son feel special. In an email she wrote, "I appreciate so much, Mr. Clark, that you gave my son something that I couldn't. I am forever indebted to you."

Jalen's mother passed away the following year. What that young man has had to experience isn't fair. He has had to bear more than his share at such a young age, and it breaks my heart.

For anyone who works with children, we often are made aware of the burdens they have to bear, but in many instances we will never know. We never have an awareness of the pain they are feeling and the struggles they have to endure. What we can do, however, is love them and see them as individuals we care about and respect. I often stop to ask myself, "How would I want another teacher to handle this situation if she were dealing with my own child?" That will more often than not lead me to the correct way I should handle whatever situation I am dealing with, and it will usually point me in the right direction when I am trying to help children, uplift them, and give them the love they need. This can be accomplished by paying attention to them, asking them how they are doing, sitting with them at lunch, or giving a small gift. In some cases, however, it might need to be a little more, and sometimes it may call for a midnight escape for French fries. It may seem like something simple at the time, but it may just end up being the most special moment in the life of a child who is desperately deserving of happiness.

Push yourself to be innovative
beyond your imagination.

I know there are times when Kim hates me. She will come to me with an idea for her classroom, and she is jumping up and down and talking so quickly I can barely follow her. She'll finish describing her great idea, and I'll go, "Hmm, you can do better."

She hates it. I know she hates it because she tells me.

In the end, however, she always comes back with an improved idea, and she'll say, "Okay, you were right, listen to this." I'll listen to her better idea, and I'll say, "Now, that is a good idea."

There is no one on earth I would rather have as the cofounder of RCA. Kim is a creative dynamo and polished professional who has a work ethic that isn't human. She has devoted her life to RCA, and she loves our students as if they are her own. The best part about my relationship with Kim, however, is that we know we can be bluntly honest with each other, because we know the purpose behind our criticism is doing what is best for our children.

I wish more colleagues could be honest about one another's ideas. People are so afraid to hurt someone's feelings or to anger someone that they will just say it's a great idea even when it may not be. I am so thankful that Kim and I have a relationship where I can go to her and she'll be flat-out honest and tell me if my ideas are just average, and I love that. I enjoy pushing myself to become better and to be more innovative than I thought possible. Through challenging ourselves, we learn our true potential and grow as educators and individuals.

Sometimes, however, I push us a bit too much.

Years ago, when RCA was under construction, the movie about my teaching experiences in Harlem, *The Ron Clark Story*, was about to be released. They filmed a segment at the construction site of me giving a tour of the empty warehouse. I jumped from spot to spot describing how vibrant and different the school would look from any school in the world. As I approached the center of the warehouse, I stated, "And right here in the center of RCA will be something you just won't believe. We are putting something here that you won't find in any school in the world, but you will have to come here in person to see what it is." After the filming was done, Kim asked me with great anticipation in her eyes, "Ron, what in the world are we putting in the middle of the school?"

I replied, "I have no idea, but we'll figure it out."

Yikes.

I told Kim that now that I had said it, that it would push us to come up with an idea. If I had not put it out there, we wouldn't have felt obligated to make it happen.

We spent the next few months running through multiple ideas: a waterfall, a merry-go-round, swings. Nothing seemed right for the lobby, but we wouldn't give up. Finally, our idea for a waterfall turned into a water slide, but since the students couldn't get their uniforms wet, we decided to go with just a slide. But it wouldn't be "just a slide," it would be a huge, two-story, electric-blue tube slide that, when waxed, would send its passengers flying through the school and rapidly across the lobby floor.

It presented us with the perfect symbol; instead of taking the stairs, why not slide? Be different, be bold, be innovative. Go for it! It summed up the mission of RCA perfectly, and it felt right. When you have been working on an idea for weeks, even months, and you finally get it all to fall into place, you just know when it's right.

As we have learned, however, whenever you try to do something unusual, you are going to be presented with problems that others have never had to encounter. And our biggest issue with the slide was getting it insured.

I asked Mehari Kassa, who at the time was a new volunteer to RCA, to work on the insurance issue. After he was turned down by five companies, he told me that we were facing an uphill battle because no one had ever tried to put a slide in a school. I asked Mehari to keep calling and to find a way to "make it happen."

Mehari came back to me after the twentieth company turned us down, and with that, I actually decided it was time to give up. Mehari had spent weeks on the process, and it wasn't fair to ask him to continue. He, however, told me that I had told him to "make it happen," and that was exactly what he intended to do. He continued to call.

The twenty-seventh person Mehari contacted, Vernie Dove with the John Hackney Agency, listened to our story. Mehari talked with passion and love for RCA and sold the company not only on a slide but also on a vision for a school that would change the world. The company was moved by his plea, and after designing a slide that lived up to their code for safety requirements and ensuring that we would carefully follow a clear set of posted rules for proper usage, we had our slide. And with Mehari's victory, he let me know that he no longer wanted to volunteer: he wanted to make RCA his full-time job. The next day he became the first employee of the Ron Clark Academy.

BIG BLUE! The first drop is a doozy.

As our infatuation with our new big blue slide grew, we decided that every visitor to RCA would be asked to go down the slide and become "slide certified"! We ordered stickers that they would wear announcing that they were "slide certified," and soon T-shirts with the slogan followed.

Word spread quickly that when you come to RCA, you have to take a ride on "Big Blue." Quite honestly, there have been times when I questioned whether visiting educators were more interested in coming to RCA to learn about our educational methods or to go down the slide. One group of ten teachers flew all the way from China to spend two days at our school and then turn around to fly right back to China. When the group walked in our doors, the very first thing they said was, "When do we do the slide?"

We even have had an eighty-four-year-old lady take the ride. (She holds the record.) She had taught more than forty years, and as I gave her the tour of RCA, she kept saying how it would have been her dream to teach at a school like ours. She said, "This is Disneyland for teachers!" She was having a great deal of trouble walking, and it was taking quite a while to give her the tour. Halfway through, Kim called me over and whispered, "Ron, don't you even try to get that woman to go down that slide."

I agreed, and toward the end of the tour, as I was helping the lady go down our grand staircase slowly, step by step, she said, "I think it would be quicker if I just went down that slide."

I looked to the left. I looked to the right. Seeing the coast was clear, I said, "Let's do it!"

I helped her into the slide, and she just sat there looking very pleased with herself. When she made no motion to slide, I asked, "Are you sure this is a good idea?"

She replied, "Ohhhh, yes."

I said, "Okay then!" and I gave her a little push, and *varooom*! Off she went! I ran over to the balcony to make sure she came out okay, and as she went flying out and across the lobby floor, her skirt slid all the way up and over her hips, revealing her granny white underwear.

One of the best teachers I know, Rhonda Lokey, demonstrates the importance of wearing pants when you visit RCA.

Since that day, we always suggest that people wear pants when they visit RCA.

After I helped the woman up, she asked if she was going to get her "slide certified" sticker. I told her that it would be my honor to place it upon her chest. As I did so, she said, "I may not be a teacher any longer, but I feel the passion of this school in my heart."

She, like thousands upon thousands of other visitors to RCA, received her sticker with pride. The idea for the slide was perfect because it not only symbolizes our mission, it also serves as a joyful addition to our school for our students.

It is cool.

It places an electrifying symbol in the middle of our learning environment.

And it is a symbol of what can happen with perseverance.

All of that happened because I challenged myself and our team to rise to the task, and we did. As always, it is miraculous what can happen when we ask ourselves and one another to be better, to do more, and to improve upon even the best of our ideas.

☀15☀

Know the name of every teacher, student, parent, administrator, and board member.

At the end of the school year in May, the students and faculty members at RCA are given a test on the names of the incoming fifth graders. We each have to know the first and last names, spelled correctly, of each new member of the RCA family. The staff members also have to memorize the last names of the parents as well and, in some cases, the names of close family members who play a major role in the life of the child.

We can't assume that the last name of the student is the same last

name as the student's mother or father. It can be offensive and annoying for a parent to be called "Mrs. Moore" just because her son is "Jay Moore." Also, it is important to know the family situation, because you don't want to refer to the aunt as the mom, just because the child might happen to be living with a relative. If you are really going to build a bond and be a family, everyone has to know one another, and learning others' names is the first step.

At RCA we pride ourselves on knowing all of our students' parents and for building bonds with them, but even when you make every effort to know every family member of all of the children, it can be a daunting task.

At the Fall Festival, I saw the father of a girl who was struggling academically. I walked up to him, gave him a hug, and started into my role: I really have to tell you, I love Cindy and I think she is a very well-mannered and special young girl, but academically she is far behind. She isn't doing her reading logs, she didn't have her homework for me twice this week, she is failing every subject except for physical education, and it's going to take all of us, each and everyone of us, working together, to get Cindy on the right track.

The father looked at me and said, "Wow, Mr. Clark, I really hate that about Cindy, and I will do all I can to help, but I'm Will's father."

Okay, as I was writing this, I had to hit "enter" three times to get away from that last paragraph because it is too embarrassing. If you are going to expect help from the parents, it certainly helps if you know who they are. That is the first step in building a relationship, and it is an easy and appropriate way to show respect.

For a teacher, that means a lot of names to learn; therefore, parents have a much easier job. They have to learn only anywhere from the one to eight names of their children's teachers. Still, as much as we do to visit homes and reach out to the parents, many will still get us confused. When they tell me they have a question about an assignment for the sci-

ence teacher or that they need to find the PE teacher, it floors me. How could you not know the name of the person who spends so many hours with your child each week? The closer you are to your child's teacher and the more of a bond you have with him or her, the better the chance your child is going to have a positive experience in that classroom.

In addition to having our students, staff, and parents learn one another's names, we also work hard to teach our students about our major donors and individuals in the community who support RCA. We present a slide show of multiple pictures of the individuals and tell the students who they are, where they work, and how they help our school. We then give our students a packet, and they have to learn each person for an upcoming test. Then, when those individuals walk down the halls of our school, we encourage our students to reach out, to introduce themselves, and to call our visitors by name. The kids do it almost instinctively because when they recognize the face of someone they have learned about, they are thrilled to meet them in person, and they also tend to show a genuine appreciation for all that individual has done to help our school.

A Side Note from the Great State of Texas!

I often say that my favorite state is Texas. I love the energy I feel when I walk through the schools and the way educators are treated and seen as professionals. It is rare to find a staff that isn't sharp in appearance and actions, and I always enjoy visiting their schools.

During one visit in Houston, I met a group of food service workers who memorize the name of every student in the school during the summer. They make it a point to greet each and every child by name and to get to know them all as individuals. They said they wanted to make the brief time they see the students as special as possible and that the simple act of learning their names made serving lunch to the students a joyful experience.

From Matthew's Mom

The most amazing thing that happened at the meet-and-greet afternoon was that every staff and student knew each new student's name—first and last! How the students and staff mastered that is still a mystery to me! Needless to say, my son has never felt so welcomed and inspired. He said, "Mom, I feel like I've died and gone to school heaven." What an incredible welcome and introduction to RCA. We knew we were truly about to be part of a family.

—Mrs. Meadows, parent, Class of 2014

⁕ 16 ⁕

Use music to excite, motivate, and inspire.

We all love music. We turn it on as soon as we get in the car, and listen to it when we get home. It only makes sense to find ways to incorporate it into our workday to provide inspiration there as well. For more traditional schools, it may just be playing classical music while students take a test or during class changes, while at more avant-garde establishments, you may have students singing songs that tie in with the curriculum or performing an all-out academic musical. Regardless of how music is used, any school looking to build an environment that students will love needs to use it one way or another.

During the presidential election of 2008, I wanted my students to understand the major issues in depth. I didn't want them to just realize that there was an African American, Barack Obama, running against a Caucasian, John McCain. I wanted them to truly understand what each man stood for and the difference he wanted to make in our country. We jumped in with both feet, learning about the Middle East crisis, offshore oil drilling, gun rights, and every domestic and foreign affairs issue that was being discussed. Soon, the students started getting into it, and we were having many hot and heavy discussions.

Over the next few weeks, the students became experts, discussing issues at will, bringing in killer points from their research on global topics, and exuding increasing confidence with each day's discussions. In order to add more excitement and energy to the lessons, I decided to get the students to write the information they had learned into a song, with half of the classroom in support of John McCain and the other half in support of Barack Obama. In a matter of moments, the John McCain supporters took life:

McCain is the man
Fought for us in Vietnam
You know if anyone can help our country
He can

Taxes dropping low
Don't you know
Oil's gonna flow
Drillin' low
Off-sho'
Our economy will grow!

The class erupted! Not to be outdone, the Obama supporters had their own reply:

But McCain and Bush are real close, right?
They vote alike, they keep it tight.
Obama's new
He's younger, too
The middle class
He will help you

He'll bring a change
He's got the brains
McCain and Bush are just the same
You are to blame
Iraq's a shame
Four more years would be insane!

The desks were certainly rockin' that day, and soon the small rap from the debate turned into a full-length song that the entire class would sing back and forth to each other.

I want Obama!   *Forget Obama!*

Stick with McCain you're   *More war in Iraq!*
gonna have some drama!

Iran he will attack!   *Can't bring our troops back!*

We've gotta vote Barack!

Obama on the left!   *McCain on the right!*

(And then everyone together)

We can talk politics all night, and you can vote however you like, I say, you can vote however you like! Yeah!

Democratic Left   *Republican Right*

November fourth we decide, and you can vote however you like. I say, you can vote however you like.

When I was asked to speak at a Coca-Cola event for college students who have received substantial scholarships from the corporation, I decided to take the students with me so that they could sing the song as a way to show how we use music to inspire them to enjoy learning. The song was written to the tune of an extremely popular song at the time, "Whatever You Like," by T.I., and as soon as the music started the audience went wild. The students truly went for it with all their hearts, and out of instinct they started to dance out into the audience, making their way between the circular tables of the crowded room. Pretty soon both sides were battling back and forth, and the audience went crazy. As soon as the song was complete everyone jumped to their feet to give a rousing standing ovation.

A few days later, Ms. Mosley called me down to the front office. Anyone who has ever called RCA or visited the front desk knows that Ms. Mosley runs a tight ship, and she puts up with no mess. She said, "Mr. Clark, why are these schools calling me about performing some song?" I had no idea what she was talking about, so she let me take the call of a lady who was on hold. The principal was calling from Lincoln, Nebraska, and she wanted to know if her entire school could perform our Obama-McCain song at an assembly. She asked me to email her the lyrics.

I asked, "Where in the world did you see our song?"

And she said, "YouTube."

I freaked out. "YouTube?!" Ms. Mosley and I pulled up the clip and realized that someone from the Coca-Cola event must have filmed the students on her camera phone. To our surprise, the video already had more than fifteen thousand hits! The next day it had more than twenty-five thousand, and by the end of the week it had surpassed one hundred thousand. The whole school—students, staff, and parents—was talking about the video. I woke up on Monday morning to find an email from an old college friend who currently lives in California. The email said, "Have you heard of these kids in Atlanta? This video of them is so cool!"

I wrote back, "Those are my students, and that is me dancing in the background!" I realized then that people were forwarding the video everywhere, and in a few days' time there were dozens of versions of the video on YouTube.com that hit a combined total of one million viewers.

The students started getting invited to perform the song all over Atlanta, and with each taped performance, thousands more were acquired on YouTube.com. Soon, the students appeared on *Good Morning America*, the *Today* show, and CNN. We thought it would be a wonderful way to share with the world the importance of using music to inspire a great love of learning in children. We were proud that our students knew so much information about the political issues, and as teachers and parents, we were thrilled to see the students being recognized.

Dasia Kirkley and Sydnei Bumpass do it up RCA style! With every performance, the students became more confident and polished!

As the video reached ten million hits, all of Atlanta was abuzz. The students were the hit of the town, and we were on cloud nine and riding an amazing adrenaline rush.

But then, something devastating happened. The students flooded into my classroom one morning in tears. Apparently, with ten million YouTube.com hits, you also get hundreds of thousands of viewer comments. Most of them were complimentary, praising them for knowing more about the election than adults. Many other comments gave words of support for a bipartisan song that encouraged people to become more educated about the issues. Tens of thousands of the comments, however, were racist and cruel. They talked about our students in a negative and hateful way that shocked us to the core. We had a crisis on our hands.

And that leads us to #17 . . .

✳17✳

Know your students.

I have heard many teachers say that when they look at their classrooms, they don't see color. They say they see each student equally and love them all the same. I think those teachers mean well, but I honestly think that we have to see color and recognize our differences, because if we don't see color, we don't see culture.

Every person in America is living a different experience, whether you are male, female, black, white, Asian American, Native American, Mexican American, et cetera. I have seen how being a white man has helped me in several situations. I see how I am treated differently when I walk into a bank or onto a car lot. I see how I am spoken to when I walk into a clothing store and how my friends of various other ethnicities are treated differently in the same circumstances.

When I was teaching in New York City, I was eating lunch with my colleagues, and I was the only Caucasian person at the table. I was a young, skinny, twenty-nine-year-old, and the rest of the educators at the table, including the administrators, were much older. When the waitress brought the check, she placed it in front of me. Now, I am goofy, so I just started laughing and said, "I don't have any money," but no one else laughed. It upset my colleagues, and they let the waitress, who was African American, know about it.

Traveling around the country with my students from RCA can be difficult at times when people make assumptions about our groups. Almost all of my students are African American, and on every trip people will either say, "Oh, this must be a basketball team. Where are you playing?" or they'll say, "Oh, this must be a singing group. Can you sing for us?"

I'll just answer, "Actually, they are just a group of really bright scholars."

In response, occasionally the individual will ask, "Oh, so how are you able to afford this trip?" I wonder if I were traveling with a group of white students if they would ask how we could afford it. Perhaps some would, but I have a feeling most would not.

No matter how much we say that racial profiling doesn't exist or that we don't make judgments about people based on the color of their skin, it just isn't true. It happens. Whether to a small degree or large, it happens. I want my students to be prepared for that and to know how to handle those situations in a positive and levelheaded way. We talk openly at RCA about race because it becomes a problem only when we try to hide it and pretend it doesn't exist. For that reason, I called a meeting of the entire school to discuss the comments that had been made on YouTube.com and to come up with a plan.

As we discussed the comments, we realized that we have some pretty sick people in our country. For example, someone wrote, "These images must be from the Atlanta Zoo." Another added, "All those people know how to do is sing and dance." The "n-word" was used freely throughout thousands of posts. One individual took images of the faces of our students and made a website where he compared each face to the species of orangutan to which he felt they belonged.

It ripped my heart out to see my students so devastated, and I finally said, "That's it, we are going to contact the people who have posted our video online and ask them to remove it. You all shouldn't have to deal with this ignorance."

But one of my students, Ahjanae, said, "Mr. Clark, remember when you taught us about how people would throw eggs at Martin Luther King and how he would just hold his head high and keep walking? You said he wouldn't fight back because he was trying to change a stereotype. Well, we want to change a stereotype, too, and show people we can do more than sing and dance and that we are intelligent and knowledgeable about the world, so we need to keep our video up there. Some people were stupid, but tens of thousands of people praised our efforts, so we are making a difference."

Another student, Willie, said, "Yeah, Mr. Clark, we are going to have to deal with racism our whole lives, so it's better that we learn how to deal with it now as kids in a positive way." We took a vote, and every student in the school chose to leave the videos online.

The next day we received a call from *ABC World News Tonight*. They wanted to do a story on the song. I explained to the kids that another news program wanted to film them singing "You Can Vote However You Like," and I told them they could say no if they wanted. As a class, they agreed to perform the song, and they commented that they hoped ABC would decide to air interviews of them talking about political issues along with clips of the song.

Well, the crew from ABC arrived, filmed the song, and immediately started packing up. I asked, "Don't you want to interview one of the kids to get a clip about the political issues they have learned?" and, while she seemed hesitant, the reporter finally agreed.

She said, "Okay, let's get a quick sound bite from this kid," and she pointed to Willie.

In my head I was screaming, *Ohhhh, yes!* Willie is like a little Walter Cronkite and I knew he was going to blow her away.

The reporter leaned down to Willie's level and in a very sweet voice asked, "So, can you tell me who you think is going to win the presidential election?"

To put it mildly, Willie went off! He was talking so fast the reporter's head was spinning, and he must have gone on for at least five minutes about his support of the Republican platform and the importance of reducing capital gains taxes.

When Willie finished talking, the reporter just stood there. She paused for a moment, and then asked, "Can I interview more kids?" Of course I agreed, and with each new interview she became even more impressed by the students' knowledge and poise. She finally said, "Mr. Clark, we're changing the story. It's no longer about the song; it's about the students. They know more than adults do about the issues in this election, and they are the ones that should have the right to vote. People need to see this."

The entire school didn't go home that day. We all stayed in the lobby waiting to watch the seven o'clock show together. Parents arrived to pick up their students but, after hearing about the show, they decided to join in. All together, we anxiously sat in the lobby and waited for the moment our students would shine on national TV.

When the powerful piece finally aired, it showed our students discussing world events with grace and ease. They were passionate, educated, and flawless. Charles Gibson from *World News Tonight* looked stunned. He announced that ABC was naming the students of the Ron Clark Academy as Persons of the Week and that we all could learn a lesson from them. The staff, the students, and the families erupted! We were hugging and screaming, and I will never forget Ahjanae Colson looking me in the eyes and saying, "See, Mr. Clark, we changed stereotypes."

She was right, and so was Charles Gibson. Never underestimate what can be learned from the heart, the determination, and the character of a young person. Oftentimes they see the world more clearly and accurately than even adults do.

"You Can Vote However You Like" went on to garner more than fifteen million hits on YouTube.com and became one of the most watched videos of 2008. When Barack Obama won, the students were inspired to write a new song for him titled "Dear Obama." It was a letter, written in the form of a song, letting him know what they wanted to see him do as president of our country. That song also soon spread like wildfire on the Internet, and the students were invited to participate in numerous inaugural events in Washington, DC. They sang their song twenty-seven times during a week that finally culminated at the inauguration where we all stood arm in arm, crying, as President Obama took the oath of office.

The students had truly been a part of one of the most historic elections in American history, and the honor and pride that President Obama delivered in his acceptance speech was evident on the faces and in the hearts of each and every RCA student.

✳ 18 ✳

Don't let opportunities pass you by, even if the time, funding, and circumstances aren't completely right.

Sometimes at RCA we realize that we have to make sacrifices to make moments happen, and we do so without a moment's hesitation. After "You Can Vote However You Like" and "Dear Obama" became so popular, we started getting calls daily with requests for the Ron Clark Academy Choir to perform. We quickly told everyone, "We do not have a Ron Clark Academy Choir; we have scholars who love to learn and who occasionally write academic content in songs."

It became a bit annoying telling people over and over, "We do not have a Ron Clark Academy Choir." That is why when the office of Speaker of the House Nancy Pelosi called on behalf of Michelle Obama and Hillary Clinton to ask if the "Ron Clark Academy Choir" would perform at the unveiling of the bust of Sojourner Truth and asked, "Don't you have the Ron Clark Academy Choir?" I responded, "Yes, we do!"

It was days before the performance, and we had no song, no dance, no hotel, and no funding for the trip. The representative said that if we'd like to participate at the ceremony, we'd need to find our own funding for the trip, and without hesitation, I said, "It's not a problem at all and we'd be honored to attend." I hung up the phone and went into freak-out mode. I wasn't sure how we'd pull it all together, but our students were not going to miss having the opportunity to participate in the unveiling of the first bust of an African American female in the Capitol Building!

We immediately announced to the parents that we were making the trip, and then we started reaching out to potential donors. At no point did we ever tell anyone that the trip was just a possibility. No one wants to donate to a "potential" trip; they want to donate to something that is going to happen and to feel that they are joining a mission that others are supporting as well.

It took dozens of phone calls and requests for help, but the support was there and the trip happened. There was one small problem: we still didn't have a song to perform at the unveiling, on national television, in front of millions of people.

The very first song our students ever performed was "I Believe" by Yolanda Adams. Kennedy suggested that we change the words of that song a little in order to talk about the life of Sojourner Truth. We played around with the lyrics, and pretty soon we realized we had a winner. We practiced for two days straight, sang the song over and over in the vans, and the very second we arrived at the hotel, we went to work to rehearse even more. RCA is all about perfection and being polished, and we knew we had to blow everyone away.

At nine that evening, we headed to the Capitol Building for a late-night rehearsal. We were so proud of the song, and we couldn't wait to rehearse it for the event planners. They let us know as soon as we arrived that we would have to show them our song quickly, because the next performer had to get in and practice as well. The next performer . . . who was . . . Yolanda Adams, singing "I Believe."

I wanted to vomit.

I let the event planners know that we were performing the same song with different lyrics, and she said that wouldn't be possible and that we'd have to sing something else. Uhhh, there was nothing else. I just stood there, pale faced and panicked, and the lady said, "Wait, oh, she's not singing 'I Believe,' she's singing something else."

I said, "Great, but do you think she would mind that we're singing her song without permission on national television?"

She said she had no idea but that at this point we didn't have much of a choice. I ran over and told the kids the dilemma, and we all agreed that since we were already in the barn we'd might as well milk the cow. We decided to move forward with the song and Willie suggested that he announce that the song was used in part to honor Yolanda Adams as well. It was a plan, and we felt we were back on track!

As we began practicing, however, we noticed we would be performing in front of the stage, and that Michelle Obama, Hillary Clinton, and Nancy Pelosi would actually be sitting *behind* the performing students, so they wouldn't actually see them singing. Argh!

We didn't want to turn our backs on those individuals, but if we all faced them, we'd have our backs to the nation. The song was high energy and had very intricate dance steps, but I asked the students who would be in the back row, "Could you possibly perform all of the song's dance steps backward, so that from the front you all appear to be in unison but those of you in the back row will actually be facing the dignitaries?"

Without a second's hesitation, they said, "Yes, sir!"

From there it was back to the hotel and back to work! Before we knew it, it was two in the morning. The kids were exhausted, but not one student complained, and we kept working, hour after hour, to get the routine perfect. At eight, we journeyed, using adrenaline and life support to lift one another up, to the Capitol, and the students took their places on the stage and in history.

As Willie stood before the crowd of thousands, he looked Yolanda Adams directly in the eyes and announced that they wanted to honor her by using the background of one of her songs to pay tribute to Sojourner Truth. Ms. Adams grinned from ear to ear, and upon completion of the performance, she was the first to give them a standing ovation.

They had performed their song "Sojourner's Truth" flawlessly, complete with the performers in the back row dancing "backward." At the end, we were meeting the dignitaries, and I saw Jordan Brown reach out to shake the hand of Michelle Obama. She just reached out, hugged him, and said, "You were my little soloist and I loved your performance." It was wonderful, it was electrifying, and it was all worth it.

The young man smiling in the back row on the left is Jordan. He turned to face the front for Jonathan's solo before turning back to face Mrs. Obama. She couldn't take her eyes off of him.

Now when we talk about that moment or countless others that were done in haste or on a wing and a prayer, we don't remember how hard it was to make the moment actually come to fruition. We tend to think how wonderful the moment was when it finally happened. To us at RCA, that is what life is about: making moments for yourself and for others to cherish for a lifetime. Does it seem impossible to make those moments happen at times? Yes. But is it worth the world when they finally occur? You'd better believe it.

✳19✳

Make learning magical.

As parents and teachers, we all know how miserable it feels to see a lack of excitement or interest in our children. When they don't enjoy learning, whether it's math, science, or reading, we need to take drastic measures! The longer they see the subject in a negative way, the more damage is done. There is always a way to bring learning to life and to place eagerness in the hearts of our children, and we owe it to them to find it.

I love the book *The Westing Game*. It's an intriguing story about sixteen individuals who are visited by an old man, Mr. Barney Northrup, wearing a pilot's cap. He gives each person an envelope that contains an invitation to the reading of a will. An old man, Sam Westing, died, and left $200 million in inheritance that each of the sixteen individuals is eager to receive.

I was reading the book with my sixth graders, and I wanted them to love it as much as I did. I want the kids to enjoy reading not only today but for the rest of their lives. I try to do all I can to show them the power of their imaginations and to teach them that images on a movie screen pale by comparison with the pictures we can paint with our minds.

As we read together in class, I put all of my heart and soul into the book, using every ounce of energy to bring the voices of the characters to life. It was useless; they didn't like it. Each day I would say, "Okay, time to get out *The Westing Game!*" I could almost hear the suppressed groans from the class. Argh!

I knew I had to do something. One miserable experience with a book can turn kids off from reading altogether, and I couldn't let that happen. I had to come up with a drastic plan to right the ship. I asked myself, "If I were reading this book, what would be the most magical thing that could happen to me?" Suddenly, I knew exactly what I had to do . . .

A few days later, while reading with the students in class, Mrs. Bearden walked into the back of my classroom joined by a very old man (an acquaintance of mine) wearing a pilot's cap. I said, "Class," and on cue the students stood, turned, and faced the guest. They stood politely at attention, but I saw eyes popping and eyebrows raised all over the room. Mrs. Bearden said, "Class, this is Mr. Barney Northrup," and with slight hesitation and bewilderment came their standard reply, "Welcome to our class, Mr. Northrup." The gentleman proceeded to pass out letters to each child before quickly exiting the room.

As soon as he was gone, the students exclaimed, "Mr. Clark, that was the man from the book we are reading! What's in this envelope?" I told them I had no idea and that they had better open them up and find out.

Inside, the students found an invitation to the reading of the will of Raymond Blood. The reading was to be on Saturday night at his mansion, Blood Manor, which was located on West Paces Ferry Road. It also stated that one of them could inherit $200 million.

"Is this real?" they all asked.

"It sure looks for real," I replied. I then added, "Ohhhh, you all are gonna have to be some kinda brave. Blood Manor? Wow, that is a 'scurry' place; I have heard about all kinds of horrible things that have happened there. Good luck with that." Their eyes grew wide with fear as they exited my room.

The next morning the students entered my class in a flurry saying, "Mr. Clark, there is no such place as Blood Manor; we Googled it!"

I told them that the stuff that happened there was so bad that they took it off the Internet. (You've got to think quickly these days.)

That Saturday night, I got a limousine service to donate a stretch limo for the evening. The students arrived at RCA just as the invitation requested, and as they piled into the limo, they asked, "Mr. Clark, where are we *really* going?"

I explained that we were doing what the invitation said, going to Blood Manor, and that I was just going along for the ride as a chaperone.

The limo driver was in on the deal, and he asked, "Uh, Mr. Clark, where are we going again?"

I stated, "Blood Manor on West Paces Ferry."

He quickly put on the brakes and exclaimed, "No way! Our insurance company doesn't allow us to go to places like Blood Manor!"

Jaws dropped.

I reassured the driver. "Don't worry, you and I aren't actually going all the way there; we're going to drop the students off a few blocks away and they can walk the rest of the way."

The students screamed at once, "Mr. Clark, you're not going inside Blood Manor with us?"

I said, "I'm not crazy. There is no way I'm going in that place!"

Of course, I went up to the house with them. Friends of RCA, Raymond and Lucy Allen, let us use their gorgeous, multistoried home for the evening, and I went there earlier in the day to set up a few items. I wrapped the house with yellow crime scene tape, and I used masking tape to make the outline of a body in the house's foyer.

"Mr. Clark, look, this is for real!" the students shouted as we approached the home.

After we were inside, Mrs. Allen, dressed all in black, greeted us at the door. She took us to the living room, asked us to be seated, and began to read the will.

The students were told, "One of you could inherit two hundred million dollars tonight, but one of you . . . dum dum dum . . . is the murderer." The students looked to the left and to the right in horror! It was great!

The students were placed in groups of two and instructed to use the clues in teams to solve the mystery (just like in the book). A clue would reveal, for example, "Go to the second-floor bathroom and look under the trash can." Under the trash can would be another clue.

Things were going extremely well as the students maneuvered throughout the beautiful home solving clues, until Dasia's group followed their clue into the kitchen. There, on the floor with blood (ketchup) dripping out of his mouth was Raymond Blood! Dasia's scream rocked the walls, and students went flying all over that house and out the front door. One kid yelled, "Call 911!"

After some quick crisis counseling, we calmed the students down and gathered them back into the living room. Raymond (Mr. Allen) stood up and explained that he was not dead and that there had been no murder. I told the students that the whole night had just been a test of their wit and skill, and that since there was no murder, of course, there was no $200 million inheritance.

The only sound in the room was a grunted "huh" from one of the dumbfounded students. We got in the limo, and the depression of losing the millions soon wore off. The kids started to laugh hysterically to the point that tears were running down their faces. They loved it. I honestly don't remember ever seeing children laugh that hard.

The next day, they ran into my classroom: "Mr. Clark, can we finish the book today?" I explained that since we had 150 pages left, it would be impossible to finish the entire book in one day. They begged, *"Please,"* and, again, I explained that we couldn't, but that I was willing to try if they were.

I will never forget the joy in this twenty-minute limo ride. I was laughing so hard I could barely take this picture.

Of course, we couldn't finish the book in that class period, but that isn't the point. The point is that they wanted to finish it. They felt as if they were part of the story, as though they had fallen into the book. They were fascinated with it, and every day that we read the book, the students were wide-eyed and excited.

Did it take time to find the house, to put up the police tape, to set out the clues, and to find a "Barney Northrup"? Yes, but it was worth it, because it gave the students something priceless: the ability to use their imaginations. Every book we read the rest of that year came to life. I didn't have to go to the extent of reenacting the entire story for each novel. All I had to do was get them to open the books, and I had them instantly. The students had learned how to pull the words off the page and to bring them to life in their minds, and that is something they will have with them forever.

You don't have to be a classroom teacher to bring a book to life. As a child, I saw my mother transform herself into a princess, an evil queen, a fairy, a witch, a human egg, and even a headless horseman, all to get me excited about reading. She wasn't afraid to make a fool of herself to surprise me into loving a story. And in doing so, she made me adore reading. That same love can be instilled into all of our children if we're not afraid to make it magical for them.

Do This:

If you want to create the magic in your classroom but you don't have time to be so elaborate, there are some quick ways to garner the same reaction.

- If you are reading a story that involves rain, storms, or other forms of weather, turn off the lights and play a recording of rain and wind in the background. If you want to carry it a step further, ask the kids to bring umbrellas and flashlights to school to really bring the scene to life. Using a fog machine also can add a great finishing touch!

- Encourage your students to participate as "active readers." For example, if you are reading a novel together and the crowd in the story begins to cheer, the students should cheer as well. If there was a loud BOOM, then everyone should shout BOOM! If a detective in the story is

(continued)

calling his friend while hiding in a closet, the person reading should do so in a whisper as if he's really in the closet. If a character sighs, the entire class should do a collective sigh. It's always amazing to me how the students will jump right into this, and, after some direction from the teacher, they will handle it beautifully. As an added plus, it encourages them to pay attention more closely to the story so that they'll know how to react accordingly.

- Allow students who make an A on their Revolutionary War history test to have their hands "tarred and feathered." The students love this! Basically, just use molasses and feathers, and the students will think it's the coolest thing ever!

- Have your class attempt to get in the *Guinness Book of World Records*. The chances are slim, but having them research to find a task you could possibly complete is a great lesson. Have them turn in proposals in the form of research papers, and then walk them through the steps of what accomplishing this feat would entail, and stress the importance of working together as a team. If you actually are successful, that is an event your students would never forget for the rest of their lives.

- If you read a book with a detective (e.g., *Harriet the Spy* or *Encyclopedia Brown*), you can collect an item from a number of teachers in the school and have the kids try to figure out what item belongs to what teacher based on clues and research.

- Add a spark to everyday events. Administrators who walk the halls each morning should switch it up one day and actually skateboard through the halls! The students will love it, it will add passion to the school day, and the administrator might actually earn cool points.

> • Give students something to look forward to. When we all have something exciting on our horizon, it makes life more exciting. One example of how you can accomplish this is to have an annual academic competition that students compete in each year. Build it up as a huge event, and point out the past winners. It will give students something to look forward to and a great goal to shoot for!

20

Teach children that the good you do in the world comes back to you.

When I travel with students, I research ways that they can volunteer and contribute to the communities that we visit. As a way to reward their efforts, I try to provide them with one big surprise each trip. When I was taking students to South Africa, the big surprise was that the students were going on a safari. I thought that was the coolest surprise ever!

As we prepared for the trip, I had the students read Nelson Mandela's autobiography, *Long Walk to Freedom*. They offered some minor complaints about having to read such a long book, and I quickly let them have it. I explained that there is no way in the world I was taking them to South Africa without their having read that book. I told them that Mandela is a symbol of freedom around the world and that the story of apartheid is one that they had to know in great detail.

They apologized and said they understood and joined with me, valiantly, in the effort to read and comprehend the entire book, its meaning, and its significance to the world.

When we finished, the students said, "Mr. Clark, we figured out what the surprise is for the trip to South Africa."

"You did?" I replied. "Well, what is it?"

To my shock, they said, "We're going to meet Nelson Mandela."

My eyes bulged as I quickly said, "No, we're not," but the kids kept at it.

"Mr. Clark, we *know* we're going to meet Nelson Mandela. Why else would you have had us read that entire book?"

All I could say was, "For real, ya'll, we're not going to meet Nelson Mandela. He is like eighty-eight years old; it's just not happening."

While we were in South Africa, we spent many days working in AIDS orphanages. One afternoon during a break, we took the students to the Hector Pieterson Memorial and Museum, which is in honor of a young South African boy who was killed during a peaceful rally against apartheid. After months of preparation, the students knew the history of the young man in detail, and it was rewarding to watch them walk through the museum with such an awareness and depth of understanding. We were the only individuals there that day, and suddenly I heard a great commotion outside. I walked to the front door and saw a series of black sedans pulling up. A black helicopter was hovering overhead, and there were children running from everywhere. I walked outside and heard the children yelling, "The king is coming, the king!"

No.

I could not believe it was happening.

Nelson Mandela. Symbol of world freedom. Former president of South Africa. Author of *Long Walk to Freedom*. It just couldn't be real. My heart was racing! Could it really be?

A swell of passion, excitement, and nerves overcame me. Suddenly my students flooded around, and we saw the back door to one of the sedans open, and out stepped Nelson Mandela. We all just about fell out. The students turned to me screaming, "Mr. Clark! We knew it! We knew you got Nelson Mandela!"

I didn't take my eyes off him as I made out, "I had nothing to do with it."

As he walked toward us, I looked at my students to see they were crying and holding their heads down. They were completely overcome. They knew the history of that man. They knew his pain and his struggles, and through his words they had spent twenty-seven years with him in prison for his attempts to gain freedom for his people. If they hadn't learned so much in-depth information about apartheid and the history of South Africa, they would have only said, "Oh, wow, there's Nelson Mandela."

In fact, it was almost too much for them to take. As he walked up to us, I said to my students, "Look up, hold your heads up, now!" They wiped their eyes and slowly looked up. Mr. Mandela walked up to one of them, a tall, skinny boy named Brandon. He looked him right in the eyes and asked, "Why do you look so hungry?" Brandon's mouth just dropped, he didn't even have an answer.

That encounter was unlike anything I have ever experienced. That night we sat in a circle as we always do each night on our trips, to discuss our day, our feelings, and the things we observed and learned. The kids asked, "Mr. Clark, did you really not get Nelson Mandela to come meet us today?"

I explained, again, for the hundredth time, "No, and I am not going to tell you again: I had nothing to do with it."

The kids weren't going to give up so quickly, and they added, "But Mr. Clark, it just seems so weird that Nelson Mandela happened to show up at that little tiny museum where we just so happened to be making a quick stop. It just seems so unbelievable."

I then told the students, "For the past week we have been working in AIDS orphanages, and you have given your heart, your time, and your spirits to uplift and help others. Sometimes in life, when you work so hard to help others, good things will come back to you. Perhaps that is why Nelson Mandela happened to come to us today."

That is the overarching message that we hope to instill in all of our students. Give back, make a positive impact on the lives of others, and the joys you feel within and the way it will uplift your spirit will provide you a lifetime of unexpected rewards.

I later heard from our tour guide, Arthur, that he found out why

Mr. Mandela was there that day. He was visiting a dear friend, the older sister of Hector Pieterson, at the museum. Arthur told me that in all of his years as a tour guide he had never had a group so blessed to be in the presence of Nelson Mandela. He also added that in all of his years traveling with groups that he had never been around such warm and wonderful children. He said he was glad that it was our group that received the honor. He said our students, above all others, deserved it.

At RCA, we work hard to inspire our students to constantly ask themselves, "How am I affecting the lives of those around me" and "How can I give back to the greater community?" We know that if we can get them into the habit of volunteering at a young age, they will continue to give back for a lifetime. Therefore, we have them volunteer at homeless shelters, sing carols at senior homes, paint community centers, run clothing drives for the battered women's shelter, and give back all over Atlanta and the surrounding areas.

If we want to raise children of character and compassion, we must instill in them a desire to help others. When I think back on some of the most wonderful parents I have met during my time as a teacher, I recall families that studied together, ate dinner together, and volunteered together. When I see a mother, a father, and their two young sons shoveling mulch around the trees of a local community center, I instantly know that when those boys are older they are going to have their families be involved with similar projects. It may only seem like a few hours on a Saturday afternoon, but it can have a lasting impact on the way our children view the world, see those who are in need, and accept their role in making a difference in the lives of others.

☆21☆

Teach children to embrace their personalities and present themselves with confidence in all situations.

When Kim Bearden and I began the process of starting the Academy, we just knew we were going to have to have a tremendous amount of support from the community of Atlanta. I honestly thought that I would walk into the major corporations here, tell them our idea and vision, and they would write out million-dollar checks with ease. I know, I can be naïve, but I just couldn't imagine that everyone wouldn't want to support a dream that could help children. The fact that we couldn't even get corporations or foundations to take us seriously hurt me. Many told us that we needed to be in operation for multiple years and have an endowment before they would consider funding our school. I thought that was the craziest thing I had ever heard, because if we had an endowment we really wouldn't need their funding. I found out, however, that start-up schools have a history of failing, and no one wants to put money into a project that isn't going to succeed. It was suggested that we work hard to build a base of community support. Through the support of numerous members of the community, we would then gain credibility in the eyes of larger donors, corporations, and foundations. To build the support and get the word out about RCA, we were advised to hold a major fund-raising gala.

I met with a lady in the mayor's office to find out the process for getting Mayor Franklin to attend such an event. Her first question was, "Who is your event planner?" and I just said, "Well, me." She smiled politely and then suggested I call Amanda Brown-Olmstead, adding that if anyone is throwing a party in Atlanta they just must, must have Amanda Brown-Olmstead as the event planner. I set up a meeting to talk with

Mrs. Brown-Olmstead, and I arrived at her house for our meeting at 4:00 p.m. sharp. I was asked to wait in the living room of her home, a mansion on West Paces Ferry Road.

Thirty minutes later, I heard a world of barking and commotion, and then, there she was. Mrs. Brown-Olmstead walked in like something out of a Disney cartoon. She was tall and elegant with a sculpted face and a dramatic fur swept around her neck and fell all the way to the floor. She carried one poodle while five others circled around her feet. She walked right up to me, stuck out her hand, and said, "You must be waiting for me. I'm Amanda Brown-Olmstead. Am I late?" I could tell she really wasn't expecting an answer.

She was unlike anyone I had ever met in my life. She sat down with me and began to tell me all the reasons why we needed to enlist her services with the planning of our party. At the end she stated, as if it were common knowledge, "Dear Ron, the main reason why you need me to throw this party for you is because I'll be there. And if any party is going to be a party, it needs Amanda Brown-Olmstead to be there."

Uhh, I didn't know what to do. The phone rang and as she went to grab it, she said, "Here, hold Poodles," and she placed the dog in my lap. As I sat there with the dog barking and snapping at my face, she talked about orders for flower arrangements and how if the color of the chairs for some event wasn't the correct color of puce that heads would roll. It was all very surreal, and my head was spinning. I finally made a snap judgment and told her that we would love to have her help us throw our party.

Her response: "Of course you would."

Over the next few months, Mrs. Brown-Olmstead said that we should attend every social event in Atlanta in order to build our reputations. She said the more friends we made, the more people would attend our gala. I will never forget our first event. Kim and I didn't know anyone in the entire room, and it all seemed so stuffy and proper. Everyone was standing in circles talking, and no one seemed approachable. Kim and I stood by ourselves and just chatted in the corner until we finally saw Mrs. Brown-Olmstead slicing through the crowd like a hot knife through butter. A string of fruits dangled behind each of her four-inch heels; I had never seen anything like it. We knew that if she saw that we weren't mingling, she would fuss at us, so we hid. Yep—we ran and we hid.

Honestly, I have never been shy a day in my life, and I am usually comfortable around everyone, but learning how to mingle with wealthy people who you are going to have to ask for contributions isn't easy. Kim and I now look back and laugh about it, but for weeks, we would go to events and waste time talking to each other instead of approaching potential donors. We were nervous and not confident, and with all I've experienced, deep down I'm still little Ron from the dirt roads of eastern North Carolina who was raised with a true Southern upbringing, where asking for money is just unheard of. I felt that there was something fake or phony about chatting up our would-be/could-be donors.

Finally, at one event, Mrs. Brown-Olmstead found Kim and me standing behind a huge hibiscus plant. She said, "What a disappointment you are. Pull yourselves together and get out there while you have some semblance of dignity left."

I said, "Mrs. Brown-Olmstead, these people are stuffy and hard to talk to."

She said, "Ron, just because these people are stuffy doesn't mean you have to be stuffy, too, in order to have a conversation with them. Don't let them dictate who you are or the way you behave. Go out there, be yourselves, and be excited to tell them about your school. Now go out there and make me proud."

We walked up to a group of ladies who were dry and boring, but I jumped into the story about the school, describing how it was going to be full of passion, color, and energy, and soon the ladies were laughing and enthralled with our stories and vision for RCA. We were ourselves and it worked. We ended up telling the ladies that we could use their help and asked them if they would consider attending our gala. Surprisingly, they said they'd love to. In the end, they, along with hundreds of others we met, attended. As Mrs. Brown-Olmstead promised, it was quite a party, and we ended up raising more than $500,000 for our dream. It happened because we overcame our fear, put ourselves out there, told people what we needed, and had someone amazing to help us, like Mrs. Brown-Olmstead. We learned quickly that the worst someone can say is no.

A couple of years later, I had our first students at RCA with me at an event at East Carolina University. The room was filled with quite a few stuffy-looking individuals, and I quickly turned to them and said, "Kids, just because these individuals may seem stuffy, you don't have to be. I want you to go around in pairs of two and meet these individuals and let your personalities shine. Work this crowd like Bette Davis in *All About Eve* [okay, they were lost on that one] and make me proud." I could see the fear in their eyes, but they said, "Yes, sir," and took off. Ten minutes later, I looked around the room to see smiling faces. The students were impressing people with their charm, their respect, and their energy. It was beautiful, and it became one of the most valuable lessons we now teach all of our students at RCA: how to work a room!

In life, 50 percent of success comes from the knowledge we have obtained, but the other 50 percent deals with how we play the game. How we present ourselves and our ideas is extremely important in the eyes of would-be employers and business partners. People want to work with those who are articulate, polished, and professional in appearance. We must work harder to teach our children the rules of "the game" and how it is pivotal to their success. "Working a room" and being comfortable in that setting is a priceless lesson to teach our young people.

Do This:

At RCA we conduct an activity that I strongly suggest that every school consider. We invite members from the community to participate in the "Amazing Shake." The community members are placed throughout our school, but it can easily be organized in a gymnasium. Each individual is at a different station, and the students are instructed to go up to each person, make an introduction, including a handshake, and then proceed to the next person along the obstacle course. The individuals present different challenges.

One person has his right hand bandaged, one is in a wheel-chair, and others are engaged in activities such as reading or talking on a cell phone. In one obstacle, a lady has dropped a stack of tissue boxes. Do the students help her collect the boxes and then proceed with the introduction or do they first introduce themselves and perhaps not pick up the boxes at all? Every move they make and the way they handle every situation is scored by the community member on a scale of 1–100. As the child walks on, they add a note or two beside the score about how the child could have handled the situation better. When children walk out of one room, they are instantly asked by a member of our staff, "Can you tell me the name of the lady you just met in that room?" If they recall the name they are given bonus points.

After every child has completed the obstacle course, we meet as a school and the visiting community members explain how each child could have handled their station perfectly in order to receive the full 100 points. They always stress eye contact, a firm handshake, and the power of smiling. Students who score the highest, they say, seem to have a confidence and a joy about themselves, and do not appear rehearsed or fake; they seem genuinely happy to meet them.

To finish the activity we announce the top twenty scores. The student coming in first place wins the Amazing Shake and receives a briefcase that is donated by the community members. Students are later given the comments about their performance so that they know specific areas where they need additional practice.

When you meet an RCA student, you can tell because they are indeed polished, but it doesn't come easy. It takes work, but it's too important to their future success not to make it a priority. As I have traveled the country meeting high school seniors I am often deeply disappointed that almost 90 percent of them can't give me a firm

(continued)

handshake, look me in the eyes, and speak with confidence. If they can't do it for us, they won't do it during that scholarship interview or when they are trying to obtain an important job. We have to make it a priority.

If you can't get the entire school to buy into the activity, you can invite members from a local business to conduct the activity with just your classroom. If that isn't possible, you can at least greet your students with a firm handshake as they walk into your classroom each day. Insist that they make eye contact, shake hands with the appropriate firmness, and smile. Encourage them to be themselves, to be natural, and to let their light shine.

Live with no fear.

As a young child, I struggled greatly when people died. I remember praying for them to come back to us. Once I realized that wasn't going to happen, I found something that finally helped to ease my pain. I decided that I could live my life in a way that would honor those who had passed away. I realized that they no longer were presented with opportunities and vowed to remember that fact as new chances and doors were opened to me. I told myself I would always go for it and live life to the fullest.

As I got older, I learned that when you "go for it," generally the worst that you come away with is a very good story.

As a bonding experience, I decided to take the students on a zip line adventure. Upon arriving at the top of the mountain, we looked around to see that clouds surrounded us on all sides. We were shown a big cable attached to a huge tree that stretched all the way across a vast gorge,

2,000 feet across; it was attached to another tree at the top of another mountain. The guide told us that we would hold on to a little bar as each of us traveled all the way across the gorge on the cable.

Okay, so I freaked. I am terrified of heights and thought I was going to pass out right there. I said, "Wow, kids, that is going to be a wonderful experience for each of you. Make sure you keep your eyes open so that you can enjoy the view. I'll be waiting for you at the bottom."

As I turned to head back down the mountain, the kids said, "Mr. Clark, you're not going to do it?"

I quickly said, "No. It's not happening."

Their eyes grew large as they huddled up to me and responded, "We're not doing it, either!"

But I said, "No. I want ya'll to do it. Come on, now."

One by one, I had to get in their faces. I said, "Come on, Brandon, you can do this! Think of all of the things you have faced in life. Think about how strong you are. This is nothing compared to what you have been through. Come on, buddy, I believe in you."

Brandon looked me right in the eyes and through sniffles he mumbled, "All right, Mr. Clark. I'll do it." He took hold of the bar, and the guide attached a rope to his waist. If Brandon did let go, he would only fall ten feet before the rope would catch him. He would then have to climb the rope to get back to the cable and pull himself to the other side.

Suddenly, Brandon was off! *Pheeeeewwwwwwww!* He went flying! I had no idea how quick it would be. I counted, and it took about forty-five seconds for him to reach the other side. As I stared intently at him, he became smaller and smaller and smaller, to the point where he was only a tiny little dot. When he arrived at the other side, 2,000 feet away, that dot jumped up and down and up and down.

One by one, I got in the face of each child, saying, "You can do it! You don't have time for fear. You don't want to regret that you didn't do this!" And one by one, they took their journey across the gorge.

And then, they were all gone. And I was by myself.

Crap on a spatula.

I realized I had to do it. I could feel the sweat building on my palms, and I felt a little faint. Please, no. I just couldn't, but I knew that if I were going to speak the words *no fear,* I had to live the words *no fear.*

I told the man I would do it. He hooked me up in half a second and told me to hold on tightly to the bar. He asked if I was ready, and I said, "No, I need just a few minutes."

So he said, "Here you go!" and pushed me with all his might. GOOD GRIEF!

I was flying, wind rushing at my face, tears pouring out of the corners of my eyes. My eyes, by the way, that were shut tighter than a tick. I just started counting, 1, 2, 3. I knew when I reached 45 that I would be there. I just had to get to 45. And then I was at 27, 28, 29, and felt myself starting to slow down. At 30, 31, I almost had stopped completely. I said to myself, "Hmm. I must have gotten to the other side quicker than the students did."

I opened my eyes to realize that I had stopped dead in the center. I was hovering 2,000 feet above the ground holding on for dear life, and about to explode from panic. I remember that the man told us that about one out of every hundred people would get stuck in the middle.

Great. Are you kidding me right now? Just great.

He also told us that if it happened to us, we should remain calm, turn around, and pull ourselves to the other side. It's at this point when I tell this story that I like to turn around, put my hands over my head, and walk backward as fast as humanly possible because no words imaginable can match how quickly I was pulling myself across that cable. Boy, I was flying!

When I reached the other side, I was met with screaming applause and hugs all around. The students were so proud of me. Wasn't it supposed to be the other way around? I guess not. I guess sometimes we have to be the ones who are vulnerable. We have to be the ones who have to face the fear because, when we do so, we're setting a different type of example for our children.

After that first zip line, I learned that I actually had to do seven more zip lines to get to the bottom. It seriously was torture, but, honestly, after that day, I seemed to walk with more confidence and more pep in my step. I just kept going back to that day and retelling myself over and over, "You really did it, and if you did that zip line, you can do anything!" I felt as though I could conquer the world, like nothing could hold me back.

Imagine how the children must have felt. That experience must still be living within them to this day as it lives within me. There is no telling how the zip line changed their outlook on life and the way they view themselves.

Not all of us can take our kids to a mountaintop on a zip line, especially with liability issues. In rare cases it might be approved, and occasionally it could be approved as a weekend event that isn't supported by the school, but in most cases you have a better chance of building the mountain than getting the event approved. What we can all do, however, each and every time we interact with children is to encourage them to live without fear, to show them that we believe in them and challenge them to go for their dreams. Whether they doubt they will make the cheerleading squad, don't feel that they can make an A on a test, or are terrified to take an honors course, we can be there to support them, to cheer for them, and to get in their faces and say, "You can do it!" Because when they finally "get across that zip line," the rewards on the other side will instill pride and confidence within them that will last a lifetime.

In January 2011, when Atlanta had a snowstorm that actually shut down the city, I was at home working hard on this book. I received an email that afternoon from a producer at CNN saying they were doing two segments that afternoon and that they desperately needed me to come to the studio to be part of the interviews. Honestly, I was curled up in my Snuggie (Christmas gift from my father; don't start), and I wasn't thrilled at the idea of putting on my suit, spiking my hair, and going out in the freezing cold, treacherous weather. I always tell the students never to pass up a great opportunity, though, and so I wrote back and said that I'd be thrilled to participate. I asked for the topic, and her email response was quite shocking: child beheadings in Acapulco and deaths due to drug-related issues in Mexico.

I sat there wide-eyed. What? All I would have to say during the interview would be, "What a shame." I mean, what else is there for me to talk about? I certainly didn't want to get into any gun control vs. gun rights debate, and I had no idea why they would even want me to discuss that topic anyway.

I wrote her back and said I wasn't sure I was the right person for that interview, but she wrote back, "Are you kidding? You are perrrrrrfect!!!!" She added that the piece was thirty minutes long, and that I was the only person being interviewed. Well, I freaked. I started running possible comments through my mind: *Perhaps if the drug lords had better teachers, they would know better.* Argh, this was going to be a train wreck . . .

I picked out my suit and jumped in the shower. Before I ran out of the house, I went back to the computer one last time and emailed her to say that I was on my way to the studio to do the interview if they really wanted me to (because I knew the exposure could help the school), but I would feel more comfortable in the future discussing education topics rather than issues like child beheadings in Mexico.

Within seconds, she wrote back, "OMG. I thought I had emailed Don Clark from the FBI! Forgive me!"

I almost showed up at that studio with bells on, ready to debate Mexican drug crimes. They would have put me on camera and introduced me as Don Clark, FBI expert, and I would have gone pale. I can see me right now, "I am so sorry, ya'll, but I'm a schoolteacher." Crisis.

The point is that I knew it was an opportunity that could help RCA, and I was willing to go for it and do it. Sometimes we just have to put ourselves out there and take a risk, regardless of how strongly our emotions are telling us otherwise.

In the classroom it may mean dressing up like a historical figure, changing your voice to sound like a character in a novel, singing or rapping a song about academic content, or standing on your head to reward outstanding achievements. The point is that we must show our children that we aren't concerned with what others think of us and we will do anything to help them succeed. If we allow them to see that we are concerned with how they think of us, we are setting a bad example and possibly placing that mentality in them as well. At RCA, because the teachers dance with wild abandon, the students follow suit. Because I become the characters in the novels, the students transform their voices as well. Because we don't care if people hear that we can't sing, the students sing loudly. And when we show them that we're not embarrassed to admit a mistake, or that our staff loves one another, or that we are excited to learn each and every day, our students take on those characteristics as well. They are watching our every move, and they are learning who to be by the examples we are setting. We owe it to them to live with no fear, because in doing so we are giving them the belief that they, too, can live with strength, courage, and the absence of concern about how they are perceived by others.

From Rebecca Price, Teacher

My visit to RCA in the spring of 2009 transformed my teaching and my life.

I teach fifth grade in a high-poverty elementary school with a high percentage of minority students. Before visiting RCA, I had been struggling with not knowing how to effectively reach the students in my class.

After visiting RCA, my colleagues and I could see that we were allowing our fears of appearing to be silly in front of our students to hold us back from truly reaching our students.

We spent the six-hour drive back home talking about and identifying key standards and concepts in math that we felt the students were struggling with. We took a few of the standards that wove together and created a song that taught the students how to turn fractions into decimals to the tune of "Apple Bottom Jeans." I abandoned my inhibitions and fears, climbed on desks and chairs, got the attention of every single student in my classroom, sang like there was no tomorrow, and taught each and everyone of them how to turn fractions into decimals. The greatest moment for me came during our ISTEP [a standardized test] when, unexpectedly and out of the blue, I looked around the room to find more than half of the students humming "Make fractions decimals around the room . . . divide the dem into the num . . . add decimals . . . bring on the O's . . . and divide it out out out out out out out." Beautiful!! :)

From that, I went on to write a song about the three branches of government and how each branch works together to the tune of "My Lip Gloss," as well as a song about the events that led up to the War of 1812 to the tune of "Soldier Boy." I continue to take every opportunity to think "outside of the box" and really dig down deep to reach the students. My work is paying off in great ways.

I also adopted seven of *The Essential 55* and call them my "non-negotiables." These seven expectations are visible throughout the room and are revisited often for clarification and understanding. The students know I'm a tough teacher. They know I don't take excuses and that I expect them to find solutions to their problems. They know I will help them with finding solutions and expect great things from them. They know that I care deeply about them and their learning and will do whatever is necessary to help them become successful learners in a challenging world.

Thank you for allowing me the opportunity to slide down your slide, meet your students, embrace the differences in us all, and know that it's okay to step outside of myself and do whatever is necessary, even if that means being silly and fearless.

—Rebecca Price, fifth-grade teacher,
Caze Elementary School, Evansville, Indiana

✶ 23 ✶

Love what your students love, whether it's *iCarly, Twilight,* or the NFL.

As parents and teachers, if you want to get closer to your children, you have to be able to have a conversation about things they care about. When I first started teaching, my students loved the Goosebumps books. The last thing on earth I was interested in reading was a Goosebumps book, but I did it anyway and actually found some enjoyment in the stories.

The next day at school I asked a group of students during lunchtime if they had read the book, and a few had and a few hadn't. The ones who were familiar with the book jumped into a great conversation with me about whether or not certain parts were scary, and the students who hadn't read the book became interested and said they wanted to read it, too. It was great, and I could feel instantly that I was more connected to those students.

My nephew, Austin, loves Rock Band Hero, and he is really good at it. During a visit home, he asked me to play it with him, he on the guitar and I on the drums. He was outstanding, but I looked like an idiot. We played for only about twenty minutes, and I had very little success. We had to play well on a certain number of songs before we could move up a level in the game, and with my poor performance we weren't moving anywhere.

When I got back to Atlanta, the first thing I did was buy one of those game consoles, and I practiced and practiced. When I went back home to visit, we played again and Austin fell out! I truly impressed him, and we went on to play for several hours and master several levels. Instead of being a nerdy adult who wasn't on his level, I improved my skills in order to earn his respect, and it worked.

When our first group of RCA students became eighth graders, I wanted to do something special for the girls. Our school is designed to appeal to our students, but as our teenage girls matured, I wanted to add something to the school that would be just for them. I asked myself, "What do these girls love more than anything in the world?" and the answer was clear: boys. Not just any boys, but "the" boys: Taylor Lautner (Jacob from *Twilight*), Justin Bieber, Trey Songz, and a whole host of athletes, actors, and singers. Hmm. How could I use their attraction for those boys appropriately as a positive thing in our school?

I thought about it for a long time and I wasn't sure if this was appropriate or not, but over the weekend a group of us gathered dozens and dozens of teenybopper photos and posters of the boys. We made sure all of the photos were proper, of course, and we hung them all over the girls' bathroom. By the time the girls arrived Monday morning, the entire bathroom was covered with photographs of heartthrobs. I wasn't sure what the reaction would be, but I know that if students love something about a school immensely, it can completely change their attitudes about the environment. I hoped the additions to the bathroom would help them love RCA even more than they already did.

After hanging every picture, I placed a note on the bathroom door that said:

> Always remember that you are strong, beautiful, and intelligent beyond belief.
> No man will ever have control of who you are.
> Know that I will always love you and see the best in each of you.
> From: Mr. Clark

I went to my room and began to get ready for the day. As students started to arrive, I waited anxiously in my room. Who would be the first to see the bathroom? What would the reaction be?

I noticed that there were students in the loft, and I wasn't sure if someone had been to the bathroom. If they had, then there certainly had been no special reaction. Then suddenly it happened. I heard the loudest unbridled scream I have ever heard in my life. I ran to the door and looked down the hall to see Krystal Morbeth running out of the bathroom clutching her chest. She bent over, breathing heavily, then, in the blink of an eye, rushed full steam back into the bathroom, thrusting herself through the door.

Hilarious. I went back to my work, and one by one I heard scream after scream after scream. Girls would run out of the bathroom, grab other girls as they arrived at school, throw their book bags across the lobby floor, and drag them with wild abandon up the stairs to the bathroom, screaming, "You will *not* believe it! *Hurry!*"

This picture shows only a handful of the more than fifty pictures that grace the walls of the girls' restroom.

Soon the girls calmed down and came rushing into my room. I was bombarded with hugs. "Thank you so much, Mr. Clark! We love it," they exclaimed.

Over the next few days, I noticed that the girls had posted a note on the door to the bathroom: "Do Not Kiss the Pictures! You are wearing out the lips and they are starting to fade!"

I also noticed a different energy from the girls. They were excited, smiling, and almost glowing. And they truly appreciated the bathroom. One of the girls, Dasia, said to me, "Mr. Clark, that bathroom showed us that you really care about us and realize who we are right now in our lives. Thank you."

As parents and teachers, we need to make sure we know who we are teaching and raising, and we need to make sure our eyes are opened wide to who they are, where they are in their lives, and the ways in which we can become closer to them through what they love.

✳ 24 ✳

Create lasting traditions.

At the end of our first year of operation, Mr. Kassa planned a grand surprise. We were meeting in Kim's office, and when we walked outside to pick up our classes for our next lesson, the school was completely empty. There was no one in the halls, the classes, or at the front desk. It was a ghost town!

We ran through the parking lot and up and down the halls, but there was no one to be found. Finally, opening the door to my class, we saw the entire school jammed in my room. *"Surprise!"* they screamed. What in the world? We had no idea what was going on as Mr. Kassa called us up to the front of the room. He began to speak about how hard he had seen Kim and me work to get the school started, and pretty soon he began to cry. And then Kim and I cried, and soon the whole room was a mess. He presented us with a plaque that stated he was naming that day "Founders' Day" in honor of the work we did to start RCA. Kim and I were touched, but starting our school was in no way a job completed by two people. We have an incredible group of board members, one of the most dedicated faculties in the world, a gem in Mr. Kassa, and parents who loved their children beyond measure. And we had a group of people who Kim and I felt were the true founders of RCA: our first class of students. The wheel, the slide, the cheers, the drums, the music, the passion, and all of the traditions were created by us all, including the children. And they were the inspiration behind it all; they were the true founders of RCA.

Osei Avril, Willie Thornton, Chi Chi Ugwuh, and Ahjanae Colson, RCA Class of 2010.

Several years later, during the week of RCA's first graduation, we took the entire school outside and had them sit on the grass where a large sheet was covering a 5-foot-by-5-foot space at the front of the building. Kim and I spent a few minutes talking about how much we loved each of the graduates, and as we told them we would be celebrating Founders' Day in their honor, we removed the sheet to reveal a plaque engraved with each of their faces. Underneath, we listed each of their favorite memories from their time at RCA.

Of course, everyone cried. I recall Jule saying, "Oh, my gosh, I feel like a civil rights leader."

We all laughed, and I told Jule, "Maybe not a civil rights leader, but each of you has made an impact on this school and on thousands and thousands of educators and students around the world. The memories you said were your favorites will remain on this wall forever, but they will also remain in our hearts for a lifetime."

Before those students left RCA, we videotaped images of them smiling and created videos of what basically looked like a head shot, although the students were moving occasionally, ever so slightly. We then hung five portrait-sized TVs above the entrance to the hallway on the first floor of our school. As those students excel in high school, and throughout the rest of their lives, we will update their video on a screen. It's almost as if they are looking down over RCA's current students, encouraging them, and giving them the hope that one day their portrait will hang above those halls, much like the portraits at Hogwarts. It's our "muggle way" of always keeping the spirits of our graduates in our school forever so that the good deeds they are doing can be shared with all. It's also our way of keeping a legacy on the wall that will inspire future generations of RCA students.

Do This:

Teachers who want to create a similar reaction can take head shots of their students who have made the honor roll for the entire year. They can place those pictures on a bulletin board in the classroom, and year after year the group will grow and grow. Students will want to leave their picture on the wall at the end of the school year as well, and it will inspire them to achieve the grades necessary to do so.

On the last day of school you can also have your students write individual letters to your next class of students. The "Dear New Fifth Grader" letters will offer words of advice and encouragement for the year and can be passed out on the first day of school.

You can also have the students write letters to themselves titled, "Dear College Graduate," and instruct them to give words of congratulations and describe the person they hope they have become when they receive their college degree. You should then add a few words to the end of the letter, letting the students know what you think are their greatest qualities. Then seal the letters and hang them at the back of the room, attach them to a bulletin board, or tape them all around your desk. Tell the students that they can only receive the letter, and read your comments, when they come back to your classroom and present their college diploma.

PART II

The Role of the Parent in the Success of the Child

No person is more important in the life of a child than the parent, and when it comes to educating our young students, the teachers and parents must work together at all times. At RCA, there are certain things we ask of our parents in order for them to help us help their children be successful. When parents take heed of this advice, we always see tremendous growth in the child, both academically and socially.

✴ 25 ✴

Be prepared for the long haul if
you want your child to succeed.

When new parents ask me what is the key to having their kids be successful at RCA, my answer is simple: work hard. There is really no magical formula, it's basically just hard work on the part of everyone involved. I try to explain to the students and their parents that we work hard and push ourselves to the extreme now so that we each can live an educated and successful life in the future.

Some parents get it, and they don't make excuses or put off hard work; they buckle down and set examples for their children. They show them what it means to study, to spend hours a week reading, to do extensive research beyond what is required, and to do what RCA expects of them. Some parents, however, aren't ready to take on the responsibility, and I have come to the realization that we, as a school, can do but so much. When the message does not seem to get through, it can be heartbreaking and frustrating.

I recall a student who wasn't passing his classes and rarely did his homework. He came to RCA as a struggling learner, and we let the parents know it was going to take a lot of work to get him where he needed to be. They told us they were on board, and the mother cried and hugged me so tightly. The father looked me in the eyes and said that our school was a blessing in the life of their family and that he would do all in his power to support our mission and help his son.

Four months later, their son—we'll call him "Joe"—was failing every subject. Our staff met with the parents repeatedly and offered multiple suggestions for ways that they could help their son. At one meeting, the mother looked at me and said, "You know what, Mr. Clark? We aren't worried about that test on Friday, because we know he is going to do well. We are putting this in the hands of the Lord, and we are going to pray." I replied that it was wonderful to pray and to have faith, but that it was important for them to also put forth the effort required and to do their parts to make sure Joe was studying each night. The mother said, "Mr. Clark, you don't understand. We are going to put this in the hands of the Lord, and He will be there taking the test with Joe on Friday. The Lord will see him through."

Again, I stressed the importance of using the study guide and reviewing the notes along with making flash cards. No response.

He failed the test.

Through many meetings after that, we heard the same response each time. The parents didn't show up to tutoring nights, and they didn't follow through with what we asked them to do with their son. In the end, he failed almost every subject, did not pass his grade, and did not return to RCA the following year.

It was a difficult blow for us. We want all of our students to be successful, and when we put forth our best effort and it isn't enough, it is devastating. There are times when the parents are not involved at all with the academic side of their child's life, and we are still able to have success. Many times, however, if the parents aren't completely on board, it can make helping the child succeed nearly impossible.

The best parents at RCA are the ones who realize that they have to make constant sacrifices for their children, and making time for their child comes before everything else. They realize that nothing you can watch on TV is more important than spending an hour with your child reading, going over homework, or playing Monopoly. Years from now that TV show, basketball game, or movie will be far from your memory, but the bonds you form with your child in those moments last a lifetime.

Do This:

Parents:

- Limit chaos in the mornings. You want it to be drama free so that your child starts school with a calm spirit. Even if you aren't a morning person, force yourself to get up early and start the day right.
- Take the time to read everything that is sent home from school. When your child isn't prepared, it causes him or her to feel stress.
- Watch educational channels instead of more popular shows.
- Develop relationships with other parents so that you can call with questions and form study groups.
- Use the time in the car to discuss what your child is learning in class. Listening to music is more fun, and you may have things to think about, but getting your child in the habit of sharing the knowledge he is learning in class will help him greatly in the long run.
- Review all homework assignments . . . do not DO all homework assignments.
- Go to school events where parents can participate— spelling bees, plays, basketball games.
- Give your child "surprise" encouragements, like a small note in their lunch box that only they will see or know what it means. You can even get the Rice Krispies treats now where there is a designated message spot.
- If your child is learning an educational song, you learn it too and rock out together on the way to school!

From Antone's Mom

As parents of RCA, we know we need to be flexible at all times and willing to do whatever it takes to help the school and our children be successful. During the presidential elections, RCA gave a new meaning to flexibility.

I was out grocery shopping with my infant daughter and received an email from Ms. Mosley via my PDA at 11:05 a.m. She said, "Parents, I need your child's dress uniform at RCA by 12:30 p.m. because our students have a potential opportunity to meet with Barack Obama."

My first thought was OMG! The people in the grocery store must have thought I'd lost my mind. I left my cart where it stood, filled with groceries, and ran out of the store, baby in tow! I got to my house in record time, grabbed the uniform, and took off. All I could do was call my cop husband and tell him to tell his buddies, "Don't stop the speeding white car down 85 South; it's a matter of national security!"

I made it down to the school at 12:15 p.m. Keep in mind, I live over an hour away.

As parents, we have to do whatever it takes, whenever it takes it, to support our children and the school. It may mean working with flash cards until midnight, volunteering to sew uniforms, talking positively about the school in the community, or sending words of appreciation to the teachers. Whatever it takes, we do it because we know it will help our children in the long run.

—Mrs. Williams, parent, Class of 2012

* I have a side note as well. When I sent out an email asking parents to submit stories like the one above for certain sections of this book, I received an outpouring of support. During the night before this manuscript was due, I sent a "tweet" that I was working hard to finish everything that night. Mrs. Williams emailed me at midnight saying that she would stay up all night if necessary to support me

and that she would send as many stories as I needed. She sent dozens of great ones, and the one above hit my email box at 2:30 a.m. That is the type of commitment we receive from our parents at RCA. It's a dedication that comes from the soul, and when you have people like that in your corner it makes us, as teachers, want to work even harder to help their children.

—Ron Clark

Don't be a helicopter parent.
You can't come to their rescue forever.

In 1983, less than 11 percent of adults aged twenty-five to thirty-four were still living with their parents. In 2010, that number had skyrocketed to almost 43 percent. What in the world is happening in our country?

Parents have a natural instinct to protect their children and come to their rescue. But as our children grow older, it can become a problem if we intervene too much on their behalf. I recall my dad telling me that when he was in school, all it took was one negative word from the teacher and his butt was torn up in good fashion at home. I think most adults can remember those days when the teacher's comments were respected and accepted without question. I wish more of today's parents carried that level of trust in their children's teacher, because what we have currently—parents who want to fight every battle with the school system and to question every action by their children's teachers—is greatly harming our education system as a whole and teaching children to expect that someone is going to save them every time.

We look at our twenty-something individuals in our country today and wonder why they are still living at home, unemployed, and not responsible for their actions. I think it is because they were raised to believe that their parents will always take care of any problem that they encounter.

I beg of those parents, *Please stop raising soft children.*

I remember meeting with a young man's parents at RCA. The boy had copied another child's homework, and the evidence was pretty strong; it was a multiple-choice sheet and both boys had selected E for question number 8. The choices ranged only from A through D.

The boy even admitted to me that he had forgotten to complete the sheet and that he had copied off his friend's paper that morning. He was given a zero on the assignment and a day of after-school detention. Well, here come the parents. They were livid and assured me that their child would never cheat on an assignment. The mother even went so far as to tell me that she completed the homework sheet with her son at the kitchen table the night before.

I explained to the parents that their son had admitted that he didn't do the work and that he copied the other boy's paper, but the father told me that he had admitted to cheating only because he was nervous. I sat there dumbfounded. I asked the mother why when they were working on the assignment at their kitchen table they had selected E as the answer for number 8, and she said that they knew the answer was D but for some reason he had written down E. The answer was B. The father told me that if I punished his son that I would basically be calling his wife a liar, because she was telling me that she had completed the work with him.

As I sat there, I could see in her face that she wasn't being honest. The child had already admitted he cheated, the other child admitted he copied his homework, and I could tell the parents weren't being truthful. I wasn't sure what to say, so I let them know that I would give the situation some more thought and get back to them within twenty-four hours but that there was a strong possibility that the punishment would stand. Well, with that comment they were furious. They told me I was being unfair and ridiculous. The father was sitting there with clenched fists, and honestly, I just wanted it to go away. As I sat there, I kept thinking about all I had done for that young man and his entire family, from helping with Christmas presents to keeping the lights turned on in their home, to tutoring them all in their home to raising funds so that he would have a scholarship to our school. And, honestly, if I did all that and they could still not have enough respect to trust me and to accept the punishment, then I can only fear what teachers around the country must be going through with their students' parents. In order to "make it go away," I know most teachers and administrators ignore problems (bullying, cheating, misbehavior) because they don't want to deal with the drama. They just want it to go away, and I did, too. I said to them, "Allow me to think about this tonight and to consider all you have had to say. I will give you a call tomorrow to discuss."

Can I please just go to Krispy Kreme now and watch American Idol *and pretend it all never happened?*

I wanted so badly to cave in, but I didn't. I knew that by going forward with the punishment that I was essentially telling the parents that I knew the mother was lying about helping with the homework, but I just couldn't let it go. I called their son into my office and told him that I would rather him make a zero on every assignment than to lie to me. I told him that his self-respect was worth more than any grade, no matter how high, if it wasn't earned. I asked him if he had ever copied anyone's homework before, and he told me that he had copied the same kid's homework once before. I followed with, "So that means you have done it twice," and he responded, "Yes, sir."

That was enough for me. I called the mother and let her know the punishment would stand and that I appreciated her respect and understanding of my decision.

She hung up on me.

Some of you reading that story may think those parents sounded insane and irrational, but when it is your child, things look a lot different. It may not be a cheating scenario, but today, parents all across our country are going to schools in droves to complain about everything from low grades to a lack of playing time on an athletic team. You may think the parents in the story seem unreasonable, but in the right situation, that parent could be you.

Why was I so adamant to make sure the punishment stood in that situation? It's because the situation and the principle are bigger than that one instance, and I don't want that young man to go through his life with the expectation that every time he is in trouble, his parents will come and bail him out. Or that his parents will be able to bail him out of every situation that does not go his way.

Parents: Sometimes you just have to let your child take the punishment. It will teach a lesson and build character. If you are always coming to the rescue, kids will learn that they can get away with anything and that their parents will save them. It happens all over the country, and it has started an epidemic where you ask a child if he did something and you get, "What? Who, me?" Yeah you! The excuse making is something that starts with the parents but it trickles down to their children quickly.

I was in a similar situation a few years ago when two young girls received their first C's in their life on their report cards. I actually thought the grades were great for the standards we have at RCA, but these girls were frantic. I pulled them in my office and explained that I wanted them to remember how it made them feel to receive the C's and told them that sometimes falling short of our own expectations can be life's best motivation. I encouraged them to work harder during the coming nine-week period and said that I felt confident they would both be on the honor roll next time.

Well, "Angela's" mom called Ms. Mosley and asked her to set up an *emergency* meeting with Kim and me. We fit it in the schedule for the afternoon and asked her what in the world was going on. She said that Angela was devastated to make a C and wanted to know what they could do for extra credit to pull the grade up to a B so that her daughter could be on the honor roll.

Parents need to learn that there is a difference between supporting and interfering. Asking for extra credit once the grading period is over, or almost over, is annoying. Deciding that you need to be involved in the education of your child only when the grading period comes around is frustrating for teachers. It becomes a hindrance instead of being supportive.

I explained that I don't give extra credit. She then asked if Angela could redo her essay answers on her last test for extra points. She said she knew that Angela understood the content because she knew the information at home. She said she had no idea why she didn't put the correct information on the test.

I explained that allowing her to redo the essays wasn't part of the school's policy and that it wouldn't be fair to the other children. She then asked if I could take one of her lower quiz grades and have it count toward the next nine weeks because Angela was actually sick the day of the test. By this point, Kim and I were done, and we told Angela's mother that the grade was going to remain a C and that, hopefully, it would inspire her daughter to try harder in the next nine weeks.

People, would you believe she came back the next day? She had found a quiz of Angela's that she claimed was graded incorrectly. I met with her and, to be honest, she had a point. Angela had numbered her answers incorrectly, and I counted four of the problems as incorrect when you could make an argument that really only one of them was incorrect. That changed her grade from a 60 to a 90. As the parent sat there pointing out the error, she looked pleased as punch and quite proud of her efforts. I apologized for the error and told her I would immediately adjust the grade. It did, indeed, change the grade to a 79.6, giving the child an overall grade of 80. She made the honor roll.

During the next nine weeks, however, she did not. She ended up making C's in three of her classes. Her mom showed up again, but I think she realized it was a losing battle when so many of her daughter's grades were low. Angela cried and cried and looked as if the world were going to end. Honestly, I don't think her tears had as much to do with missing the honor roll as they had to do with her anger that her mother wasn't able to get the grades changed. She probably didn't work that hard that nine weeks, either, because she expected her mom to come in and save the day.

What happened to the other young lady who also received her first C?

She made the honor roll, and I have a strong feeling she did so because she realized that no one was coming to her rescue, and so she found a way to be successful.

I know we have to support and defend our children, but if we do it every time and while wearing "perfection blinders," then we are building our students up not to know how to handle failure. They will be twenty-five years old, jobless, and still turning to their parents to make excuses for them and to bail them out.

From Robin's Mom

Parents must always take the teacher's side (unless they have physically hurt the student). I think one of the biggest problems we have today is that the parent always takes the child's side immediately, and there is not enough support for the teacher. I think we as parents do our children a big disservice when we do this, because then we send them out to the workforce unprepared to deal with a boss. Much to my children's chagrin, when they have come home with stories about a teacher not being "fair," I have always taken the teacher's side. Of course, if I ever heard a story where I thought my child was right and the teacher was wrong, I would intervene. But let me say this: my oldest daughter is twenty-three years old, and I haven't intervened on behalf of any of my children yet. For the system to work, we have to put our faith and trust in our teachers.

—Mrs. Okunowo, parent, Class of 2013

✳ 27 ✳

Realize the power of gratitude and appreciation.

Parents I meet around the country will often ask, "What do I do when my child is stuck in a classroom with a horrible teacher?"

The quick answer is, "Give presents."

Seriously, I am just keeping it real. When people feel appreciated and that their efforts are noticed, they work harder and do a better job.

I remember that I couldn't stand my eighth-grade history teacher. He would sit behind his desk and chew tobacco while we worked out of textbooks. He was only interested in talking about shooting deer and the upcoming NASCAR race, and I just could not relate. When he would give grades, everyone would receive effort grades of A or A+, and I would always get a B. That was completely ridiculous, because I worked just as hard, if not harder, than everyone else. The kids who were barely passing other classes but were well versed in NASCAR and hunting were getting A's in effort. I felt as if the universe had been turned on its axis.

The teacher also loved the Duke University Blue Devils, but I, as a Tar Heel fan, utterly detested them. However, I knew that for Christmas, I had to get him a good present and do my best to try to form some sort of relationship. I told my mom, and we bought him a Blue Devils cup set along with a Duke hat. (Forgive me, Tar Heel Nation!) I made a point of handing him the present personally and saying, "Thank you for being a good teacher. I have learned a lot from you this year."

When I walked into his class the day after the holiday break, he slapped me on the back and said, "What's up, my man?" I was so shocked I just said, "Nothing much," and sat down quickly. It stung, people! But it was his way of interacting positively.

During the next six weeks, he became much nicer to me and my effort grades suddenly became A's. My effort, actually, did not change. The only thing that changed was that gift. Perhaps he perceived that I didn't like him or that I wasn't trying in his class, but by giving him the gift and telling him I appreciated him as a teacher it made the relationship much better. I am not saying this strategy will work in every situation, but appreciation goes a long way, and it can never hurt.

Each year, I take my fifth graders to Washington, DC, before the Christmas break. On the final night, we usually do a "reward trip" where the students who have been the best behaved and who have worked the hardest go on a final night on the town with a few of the chaperones.

One year, we decided to take the group to see the White House Christmas tree one final time. The students had seen it from afar, but I thought it would be cool for them to see it up close. It was getting late, however, and by the time the sixteen of us walked all the way to the White House, it was past ten. In an effort to save energy, the Christmas lights had been turned off early, and there we stood at the foot of a plain, dark tree.

The students looked devastated, but I said, "You know what? This is a wonderful opportunity for us to walk over to the White House gate and to look at the home of our president one final time." We walked to the gate and began to reminisce about all of the history we had learned throughout the year.

As we looked up at the White House, one of the students, Tiara, said, "Mr. Clark, they really should get some security out here. Anyone could just jump this fence and run right up to the front door of the White House." I laughed and explained that I was sure there were fifty to one hundred security guards out there. I told her that if we jumped the fence, that Secret Service agents would appear out of the trees, from under the ground, out of the bushes, and from every which way.

Tiara said, "Well, Mr. Clark, that is some kinda nice of them because it is cold out here, and I wish I could thank them for staying out here so long in the freezing cold to protect the president."

I said, "Well, Tiara, I am sure they heard you because I have no doubt that they have bugged this entire fence and that they are listening to us right now."

Tiara and all of the kids went wide-eyed and their mouths dropped. Then suddenly, they all leaned into the gates and started talking, "We just want to thank you for all you do to protect our country," and "It's wonderful for you to be out here in the cold," and "Thank you for protecting our president, even though a lot of people don't like him right now." I stopped them and told them not to mention anything negative about the president, because we wouldn't want anything that we said to be perceived as a threat.

The kids said a few more thank-yous, and we started to walk off, when suddenly, a man in a long black trench coat appeared and said in an authoritative, deep voice, "Everyone turn around and face the fence."

My heart sank. Darn, what did one of these kids say? We turned to face the fence and many of the kids took hold of the bars. Wow. I just dropped my head. Our reward trip night on the town suddenly seemed like a very dumb idea.

Then the man spoke again, "Wait . . . wait . . . wait . . . okay, look up on the top of the White House." We all looked up to see more than a dozen silhouettes of Secret Service agents who were on top of the White House stand and wave at us. All of our mouths dropped in shock. The guards then turned on a huge spotlight from the roof, and the kids and I were suddenly surrounded with bright light as if it were the middle of the day. We slowly raised our hands to wave back, and we all tried our best to force smiles.

In an instant, the lights were off and the silhouettes were gone. We turned around, and the man in the black trench coat was no longer there. We turned to one another and immediately huddled together in shock. We remained attached as we hustled quickly back to the hotel in one big shaking mass! We must have walked for four blocks before we finally stopped, looked at one another, and burst out laughing! The kids screamed, "Mr. Clark, did that just happen?" and, "That was amazing! This was the best night of my life!"

I turned to Tiara and said, "You caused that. By showing appreciation and how much the effort of the Secret Service agents meant to you, they

gave us that wonderful holiday 'hello' in return." Tiara smiled from ear
to ear.

Do This:

If you are in a situation where your child has a teacher you are unhappy with and showing appreciation doesn't work, there are other
strategies you can try.

- When you are upset, avoid contacting the teacher by
  email. The tone can be misconstrued and lead to bigger
  issues. Schedule a meeting in person.
- Document attempts to reach the teacher, especially if
  they do not respond. It will be easier to plead your case
  if you have documented communication attempts.
- Speak with the teacher first before contacting the principal. The first question the principal will ask is if you
  spoke with the teacher about the matter, and if you didn't
  it will reflect negatively on your part. Follow procedure
  and give the teacher a chance to remedy the situation
  first.
- Never speak negatively about the teacher in front of your
  child, because if he sees you don't respect the teacher,
  he will feel it's okay for him to show disrespect in the
  classroom.
- If your child complains, remind him that he will have
  many different types of teachers in his life and that part
  of the journey is learning how to be successful no matter
  what the circumstances.
- Maintain a joy of learning in the home. Find ways to
  supplement the curriculum and make sure the light for
  learning does not dim in your child's eyes.

> • Consider having every teacher in the school fill out a survey of their favorite things and keep a book of them in the front office. Check it often to find ways you can surprise, support, and show appreciation for your child's teachers.

✳ 28 ✳

Remind children of their blessings and stress the value of a strong work ethic.

Parents and teachers can never do enough to teach children about gratitude. Children need to be reminded constantly of how fortunate they are to live in a country where they have the chance to get an education, live in a free society, and have an opportunity to be successful through hard work.

Whenever our students at RCA want to tell me something isn't fair or that another child got something better than they did, I tell them that if they really want to talk about fairness, then we should compare the situations of all fourteen-year-olds in the world to make sure that everyone is being treated fairly. Then we discuss areas around the world where children don't have enough food to eat, education is not provided, children are working in sweatshops, and some children have been separated from their families. I point out that it appears we are doing quite well and really should be embarrassed about having any complaints at all.

Children need to be reminded of all they have to be thankful for. A family friend's son was using his iPhone at Christmas. I commented how lucky he was to have one, and his response was, "Oh, my parents were cheap and got me a used one, and it's only sixteen gigabytes." I told him that that was the most ungrateful comment and that if I were his parent, I would take the phone away from him immediately. The parents were sitting right there. They said nothing.

What is going on with our society? Seriously, if we allow children to be ungrateful and to expect too much, then we are setting ourselves up for failure and disrespect.

One way to get children to recognize the need to appreciate what they have is to have them volunteer in the community. Another way is not to allow your child to have TV, telephone, video games, or other luxuries for a certain period of time. It is as if parents are afraid to punish their children or to take away any luxuries. Doing so doesn't make you a bad or a mean parent; it makes you a strong parent who is setting expectations and doing what is right.

Parents, remember, you are in control, and you dictate what happens in your home. If you don't want your child to be disrespectful or rude to you, then you have the power to stop him or her. You need to put your foot down, to lay the ground rules, and to stick to your guns. Don't tell your son that you are going to take away the phone for a week and then give it back in two days because his behavior improved. Even worse, don't threaten to take the phone away for the rest of his life because you know that isn't a threat you are willing or able to carry out and your child will see right through the empty threat. If you want to earn respect, you have to show that you are in control. If you let your ten-year-old have authority over you, then your opinions, demands, and rules will seem meaningless when he or she is a teenager. Stop being afraid to be in charge of your house, your child, and your life. Sometimes doing what is right isn't doing what is easy.

We implemented a tradition at RCA to instill the ideals of hard work and appreciation in our students. When we first started giving our students RCA sweatshirts, we found that they didn't appreciate them at all. They didn't have to work for them, and they didn't have to buy them. They were given to every student, and we ended up finding them lying around all over our school. The students showed no appreciation or ownership of them at all.

Around the same time, we had an idea to order RCA letterman jackets for our students, but we wanted the students to have to earn the jacket, much like varsity sports players earn them after being a solid member of the team. We approached two of our donors who we love dearly, Tom and Alicia Maxey, and suggested the idea. They quickly agreed, saying they especially loved the idea of having the students earn the jackets.

A jacket for every child was purchased, and in November we started the tradition of having "jacket days." At the end of school each Friday during our school-wide meetings, we would announce that certain students had earned new RCA jackets. We would then make a brief speech about each child. (Whenever you are about to praise or give something to a child, such as an award or recognition, it's a great idea to tell wonderful things about the student, building up the suspense, and then to say the child's name in the end.) The speeches would go like this:

"This young man has impressed us so much this year. He has not only displayed academic excellence, but he has also shown us that he has great character, determination, and compassion for others. He is a shining star at our school, and we are so proud of him. Please join me in honoring him as we present him his jacket. For your heart, your effort, and your contributions to this school, we present you with your jacket . . . Mr. Derius Hulbert."

We usually give five jackets on the first "jacket day," and the students are thrilled. They run to the front, give Mrs. Bearden and me hugs, and we place the jacket on them as the rest of the school cheers. The first day is special, but it pales in comparison to the days that are to come.

After seeing the first group get their jackets, the other students are very eager to get theirs, so much so that it seems to consume their thoughts. They become very intent on finding out exactly what they have to do to earn their jackets. We tell them that each week everyone of their teachers vote, and that for a child to receive his or her jacket, every

teacher must have voted "yes" that the child has put forth tremendous effort and deserves the jacket.

The second week, around another five kids will obtain their jackets,
and, usually on that day, several of them will cry in joy. They will run out
to carpool at the end of the day, thrilled to show their parents the jackets.

By the third week, I look out at my fifth-grade class to see ten students proudly wearing their jackets and the other twenty students trying
to do all they can to pay attention, work hard, and earn their jackets. On
that Friday, another handful of students receives their jackets, and by this
time, tears and snot are all over the floor.

Many parents will tell us that the kids refuse to take off the jackets
and that they sleep in them. The students glow with pride as they wear
their jackets, and not one is ever left behind or thrown idly around the
school. They are symbols of pride and quickly become the students' most
prized possessions.

In the following weeks, there were times when a few kids earned their
jackets and there were times when no one received one. We don't cave to
pressure and just give the kids their jackets because we feel sorry for them
and don't want them to feel embarrassed. We want the students to truly
earn the jackets. If we just give it to a child who hasn't earned it, it means
so much less.

There have been times when I know we gave certain students their
jackets too early. How do I know? I can tell because when they come
up to get their jackets, I can see it in their faces. They aren't crying, and
their smiles aren't completely full. They just seem pleased. When other
students, who I know have truly pushed themselves and given all they
have, get theirs, however, the look on their faces is priceless. It's one of
accomplishment, honor, and pride. It is impossible to describe. At times
they will hug me so tightly and hold on for what seems like an eternity.
They cry into my chest and shake with joy.

It has taken some kids more than a year to earn their jackets. One
young man just couldn't get it together in terms of academics, respect,
discipline, and treatment of his classmates. He was, quite honestly, a
handful. Each week I would meet with him briefly to tell him the ar-

eas he still needed to work on, and I would give him words of encouragement. It took him so long to earn that jacket that I didn't want him to lose hope. Eventually when his name was called, that young man had truly earned that jacket, and he cried. I expected that. I cried, too. Also expected. What I didn't expect was that I looked around to see his classmates, boys and girls, crying for him as well. It was beautiful.

That boy received his jacket during the first week of June, but, sure enough, he showed up the next day sporting that jacket, in 90-degree weather.

To be honest, we still find RCA sweatshirts all over the place, but we never find RCA jackets lying around. They are treasured because they were earned, and that makes them become irreplaceable and precious. Some may say it's cruel to have students go so long without receiving their jackets. They will say that if some students don't have their jackets and the others do, it will hurt their self-esteem and demoralize them. When those children are older, however, they will find that all adults don't receive the same paycheck and the same rewards. Those who work hard are the ones who benefit, and that is the lesson we are teaching our students at RCA. Is it a difficult lesson? Yes, but it creates a lasting impression and the results equal hard work, appreciation, and a true understanding of what it means to earn what you receive.

Do This:

Make an effort to tie items you purchase for your child to his behavior at home. If the room isn't clean, the chores aren't done, and there are disrespectful moments, you shouldn't feel the need to purchase anything special for your child. I know of one parent whose child was being lazy during the summer. As a punishment, she said her child would not receive new clothes or shoes for the upcoming school year. As parents, we all know we have to buy new clothes for our children for the school year . . . or do we? If they don't earn

(continued)

it, why not let them wear what's already in their closet? One mother I know, Ms. Saab, bought new clothes for her daughter's first year of high school. When her daughter talked to her in a disrespectful tone, she told her daughter to take off the clothes she wore to school, wash them, and wear them again the next day. She said, "You can wear that same outfit every day until you learn to be respectful." I saw her a week later and she said, "Mr. Clark, things are lovely in my home, no issues at all." Sometimes it takes being tough, and we can't feel guilty for taking back the authority from our children.

One of our parents was frustrated because her son didn't want to study at night. She was a wonderful mother who always had a home-cooked dinner on the table. Her son, however, was given a hot dog to eat each night until he decided he wanted to study. If he worked hard that afternoon, he ate with the family. If he did not, she warmed a hot dog.

Parents, do what you have to do. You are in control, and we have to teach our children that in order to receive rewards, they have to put forth the effort and have an attitude that is respectful and appreciative.

29

Nip it in the bud; small issues can grow into big problems.

It can be very hard as a parent to take advice from teachers on child rearing. You have your own beliefs about how to handle certain issues and I understand that. But I do wish parents would be more open to suggestions as we sometimes are the first to see the problems.

When a child is ten years old and she is already responding with comments like, "I know, Mom," in a sarcastic tone, and getting away with it, that child is going to be a handful when she is thirteen. Children will get away with as much as we allow, and if parents don't maintain strict discipline with children as they are approaching their teenage years, they will surely be in for a challenging experience.

I recall a student named Robert, whom I taught before I started teaching at RCA. He was so disrespectful and short with his parents. During a home visit, I recall seeing him roll his eyes and mumble when his parents would ask him to sit up straight or speak up. They looked like it didn't really bother them. I told them that they shouldn't allow that type of behavior, but they said that they had pointed out to him that he was being disrespectful and they weren't sure what more they could do. I told them that they had to show him that they are the bosses of their house! They had to punish their child and show him that the level of disrespect he displayed would *not* be tolerated. They told me they didn't think it was that bad.

I had success with Robert in fifth grade, but he showed minor tendencies toward disrespect throughout the year. I told his parents, but they did not react or seem to take it seriously. In my class he had success, however, because he knew in my room it wouldn't be tolerated. I set the boundaries and he didn't cross them. In his home, however, there were no boundaries and he was free to do as he pleased.

Over the course of the next few years, Robert ended up being suspended multiple times for being disrespectful. I watched him get into a fight when he was in the seventh grade for being arrogant with other students, and that boy almost had his nose beaten off his face. I, along with other teachers, had to pull other boys off him. I still remember sitting in the principal's office with him, holding a wet cloth to a cut on his forehead as blood streamed down the whelps that covered his face. He was trembling, sweating, and a complete wreck.

Robert ended up at an alternative school and did not graduate. As the years passed, I saw his parents several times at the grocery store and in passing in town. They looked worn and tired. They always smiled, and we would hug. I recall his mother telling me that Robert was running with the wrong crowd and in trouble with the law. She said that they tried to talk sense into him, but he didn't pay them any mind. I told her I would reach out to talk with him and that I was sorry for what they were going through, but I really wanted to say, "The reason he doesn't listen to you now is because he didn't listen to you when he was ten years old and you did nothing about it. You let him run your house and disrespect you and, therefore he isn't about to listen to you, respect you, or care what you or anyone else has to say now."

I know that sounds horrible of me, but it's the truth. We are the adults. We are supposed to be in control of the situation, not the children. We have to guide them, to teach them respect and manners, and to keep them on the right path. And if they start to rebel and show signs of disrespect at a young age, we have to put an end to it quickly and make sure we are establishing a relationship where it is indisputably clear that it will not be tolerated.

When I tell parents now that I see disrespect creeping in and that we need to put an end to it at home and at school, I am so grateful when I have parents who support me and are on top of it. I know that not every child is going to turn down the road Robert took, but I also know that kids will get away with as much as we allow, and if you enable kids to have authority over you with sarcastic and rude tones and words, then you are opening yourself up for much more. When parents don't take my advice and continue to allow their children to have so much control and to talk back and show disrespect, it just breaks my heart.

As parents, you are in control, and you have the ability to get your children to treat you, and others, with dignity. The key, however, lies with stopping the behavior before it grows into a demeanor that is too habitual, accepted, and ingrained to reverse.

Behavior is a learned habit, and how your children treat you is caused by what you teach them is acceptable. Practice makes permanent in the mind of a child, for better and worse.

From Kylie's Mom

I recently had someone ask me my thoughts on having my child attend a school that placed so much focus on respect, manners, and discipline. Without hesitation, I said I was completely for it. He was a little surprised and asked me why I didn't contemplate the question before answering. I thought briefly and explained that in my family, the teachers see my child more than I do and I have to trust that they are looking out for her best interest. In the same way that my ex and I co-parent, I feel that the school is the unrecognized third parent in the co-raising of my child.

After this conversation, I really started to think about how Kylie's time is broken down and here it is:

On average, Monday through Friday, Kylie spends ten hours a day at school, including after-school activities. For the same days, she spends three to four hours a day with me. On the weekends, her time is split between our house, her father's house, and friends' houses. All in all, my child spends fifty waking hours a week at school and about thirty waking hours a week with me. Knowing this, it thrills me that during the majority of her waking hours, there are twenty teachers, staff, and faculty members that are all teaching my child not just the basics of reading, writing, and arithmetic, but life skills—things that will help her long after she graduates from this school, high school, and college. Things such as honesty, manners, respect for herself and others, kindness, compassion, and the ideas of giving back to others and your community are but a few of the life lessons that I try to instill at home that are reinforced at school. These things don't cost a dime, just a little bit of time, but the investment is priceless.

—Mrs. Andrews, parent, Class of 2013

✳ 30 ✳

Don't get your kid a video game system
unless you are ready to be a prison guard.

Video games are no longer just a reward or an occasional form of recreation; they have become an integral part of our culture. Our children are consumed by them, and this can have a negative effect on every aspect of their lives if we aren't supervising them closely.

When kids are young, they are so eager for school. Getting them to do homework can even be effortless and enjoyable. They see school as fun and exhilarating. Then the battle begins. When children obtain video game systems, that suddenly becomes the definition of "fun." Nothing can compete with it, and school and homework quickly become things that stand in the way of the enjoyment. Everything else becomes boring, and trying to get a child to go from playing in a virtual reality world with wizards and machine guns to sitting in a chair reading a book is like trying to get a cow to walk backward. You might accomplish it, but it's going to take some effort, and you definitely aren't going to make friends with the cow.

It can be an overwhelming challenge to teach our children that their imagination is far more powerful than the images they see on TV or in a video game, but with the way the games are looking these days, that is becoming a tough argument.

I am not saying that children shouldn't have video games because, honestly, if you had taken my Atari from me in 1984, I would have ripped all of my Michael Jackson and Cyndi Lauper posters off the wall and cried into my Millennium Falcon pillow for days. The important point to make, however, is that I was making straight A's. As long as students are performing well in school and only playing the games in moderation, there isn't really a problem. The issue I have is that the students who are playing the games the most are often the ones who aren't successful in school. And those who are playing video games while still being successful in school often aren't choosing to try out for athletic teams or to volunteer for community service.

I taught one student who is probably one of the strongest academic students I have ever encountered. He never earned anything less than an A in my class, but all of his other time was spent playing video games. His mother told me that they have a deal that as long as he is making straight A's, he can do whatever he wants in his free time. When that student became an eighth grader, we started filling out his paperwork for scholarships to private high schools. When we got to the page where we had to list extracurricular activities, we had to struggle to think of anything to write at all. There just wasn't a category for "Super Mario: completed level nine." When I tried to talk to prospective schools about giving the child a scholarship, most of them said they were looking for children who were more well rounded.

Honestly, I know we are all fighting an uphill battle if we try to take away video games completely. For those of you who have managed to keep them out of the hands of your children, I applaud you and thank you for your willingness to be the bad guy for the sake of your children. For those of you who have allowed video games in your homes, you have to be strong and lay down the law. Don't assume that because your child is polite and doing well academically that the countless hours your child is spending playing the games is okay. You have no idea the opportunities your child is missing because of the time in front of those games. By having the games do so much of the thinking for our children, we are not giving them the opportunity to use their own imaginations, and the worst part is that we'll never know where their own thoughts would have taken them.

If you are a parent who feels like this is a battle you just can't win with your child, remember that any tool that can be used to distract can also be used to engage. Perhaps encourage your child to enter a video game tournament; that would promote interaction with other students his or her age and provide the opportunity to discuss sportsmanship. Sign your child up for workshops that discuss the industry behind video games and inform your child about how video game technology is being used in operating rooms, on the space shuttle, in the military, and in science labs around the world.

The types of games you allow your child to play are also important. Studies have shown for years that playing a musical instrument can improve memory retention, test scores, and academic success. While playing Rock Band Hero isn't exactly the same experience, it can help children with hand-eye coordination and how to understand rhythm.

When selecting the games your child plays, make sure to avoid the games that are violent. Studies show that teens who play violent video games for extended amounts of time:

Tend to be more aggressive

Are more prone to confrontation with their teachers

Engage in fights with their peers

See a decline in school achievements

An alternative would be one of the dozens of games on the market today that deal with ancient times and the history of the world and involve strategy and understanding the culture of the time period. When a child wants a certain game, it can be challenging to steer him toward another choice, but this is when it is important to remember that you are the parent. You are in charge, and you are running the show, not your child.

✳ 31 ✳

Show them how to study;
don't expect it to come naturally.

Some years ago I realized that although I spent a tremendous amount of time preparing students for the upcoming test and encouraging them to study each night, I was often desperately disappointed with the test results. When my students do poorly, I always look to place the blame on myself and ask, "What could I have done better?" This time, however, I felt as if I had done everything I could to prepare them, and if they just would have studied at home, they would have been fine. I decided to ask the students to show me exactly how they studied. The results were a crisis. Students said they just looked over the notes (translation: they just stared at the page), and others said they copied the notes over (translation: they just copied word for word from one page to the next without paying any attention to the meaning), or they admitted they really didn't study very much (translation: they didn't even remember there was a test).

I decided that it was worth the time to spend an hour actually teaching my students how to study. The first step was to show the students how to study one page of notes at a time. I placed a page of notes on the document camera so that the entire class could see it. I then read through the notes with the students and told them to turn to a neighbor and try to tell him or her as much as they could remember from the page we just read. Well, the students looked at me like I was crazy. They said that when we read it as a class that they didn't know they were supposed to be remembering the information. Good grief. I asked them what they were doing when they were "looking over their notes" at home, and they let me know that they were doing just that—"reading the notes" with no expectation of really retaining the information. To me, that was a no-brainer; to kids, it isn't always so obvious. Regardless, I asked the students to tell their neighbors as much information as possible, and after they had finished, I suggested that we read the page again together. Now that the students knew that the expectation was to retain as much information as possible, I wanted to see if they could improve. When the students turned to their neighbors the second time, there was a tremendous improvement in the amount of knowledge they were able to share.

The students learned that a great way to study is to read over the notes (one page at a time) and then to share the information with a family member or study partner. Some of the students told me that it was hard to get someone to help them study, so I told them that they could use the same strategy on their own. They were told to read half a page of notes and to then turn to a blank page and jot down all of the key points they could remember. They were then asked to turn back to the original page to see how much they were able to remember. If something was left out or wasn't jotted down correctly, I told them to highlight that information and then to try again and again until all of the key facts were recalled and translated to the blank page correctly. They were told to continue the process throughout all of their notes.

Another strategy that I suggest is to use as much color as possible, drawing pictures and highlighting information in various shades to help them recall the information easier. For example, if a child is studying the battles of the Revolutionary War, they should write each battle and all of the subsequent information in the same color. For example, the information about Lexington and Concord would be all in blue, and the page on the Battle of Yorktown would be in red. When the student tries to recall information about the Battle of Yorktown, he then only has to recall all of the information that he wrote in red. Anything in blue wouldn't even register as being associated with that battle.

If students are learning information that comes in a certain sequence, such as the events in one of Shakespeare's plays or the time line of a president's life, I encourage them to write each significant event on a flash card, then shuffle and try to place them in the correct order on the floor or the table.

These strategies may seem like common sense, but they aren't so obvious to our children. Taking the time to show them how to study and retain information is a valuable lesson that when mastered will help them for the rest of their lives.

Do This:

Parents, you can also make the process of studying fun. You can tape key bits of information underneath the toilet bowl seat, on the milk carton, and in the sock drawer. Organize study parties where you invite the four smartest children in your child's class over to your house. You want your child at their level, so by surrounding him with the best in the class, you are helping to push him to that expectation.

Of everything you do as parents, the most important aspect of helping children study at home is to remain positive and upbeat. If you approach learning the information with a fun and confident attitude, your children will follow suit. If you act defeated, tired, and impatient, you are in for a long night and a horrible experience for you both.

From Cameron's Mom

RCA is constantly opening Cameron's eyes to new and exciting things, and it seems to give him energy and ignite all his senses. I decided to raise the bar at home as well, and, instead of making study nights and homework boring, I decided to find my own way to "fire it up." So, when big study nights come, Instead of staying home, we try studying at coffeehouses, parks, and even an old, historic church. We've been to the Carter Center, Morehouse College, Emory University, and lots of other, nice, free places that are a wonderful change of scenery for the whole family. We look forward to those evenings and weekend study dates. Most times we start out not knowing where we will end up. Sometimes we end with a treat like ice cream or a ten-flavored slushy from QT. It's our own version of a reward trip.

—Mrs. Nesmith, parent, Class of 2012

From Kylie's Mom

This year Kylie has Mr. Clark for global studies, easily her worst subject. She struggled all last year with this subject and is again struggling. She studies and we engaged the help of a tutor, but still, she struggles. I contacted Mr. Clark near the end of the first quarter to ask for some study tips because she was really not doing well at all. Instead of simple tips, he offered to come to our house to see how she was studying and offer improvement strategies. I'm not sure why this surprised me so much, but given his extremely tight schedule, time has got to be a most precious commodity.

When he arrived, we offered some dinner and Kylie pulled out her notebook and they began to study, and I watched. I watched him interact with my child. I have been studying with her nightly, creating flash cards, reviewing her notes, sending her off to a tutor (who is also part drill sergeant)—all having little impact. They sat opposite each other and I watched him listen to her. They talked and joked, but mostly, he sat patiently. He asked her very simple questions relating to the subject matter and listened to her. It seems like such a simple thing, but as a parent studying with a child, I don't think I ever stopped to listen to her. How does she learn? What things did she think of that might help her remember the subject matter? Colors? Pictures? I never thought of these things as a way to help her retain information. I felt very inept and was keenly aware that no matter how hard I tried to help my child, I lacked some essential tools, one of which was the simple skill of listening. That's why he is a teacher; he not only teaches the child, but he will also teach the parents or anyone else who is willing to learn.

Aside from listening, he allows kids to be kids, another trait that is sometimes lacking in the world. As he allowed her to come up with her own associations for the material, they came to Claudius (a Roman emperor supposedly murdered by his wife). He asked Kylie for a way to remember the story. After a moment of silence, she had that lightbulb "aha!" look and said, "I got it! Your name starts with C-L-A and Claudius starts with C-L-A and you just ate dinner with us, so I can think that we poisoned you just like Claudius's wife did with mushrooms." She was so excited, and I think Mr. Clark and I were slightly stunned, and then we laughed. I promised him that we did not poison him, and he took it all in stride and said, if that's a way she can remember, then that's fine.

Kylie and I still laugh about this, but it also reminds me to slow down and listen; to wait for her to develop her own system of learning and work with her in that way.

As parents, we often want to dictate how our children will study, but, as Mr. Clark showed me, sometimes it's best to sit back, to observe them, to listen, and to let them be the guide.

—Mrs. Andrews, parent, Class of 2013

32

Realize that even
very good children will sometimes lie.

Come on, now. As a child, you lied to your parents to get out of trouble. I lied to my parents to get out of trouble. We all did. Why then, do so many parents these days find it beyond belief that their own child would lie? It blows me away.

I have experienced countless parents who are determined to stand up for their children, even when it is obvious that their child has lied. The typical phrases are:

"But my child doesn't lie."

"It's not like my child to lie."

"Well, he's never lied before."

And, my personal favorite:

"I know my child, and I can assure you that he wouldn't lie about something like this."

Okay. Wow. Really? Kids lie, people. And when they are backed into a corner, they can be extremely convincing. The stricter the parents are, the more likely it is that their kids will lie to get out of a situation, because they know the punishment is going to be severe.

I hate when I tell a parent things that I saw students do at school, and the parent turns to the child and says, "Is that true?" That is completely undermining the teacher's authority. I will tell some parents things that have happened and they'll say, "That's all I need to know," and they are off to the car with the kid, and I can tell that child is in a world of trouble. Some, however, will sit there and want to hear the story from the child, and then they want me to get any other kids who might have been present so that they can hear their versions of the story as well.

Listen, teachers have no reason to lie. They are not at risk of being punished. We are telling you about a problem in order to help you and because you need to know what your child has done. Please understand that going to you with unpleasant situations that involve your child is not easy for us because we know what your reaction is most likely going to be. Given that knowledge, if we still feel strongly enough that we need to sit down and share the information with you, it's something we feel is important for you to know. Unless you have a concrete reason to think otherwise, believe us and then please handle it at home.

We had a situation at RCA where two students were apparently holding hands while heading to a basketball game in one of our vans. Now, that seems like nothing, but at RCA, it's a crisis. We are 100 percent focused on education, respect, and self-discipline, and even handholding is going to receive punishment. Both of the students admitted to us that they held hands for about thirty seconds. They both told all of their friends that they had been holding hands as well; it was common knowledge. Three other students even admitted that they saw them holding hands. I called the parents and let them know what happened and what the punishment would be.

I thought it was over, but the next day, the boy's parents came in *furious*. (If I could make that word in 20-point font, with red fire and horns coming off it, I would. That would be a more accurate description of their demeanor. Just italicizing the text is in no way cutting it.)

They said that their son told them that they never were holding hands and that everyone was lying. (I can see it right now. He walked in that house terrified and when the parents went to punish him, he lied right through his teeth.) I told the parents that I was 100 percent sure it happened because even their son had admitted it, but they told me they know their son and that he doesn't lie to them and that only God can know things at a rate of 100 percent.

They said that since I didn't see it, I couldn't punish him for it. I tried to tell them that they needed to realize their son wasn't being honest, and the father looked at me and said, "The way you are handling this is pitiful! *Pitiful!*"

I felt as if I had been punched in the face. I just took a breath and continued to listen as the father ranted on and on about how his son's character and the character of their entire family were in question. I waited, patiently. When he was finished, I waited a second and then calmly said, "I understand your concerns, and I would like to talk with your son again. Give me some time to give the situation greater consideration." I also told them, as I often tell students and parents, that I would rather take some time and make the right decision than jump to a decision that isn't fair or appropriate for the situation.

So I talked with the child again, and when I asked him if they had really been holding hands, he just dropped his head and said, "No, sir." He couldn't even look me in the eye.

Not only had he lied to his parents, but their influence in the situation had caused him to lie to me, too. The child had been honest with me the first time. His character was spot-on. The parents, however, caused him to be dishonest and in the process damaged his character.

You love your children, I know, and it kills you to think that they would lie to you, but it happens. It doesn't mean they don't love you. Actually, sometimes it means that they love you so much they can't bear to hurt you, but it does happen. Trust your child's teacher. They are with him or her every day, and they have no reason to lie.

33

Be patient.

I was in the middle of writing this book, and I had a ton on my plate. I was at my parents' home, and my mom asked me to go with her to spend the afternoon visiting a friend of the family who has a tendency to be a tad bit annoying. I quickly told Mom that I couldn't possibly go because I needed to devote every possible second to finishing this book. Mom realized that she would be fighting a losing battle with me, and so she quickly turned to my dad and said, "Ronnie, I guess that means you'll have to go."

"Oh, hell no," he replied, and then added, "Ron, you go with your mom, and I'll write the damn book."

Good grief. We all laughed, but then I finally gave in and said I'd go with mom. To my surprise, when I returned home, my father, who loves NASCAR, poker, Westerns, and Fleischmann's gin, had kept his word. My laptop was open on the kitchen table and he had actually gotten on there and typed out a full page, and I decided to leave it in the book. And here it is:

When Ron told me all he had going on, being the good father I am, I asked if there was anything I could do to help him. Maybe go to Las Vegas, host a party, or make a speech?

"Well, yes, I want you to write a page in my new book."

What have I done? Foot in mouth again! I told him I would try.

Dedication and patience are two things I think a good teacher must have. Patience is one thing I didn't have when I was younger. Ron was about seven when I thought I would teach him how to mow the yard. I remember him telling me it was 95 degrees outside and 70 degrees inside and that a certain episode of *Guiding Light* wasn't going to watch itself.

Oh, hell.

Well, I told him I didn't care and he better get out there on that lawn mower right that minute. I picked him up and put him on the riding lawn mower and showed him how it worked and how to mow. He took off doing fine. I was so glad because now I had someone to help me with the yard.

So I went in the house to get us something to drink. When I came out, something didn't look right. He was going up and down like I told him, but he was leaving about a twelve-inch streak each time. I stopped him and showed him again. He took off still leaving twelve inches each time. He knew I didn't have any patience. I finally made him get off and go in the house. I could see him smiling through the back of his head.

I went on mowing the lawn myself for years. There were many days I was tired and didn't want to bother with it, but I just did it myself. I didn't want to take the time to have to be patient with Ron, and because of that, I made a lot more work for myself.

As I got older, I realized that if I had used thirty minutes of patience that first afternoon, it would have saved me countless hours over the next ten years. Ron would have known how to mow the lawn, and he would have known the consequences if it wasn't done as I instructed.

I wasn't able to really hold him accountable that first day because I had never really taught him properly. I learned that taking the time to be patient and to show your expectations is valuable.

Later, I got a job that required me to instruct others. I tried to be patient because these were people who worked for me and if I wasn't specific with them about what I needed them to do, it was going to cause more work for me. I remember standing up there and being as patient as I could be, and I think I was a pretty darn good teacher, too.

I guess if I had gone to college to be a teacher I could have been Disney's American Teacher of the Year, too, as long as I remembered to be patient and get the teaching right the first time.

Ronnie Clark Sr.

P.S. I need people to help upkeep my farm on Facebook. If you are reading this, feel free to come on and feed my chickens, fertilize my crops, and milk my cows.

You gotta love my father. He makes a good point about patience, and I think it's important to note the value of being patient in the long term as well as the short. I have taught students who as children had low test scores and barely passed my class. They lacked study skills, common sense, and critical thinking ability. Those talents, however, will come in time, and it's important for parents not to feel as if they are fighting a losing battle with their children. Some of those same students who struggled in my classroom went on to graduate college and obtain great jobs. It just takes some kids longer to pull it all together. The one thing, however, that those successful students all had in common is a desire to do well and a never-give-up attitude. As parents, you can set that example for your children, and in many ways, you will be giving them the main component they need for a successful future.

From Matthew's Mom

When my child and I would get frustrated with his schoolwork, I learned the best way I could support him was to simply walk away for a few minutes. That way, I would "walk myself off the ledge" (so to speak) before getting even more frustrated, and then go back and "walk my child off the ledge" with tons of encouraging statements and support. Sometimes it meant I might even have to bake some chocolate cookies to help us get through studying. The constant praising, reinforcement, and encouragement that he could do it while remaining calm began to pay off for both of us—big time!

I remember early on getting so frustrated (shouting and fussing) and then my child would get even more frustrated, and finally I made a promise that I would not let the work stress us to that point. Rather, we would agree to work hard, study hard, and stay committed to staying on task. Our philosophy was "We are in it together!" We found creative ways to study, which often included getting the whole family involved or snuggling up in my bed to study. And, most important, I prayed for him daily and for the staff of RCA, "Lord, please increase the learning capacity and passion for learning for my child!" The moral of this story is that if we support and encourage our children and let them know they can do it, then they will begin to believe it themselves.

—Mrs. Meadows, parent, Class of 2014

34

See the potential in every child.

My mother has often said that my great-grandma Maude Nola-Mae Midyette was the finest lady she has ever known.

She read her Bible daily, taught my mom to sing "The Old Rugged Cross," worked hard on the farm and in the kitchen, and sewed the clothes for the entire family. At night Grandma Maude would let my mom sleep with her and put her cold feet between her legs in order to keep them warm. She was a fine lady.

In the early mornings my mom would join her grandma Maude and the entire family as they headed down to the tobacco barns. At the break of dawn in rural North Carolina the air is thick and sticky, and when you open the door to a tobacco barn you are met by the strong stench of cured tobacco leaves hanging in the rafters. When my father and I were each boys, we primed the tobacco in the fields, breaking the leaves off the stalks and throwing them on a cart that a mule would then pull to the barn. When my mom was a little girl she would "hand tobacco" faster than any of the adults; it was her job to take the leaves off the cart, turn them in the same direction, press them down, and hand them to the looper, who would tie them up with tobacco string before passing them up to be hung in the rafters.

Come break time, if you had worked hard for the first few hours of the day, Grandma Maude would bring out a brown paper bag that was filled with her cold homemade biscuits. After hours of hard work, every crevice of your body is filled with dirt and juice off the tobacco leaves, and nothing tastes better than a cold homemade biscuit.

When the bag is passed to you, the first thing you do is take out a cold biscuit and stick your finger deep in the middle, making a sizable hole. The next step is to take the bottle of Grandma's molasses and pour the slow, sweet syrup deep in the middle of the biscuit. You then smash it together, and place the best tasting thing on earth in your mouth. It's like heaven.

My mom told me that the biscuits tasted good to her because she knew she had to earn it, and she said that she wanted nothing more in the world than to make Grandma Maude proud. She said Grandma told everyone, "That Barbara Jean is the fastest hander I've ever seen," and because she said it, Mom wanted to live up to that expectation. Knowing that her grandma thought so highly of her was her inspiration for working hard and pushing herself every day. She wanted Grandma to recognize her and to be proud.

To this day, I have never seen anyone with a work ethic like my mother's. My entire life I saw her bring home the payroll from Beaufort County Schools and sit at the kitchen table going over and over the numbers. She was determined never to make a mistake, reminding me often about the importance of taking pride in your work. In the middle of doing an outstanding job at work, she cooked a full meal daily, served as den mother for my scout troop, and volunteered constantly at school. She also kept our home meticulously clean; Mom is the type of person who washes the dishes completely before putting them in the dishwasher. Everything she did she strove for perfection, and I could tell she always gave her best.

Why is she like that? What makes her take so much pride in her work and apply herself in all that she does? There are a lot of factors that contribute, of course, but when you ask my mother about her childhood she always talks about working in the tobacco barn and her efforts to make Grandma Maude proud. Her love of her grandma and her desire to become what Grandma saw in her led her to work so diligently. I believe that experience caused her to have the work ethic that she does to this day.

When we raise our children, we need to remind ourselves that they will become what we see in them. If you tell them over and over that they keep a messy room, they will begin to believe that they will always have a messy room. If you say over and over that they aren't good at math, then they will label themselves a bad math student, and they will possibly grow to hate the subject. And if you tell them that they are spoiled rotten, they will begin to believe that as well.

One particular area where this bothers me is science. If we act like young girls aren't supposed to like dissecting frogs, holding snakes, or doing lab experiments, then we are steering half of our population away from various scientific fields, and we can't risk losing some of our greatest minds in such important professions. We could be passing on a cure for cancer, top brain surgeons, or someone who could revolutionize the science field, all because we are sending the message that girls shouldn't enjoy science.

Speaking of science, I encourage you to try your own experiment. The next time your child exhibits a behavior that you'd like to see repeated, such as holding a door for you or offering to help bring in the groceries, say to him, "You always make sure to hold the door for me. I can always count on you for that." Then, take note of how hard your child will work to hold the door for you in the future.

When students smile at me in the morning or say hello in a kind way, I will often say, "You always make my morning with such a bright greeting." Every morning for the rest of the year those kids will say hello with the biggest grins. Kids look to us to learn about themselves, and we need to remember that they will strive to become the individual that we see in each of them. See greatness, tell them the wonderful qualities they possess, and avoid any statements that will place a negative label in the mind of a child. The behaviors we teach them at a young age will help mold who they become as adults, and we need to remember that our words, and our influence on our children, are paramount in the formation of their habits, personality, and personal view of themselves.

35

Punctuate the power of words!

I can't stress enough how important it is for those of us who raise and educate children to place a dedicated emphasis on vocabulary development. Parents, when reading with your young child, you want to stop often to ask your child if he knows what certain words mean. You want to see if he can use the word in another sentence, and depending on the words you are discussing, you might want to make a game out of the new vocabulary. Ask your child to see if he can find the words in another book or hear them used on TV. Tell him that if he hears you use one of the words in a sentence, you will jump up and down three times and snort like a pig. Tell him that if he can use one of the words in a sentence accurately while talking to someone other than you, you will call him "prince" for a day. The point is, we have to find a way to improve our children's vocabularies because if we don't, it is going to be a roadblock to reading comprehension for years to come.

One day I was talking with my global studies class about Anne Boleyn and how she was beheaded by order of Henry VIII because she had supposedly been unfaithful to him. I told them that it was considered to be an act of treason against the king and the nation. I then asked, "So, therefore, can anyone tell me what Anne Boleyn was accused of being?" No one raised a hand. I said, "Come on ya'll, she was unfaithful to the king and therefore she betrayed the nation, so she was a . . ."

I started to spell it for them on the board: "She was a T . . . R . . . A . . ." and all of a sudden the entire class yelled, "Tramp!"

Oh, me.

The sad part is that they had no idea what "traitor" meant, but they all had a complete understanding of the word *tramp*.

I explained that the word was *traitor* and was shocked to find that not one sixth grader knew what the word meant. I think as teachers and parents, we take for granted that our children know many common words, but I am often reminded that this isn't necessarily the case.

Discuss vocabulary as often as possible. Point out words on TV, in songs, in novels, and in schoolwork. Don't expect kids to let you know every time they don't know a word. We have to assume they don't understand completely until they prove differently.

36

Don't be a Penny Parent.

A penny has two sides; heads and tails. As a teacher and a principal, I sometimes encounter parents with two sides when they feel that they can't be honest with me. Of course, I love when parents are supportive and agreeable, but not when it's only a facade. I always ask parents to please come to me with any problem, issue, or concern. They tell me they will, and when I see them in person they will give me a big hug and say all is well. I will later hear through the grapevine that the parent is unhappy about something, and I can't help but feel a little betrayed. I am a perfectionist, and if someone is upset about something I would like to know about it so that we can come to an understanding. We're all on the same team. If parents are comfortable enough sharing their unhappiness with others, I wish they would share it with me as well.

At RCA you are given an after-school detention if you don't have your homework. I gave Trey Williams a detention for not having his math homework, but his mother called me to say she had actually dropped it off to Ms. Mosley that morning after he left it in her car and that Ms. Mosley said she would give it to me. Now, Ms. Mosley does not play like that, and when I checked with her she told me that she had already told Trey's mom that she wasn't going to give it to me because it was the student's responsibility to have the work. I met with Ms. Williams and let her know that she can't bring homework to school late and that the detention would stand and she told me she understood and supported me 100 percent. She was lovely.

As I walked through the lobby Ms. Mosley asked me what had happened in the meeting, and when I told her, she said Ms. Williams had stormed through the lobby in front of the students mumbling under her breath something about "stupid." I assured Ms. Mosely that whatever she was upset about, it wasn't me or the meeting because she had been lovely. Ms. Mosley just looked at me, in her way, and said, "Okay, Mr. Clark."

The next night I got a call from the head of our parent organization, RCAP, and was told that Ms. Williams had been calling other parents trying to see if they would join her to change the detention policy at RCA. She had also started calling parents she knew at other schools to find out what their policies were for parents dropping off work.

I was shocked. Why would she have supported me earlier if that was clearly not how she felt?

I had to call Ms. Williams back in, and again she was lovely, but I called her on the carpet on the things I knew she had done. She finally said, "Well, I was upset but I didn't want to tell you because I thought you would take it out on Trey."

I was insulted. To assume that teachers would punish children because of the actions of their parents is to think very little of them. Anyone who works with children learns to make a distinction between the child and the parent quickly, and holding one accountable for the actions of the other is unprofessional.

I explained to Ms. Williams that I would never be upset with Trey because she was unhappy with an RCA policy, but that I really needed her to trust me on the responsibility and detention issue. I told her that in life she won't always be there to rush the homework to school when he forgets it and that we have to teach him to be organized and accountable at a young age. The younger it is ingrained, the better.

Penny Parents don't realize that they can be hurting their own child by talking negatively in the community as well. My grandma always says that you don't want to hang your dirty laundry on the line. In other words, when you have a personal family issue, you want to handle it in your home without letting the whole neighborhood know about it. If parents are speaking negatively about the school, that spreads quickly, and people who perceive the school negatively will also perceive its students negatively. It ends up hurting the children in the long run.

I encourage all parents to let the teacher or administration know when they are unhappy. Don't be afraid to talk *to us* directly, rather than *about us* in the community. We need you to be the front side, Honest Abe. When that happens, we become informed and then we can address your needs and work together to strengthen and improve our school.

PART III

Creating the Right Climate and Culture

As adults who work with children, we have to make sure we have created the right environment, set the correct expectations, and modeled the appropriate excitement and energy within ourselves. We want our children to see that there is no greater joy than learning, and it is up to us to create the best possible climate and culture where every child will enjoy learning and have a curious passion for knowledge.

✶ 37 ✶

Welcome students and families to your school in style! Roll out the red carpet—literally!

Approximately four hundred students apply to RCA each year, and it presents us with the daunting challenge of interviewing almost all of them over a two-month period. We are very intentional about the students we accept because we need to make sure we have a very diverse group of learners. If we accepted only students who are academically strong, people would claim that our success was based on their abilities and not our methods. If we worked only with challenging learners, people would say that our methods work only for those with special needs. Therefore, we accept students of all abilities, from kids who have never had academic success to kids who are gifted to kids who have caused discipline problems in the past.

After we select our thirty students out of the four hundred who typically apply, we mail out three hundred seventy letters to parents, expressing our regrets that their children will not be able to attend RCA. It honestly makes me sick to my stomach, and I worry about it for weeks. There are still some kids we didn't accept that I remember to this day. I can still see their faces and wonder where they are and how they are doing. It would drive me crazy if I let it.

However, the other thirty students receive a very special note. It's a super thin envelope that contains a shiny sheet of a paper, a Golden Ticket, à la *Willy Wonka and the Chocolate Factory*.

The letter reads:

A fond hello to you, the lucky recipient of this Golden Ticket, from the Ron Clark Academy! It would appear that congratulations are in order! You have been accepted as a rising 5th grader at RCA! Bravo! Unique, amazing, and unimaginable things are in store for you—many wonderful surprises at every

turn! Be patient, your time as a student at the Ron Clark Academy is just
around the corner, and on September 1st, your magical journey will begin.

For now, we do invite you to come to our school and be our guest for
one entire afternoon—you and all others who are lucky enough to receive a
Golden Ticket.

Your instructions: Arrive at our school on May 2nd. On this day, and
it must be this day and no other, you are to arrive promptly at 12 noon. Do
not be one minute early, and do not be one minute late. We are all watching.
You are allowed to bring one or two members of your family to make sure
that you don't get carried away in the excitement of RCA's Grand Welcome to
the new 5th-grade members of the RCA Family.

And . . . please do bring this ticket with you. It is your entry into the
beginning of the educational journey of a lifetime.

When the new students arrive at RCA, we have quite a surprise in
store for them. We drape the gates of our school so that no one on the
outside can see inside our courtyard. The families are asked to line up
outside of the gate in a single-file line. Suddenly, the gates open to reveal
the entire RCA family, our students, their parents, our staff, board members, donors, and friends, all rockin' it out! We have a band and singer
belting out tunes such as "Celebration" and "We Are Family," and a long
red carpet cuts through the crowd. We invite the parents to accompany
each new RCA fifth grader and walk down the red carpet as we cheer,
dance, and shout from the sidelines! It is a wild and rambunctious time!
At the end of the red carpet, we have ten to twenty of our current RCA

parents acting as paparazzi. They take pictures, ask for the autographs of our new students, and treat them like rock stars.

Tessema Haskins walked the red carpet like a professional!

After every child gets to the end of the red carpet, we all begin to dance. The new RCA fifth graders seem terrified, but the upper classmen take the lead, pulling the new young ones into circles with them to dance and laugh. We make it clear to our students that this day is about our new RCA students and that they should do all they can to shower attention and love on them. Our students never disappoint.

After a few songs, we have a ceremony in which our current students introduce themselves, and then we have a cookout organized by our current RCA parents. It's a beautiful day and it sends a message that our school is a family: it's a place where you will be loved and accepted, and it is a place where magic can happen.

From Darius's Mom

I will never forget the day we walked out of our initial interview with the team at RCA. I looked into my son's eyes and I saw a light that I had believed had gone dim inside. I saw such Excitement, Hope, and Confidence. I saw a Strong Desire to Win!

This alone was so encouraging to my husband and me because Darius had really begun to lose interest in school.

So, as Darius walked out of his interview and gave us a Big Hug, we anxiously asked him, "How did it go, son?" He smiled with confidence and said, "I'm in!" My husband and I just looked at him and sarcastically said, "Oh, really?" We all just laughed it off and headed out to the car.

As we began our drive home, Darius immediately began to thank me for bringing him to RCA. I nervously explained to him that there were more than four hundred applicants interviewing, and RCA only had room for thirty new fifth graders. He kind of lowered his tone and said, "I know, Mom, but you don't understand; what I am trying to say is, it doesn't even matter. This experience alone has changed my life forever."

He continued to explain, "Mom, I just appreciate you trying to get me into this amazing school, even if I don't get in."

I thought to myself, *If this interview impacted him this much, then getting into the school is going to be like a dream come true!*

After that day we went home, said a prayer, grabbed a hold of Darius's belief, and waited to hear back from RCA.

A few weeks later, Darius ran out to the mailbox after coming home from school; he said he had a feeling. He suddenly ran into the house jumping up and down saying, "It's here! It's here! My letter from RCA!"

He ripped into it, and it was beautiful! A golden sealed envelope like something only royalty would receive!

He began to read a few lines, "Welcome to RCA, your journey begins!"

He instantly fell onto the floor on bended knees and began to cry.

I will never forget that look on his face, crying and thanking God for this special blessing he had just received. We all began to pray and cry with him. We knew that this would be an amazing journey that would change all of our lives forever.

When I look back on that day, I remember that it all began with his belief; he never doubted that he was going to RCA for one second; he knew it was the place for him.

Now he loves his school so much. He loves poetry and spoken word. He loves speaking and performing. He loves history and reading, and he thrives on having intelligent conversations with adults on every topic, from politics to current events to the global economy. If it weren't for RCA, we may not have ever known all of that was inside of our son.

RCA has not just changed his life, but the entire family has been impacted by the school as well. There are so many things that have changed in our home. You have given us more than you will ever know.

—Mrs. Emmanuel, parent, Class of 2013

Believe that every child can learn, regardless of ethnicity, learning disabilities, emotional or behavior problems, or the economic situation of the family.

After I speak for audiences around the country, I will occasionally have teachers come up to me and say things like, "Yeah, that stuff you do may work for your students, but you haven't seen my students. I have all the discipline problems in my class, and they gave me all the low kids. I don't know what I did to that principal, but she has socked it to me this year."

It breaks my heart. If we, as adults, don't see potential in every child and truly believe that every child can learn, then how can we expect them to have hope and see the potential in themselves? As parents and teachers, we have to approach working with our children in a positive and uplifting manner.

We have to look at our children and see what we want them to become.

One of my former students, George, whom I taught prior to teaching at RCA, was a handful, to put it lightly. He came to me scoring in level 1, the lowest possible level, in reading. George was not only a low reader, but he was also a discipline problem. He would speak out of turn, bully other students, and cause problems daily. When I would call on him to read, he would defiantly say, "I don't want to read."

I had to do something. It was getting to a point where I couldn't stand that child, and children aren't stupid; they are keenly aware when someone likes them and when someone doesn't. I knew I had to change the way I saw George.

The next day I kept him after school and asked him to read a paragraph out of the novel we were reading. He refused, and so I said that I would gladly read it with him. He agreed, but as we read the first sentence I could tell he was only mumbling and trying to say the words he heard me reading. I remember thinking, *How in the world did this kid get passed on to the fifth grade?* but I already knew the answer; he was a discipline problem and the teachers just pushed him on, despite his academic shortfalls, so they wouldn't have to deal with him again.

Even though I was upset, I didn't let it show. I remained upbeat and happy, and I said, "Okay, buddy, I have a plan!" I was bouncing around the room gathering markers and flash cards. I must have looked over the top and a little too excited, but I was doing all I could to show George I was thrilled to be working with him and overjoyed with my new plan.

I told George that we were going to make flash cards for the words in the book and that we were going to knock that paragraph out together. I told him that I knew he was a great reader and that I could tell he was going to really shine once we took care of a few vocabulary issues. We used the colored markers to write the words on one side and the definition on the other. I would first tell him the word and its meaning, and then I would ask him what color he felt that word should be.

We would use that color to write the word. I would then ask him why he felt that color would be appropriate, and it would usually be because it reminded him of something associated with the definition. For example, we wrote the word "strife" in red, because he said that sometimes disagreements can turn into fights, and when people get mad their faces turn red. I told him to take a red marker and draw a face that looked upset on the card.

After we completed all of the cards, matching the words with colors and adding pictures and definitions, we began working on pronunciation. So many parents and teachers make the mistake of focusing only on learning the meaning of words. If students know what the word means but they have no idea how to pronounce it, then all of their work is basically for nothing.

During my first year of teaching, we had been learning vocabulary words for months when I decided to play a review game with the students. They all did miserably because to be successful in the game, you had to know how to pronounce the words correctly, and while half of the class could, the other half was clueless. Learn pronunciation first, and then work on the definitions. The words you are learning will then stick longer and have more of an impact on the child's reading ability and comprehension.

That is what George and I did. For a few days after school, we worked on pronunciation and then vocabulary. It was actually fun, and I saw George in a different light. In almost every case, the kids who are discipline problems and who can be so annoying actually can be quite lovely and pleasant when there is no crowd watching. If you can bond with that child and show him that you see who he is when no one is around, you have a much better chance of getting him to display that side of himself in the classroom as well.

After he could pronounce the words and knew their meanings, we began to work on fluency and how to read with the proper inflections, pauses, and emphasis for dramatic effect. I wanted George to appear to be a master reader, and after about a week, he did, for that one paragraph at least.

A couple of days later, we finally reached that paragraph as a class. I took a breath and said, "Next to read, please . . . George." Now, the rest of the class knew he refused to read, so I could see on their faces they thought that this was a waste of time. I looked at George, and he didn't read. He was just staring at the page. He realized, "That's my paragraph," and he just sat there.

I said to myself, "Please read. Please read. Please." Suddenly, he began:

"The period of time after the Civil War is known as Reconstruction. It was a time period that was filled with much pain and strife but also much progress."

He continued to read the entire paragraph without making any errors, and when he finished, the entire class erupted in applause. Students said, "Wow, George, you are a good reader," and "You should read more often."

George held his shoulders back and said, "Yeah, I know, I just don't like to read all the time."

Heaven help me.

After class, George walked up real close to me, leaned in, and said, "Mr. Clark, can we do some more of those paragraphs?"

"Of course," I replied.

George and I worked together off and on for the rest of the year, and, quite honestly, I did spend a lot of one-on-one time with him. At the end of the year, however, he scored a level 4 on the end-of-grade tests, the highest level possible. He actually only made level 4 by one developmental point, but I don't care; I'm claiming it.

George went on to be a decent student. He never was on the honor roll, but he held his own. He graduated high school and then entered the navy, and he is still there today serving our country.

He came back to my classroom to talk to my new fifth graders, and when he did, he left them with one word of advice. He said, "Work really hard to be the individual that Mr. Clark sees in you. Even if you don't see it in yourself, sometimes adults just know us a little bit better than we do."

As adults, we all owe it to our children to know a little bit more than they do, and to be willing to dig a little bit deeper and look a little bit harder in order to see their hidden gifts. It is there in every one of them, and if we can see past excuses and hard exteriors, then we can begin to help them each become the wonderful person whom we see inside.

☀ 39 ☀

Open your doors to the parents.

Once a year at RCA, we have an open house day where the parents are invited to spend the entire day at our school. This isn't a one-hour visit; this is an 8:00 a.m.-to-4:00 p.m. daylong deal. The parents arrive with their children in the morning, and they actually spend the entire day going from class to class just as if it were a normal day. They sit beside their child, participate in lessons, and have to do everything the kids are expected to do.

As teachers, we try hard to make the lessons reflect what the students experience every day so that parents will have an accurate picture of what their child experiences. At the same time, we are also aware of the need to make the day fun and filled with activities that will enable the parents to be engaged with their children.

We make sure the parents get the full experience, and even if children have physical education, the parents are expected to participate. When parents leave at the end of the day, they look as though they have been hit by a train. RCA is not a typical school, and after a day of dancing on desks, blowing up things in science, playing Scramball, and rapping about prepositions, they are worn slam out. The opportunity to sit in all of their child's classes, however, is priceless.

I tell our staff that this is a tremendous opportunity to let every parent know what we expect from their children, and I encourage them to make the most of every moment. Our staff always says that the day not only allowed them to convey the information to the parents, but that it also bonded them together as well. They say they feel so much more comfortable calling the parents to discuss issues their children are having in class because the parents have a frame of reference in which to understand the problem. It is a valuable step in improving any school, and is one of the most powerful things we do at RCA to achieve success from our students.

✳ 40 ✳

Dress the part; attire matters!

One of the most common questions I receive from educators who visit the Academy is, "Do you all really dress like this every day?" They are referring to the professional attire that our staff wears at RCA. Every man is in a suit and tie and every female is either in a suit or professional dress. We look sharp and impressive, every day.

Educators will often complain that we don't receive enough respect or praise in our society, hence the lower pay that is received. But I feel if we are going to be treated as professionals, we must dress like professionals. As I have traveled around the country, I have seen teachers in sweatpants, jeans, and T-shirts; and women with underwear showing over the top of their pants when they bend over, women wearing four-inch heels, miniskirts that leave nothing to the imagination— you name it. When I mention to the administration that they should have a stricter dress policy, they will often tell me that they can't expect teachers to go out and purchase professional clothing. I find that laughable, because if you work at a bank or any other professional business, regardless of your role, you are expected to dress in a suit and tie. Why can't we hold teachers to that same standard? In the end, we get what we expect, and if you have low expectations in terms of the attire you expect from your employees, you will get teachers who dress down.

The reasons for dressing professionally are endless:

1. Discipline problems are reduced, and students treat the staff with more respect.
2. Teachers are seen as intelligent and sharp experts in the eyes of parents.
3. The staff feels a sense of pride in their collective appearance.

This is a daily expectation, and makes us feel like we can conquer the world.

4. People who dress well feel more confident and walk with a pep in their step! The energy can be felt throughout the school.

Just look at this picture of our staff. We dress this way daily. We are a professional team that carries itself with pride in our appearance and actions. We dress this way because it is expected, and it should be expected everywhere.

During preparations for our first year at the Academy, I knew that having a staff that was professional in appearance was a necessity. I contacted some potential donors and the Macy's store in Atlanta to see if they would be interested in helping with a magical project. When I ask for help, I always begin with the phrase, "I'm not sure if you can help me or not," because that usually inspires people to want to show that they can help. It took an afternoon of phone calls, but eventually all was set. During the first week of staff training, we loaded all of our teachers and staff into the school vans, blindfolded them, and drove them to the mall. They had no idea where we were going or why we were going there.

Upon arrival, we led the group to the front doors of Macy's. We then told them to take off their blindfolds, and when they did, we announced that we were going on a shopping spree for professional attire, and that each person was going to be given a $1,000 Macy's gift card! They went bonkers! Everyone was hugging and jumping up and down. We headed inside and spent the next three hours trying on suits, giving advice to one another, laughing, and truly bonding. It was a fabulous afternoon that pulled us all together in a very unique and special way.

On the first day of school, we all walked in with our new attire, and boy, we looked sharp! It honestly looked as if our staff was ready for the runway and that there was nothing or no one who could hold us back. We went into that first year on fire with our heads held high. We felt polished, we looked amazing, and we gave off an appearance of professionalism, dignity, and unity. It was the best way to start off the year and to send a message to all of our students and their parents that they were dealing with a world-class faculty that could be trusted and should be respected.

Susan Barnes, language arts teacher at RCA, making her
entrance on the first day of school.

41

Make the most of every moment! There should be an urgency in education!

For years there has been a debate about lengthening the amount of time
students spend in school. Many charter and private programs now have
the students stay until 6:00 p.m. during the week and all day on Saturday.
I think those programs are a blessing for those students, who would tend
to fall into mischief during the crucial 4:00-to-6:00 window. That's when

most crimes, sexual activity (leading to pregnancies), and delinquent behavior occur. As for the question of whether students really learn more if you lengthen the day, it all depends on the level of instruction occurring during that time.

Unfortunately, as I have traveled around the country visiting schools, I have seen more "dead time" than real instruction. I see teachers sitting behind their desks as students do silent work, chaotic environments where teachers have lost control, and students who seem barely able to keep their heads off their desks. If you increase the length of the school day in those environments, all you are doing is prolonging the misery.

At RCA, we decided that we needed to create in our students a sense of urgency and the idea that every moment is valuable. The next seven tips outline the steps we have taken at RCA in order to put the sense of urgency in place.

Elizabeth Scott, RCA's director of child services.

⭒ 42 ⭒

Can the intercom.

(Teachers all across America just shouted, "Amen!" when they read that.)

When I am teaching a lesson and the students are at full attention, the last thing I want to hear is someone over the loud speaker calling Andrea Sage to the office. It's annoying and it sends a message to the students that the intercom announcement is more important than the lesson. Just don't do it! (Also, at times when the intercom is absolutely necessary, whoever is on the intercom should always be direct and speak in a professional tone.)

⭒ 43 ⭒

Please don't interrupt a teacher's lesson to deliver a note, ask a question, or disturb the class.

I want my students to recognize that every moment is valuable and that we don't have time to waste. When parents show up at the door to give their child a lunch box, or when staff members walk in to pass out letters that are to be sent home for other minor reasons, it sends the message to the students that all of those little interruptions are more important than the lesson at hand.

At RCA, we make a point never to enter a teacher's classroom in the middle of instruction unless it is for an essential reason. I will go weeks at a time before anyone ever walks in during a lesson. I find that the students and I get a great deal accomplished and we are able to focus without any interruptions at all.

When we first try to explain this to our students' parents, they feel as though they are being left out. They will show up at Ms. Mosley's desk, and she will tell them that they can't go to their child's class to hand them their p.e. shorts that they left on the kitchen table. They aren't happy about it, but eventually they come to realize that it's in the best interest of the students to respect and honor the academic time at the school.

✳ 44 ✳

Avoid sitting down while
students are in the room.

The teacher is the supreme focal point of energy in the classroom, and when he or she sits down, it sucks the life right out of the room. Educators should never grade papers, work on lesson plans, or spend time on their computers preparing for the upcoming lesson while students are in class. Teachers should sit down only if they are participating in a group activity, conducting a writing conference with a student, or sitting in a reading corner with the class. One of the greatest things about our staff at RCA is that they are always on their feet and on fire! They realize that when they sit down, energy goes down—so they remain on their feet and engaged constantly.

How can you adjust if physical limitations keep you from standing? I know the most amazing Spanish teacher, Amy Dunaway-Haney, who is wheelchair bound. She exudes energy with her voice and her facial expressions, and one cannot help but be motivated when watching her in action. She cannot stand, but she gets the kids on *their* feet—often! Her classroom is full of engaging kinesthetic activities, and the energy is contagious.

Adam Dovico, current events and math teacher at RCA.

☀ 45 ☀

Do not use cell phones or computers while the students are in the room, unless the device is part of the lesson being taught.

One of my students, Misaiah, asked me this year, "Mr. Clark, why don't you have a Facebook page?"

I replied, "I do, buddy."

He then said, "Oh, I figured you didn't have one because my teacher at my other school had to update hers throughout the day, and we had to read silently so she could concentrate."

Unfortunately, that happens more than people imagine. When we accepted our first group of students to RCA, we asked them what things they liked and didn't like about their previous teachers. The most common complaint was that they didn't like when teachers talked on their cell phones or texted throughout the day. They said that when the teacher wasn't paying attention to them discipline problems would happen and that it was boring having to sit at their desks doing work all day.

The teacher's priority needs to be the students, and while they are in the room together, the rest of the world should vanish. The classroom time between teachers and students is magical, and the children deserve to feel that in that moment there is nothing more important in the world than their quest for knowledge.

☀ 46 ☀

Make homework for home, not school.

Don't give the students an assignment for homework and then allow them to work on it in class. Every minute the students are in the classroom is valuable and should be spent with active, high-energy instruction.

I know that teachers will often come to the end of their lesson and decide to allow the class to work on their homework. At RCA, our teachers have committed that the lesson never ends. We "overplan" and always are ready to keep the energy going with exciting and engaging content. Don't waste precious classroom time with homework!

✳ *47* ✳

Make sure you do your homework, too!

Teachers need to be organized and crisp, and they should maintain a classroom where time isn't wasted. I would predict that 90 percent of classroom behavior issues occur when the teacher isn't teaching. That is when students become bored and take the opportunity to goof off. If the teacher is teaching and keeping the kids active every moment, discipline issues will decrease.

Do This:

Have all materials that you will need for your lesson at the front of the room and ready before the students enter.

As soon as the students enter you should immediately begin the lesson. If you give them too much time to get settled, they will take longer and longer each day. Keep teaching until the very last second. If you stop a few minutes early, you are creating a dangerous space of time where discipline issues are going to occur. Make sure any flip charts or PowerPoint presentations are ready to go before class begins. When teachers have to go to their computers to pull up information for the lesson, students will take the opportunity to talk and get into mischief.

✶ 48 ✶

Begin each class on fire!

When I look down the hall and see my next class of students heading toward my room, I instantly *jump* up on the desk and begin teaching. I'll be in full "teacher swing" as the students approach my room, and they'll hear me going at it:

"And then, the final bomb sealed the victory! And that, my friends, is the greatest story I have ever told . . ."

The students enter to see me standing on a desk, arms raised high as I teach the dramatic lesson to an empty classroom! They come running in and ask, "Mr. Clark, what are you doing?" and I'll reply, "You were late so I started without you!" I honestly think they believe that I am always in there teaching whether students are in the class or not.

The system works, however, because Mrs. Bearden tells me that when it is time to leave her class, the students pack up with more efficiency and quickness than she has seen in all her years as a teacher. They know that they need to get to my class quickly because if they don't, they'll miss something! In all honesty, they probably think I am a little crazy, but that's okay, too. When teachers are a little out of the ordinary and quirky, it endears them to their students and helps to add a special spark to the relationship.

And one thing is for sure: they know I make the most of every moment I have with them to give them the best education possible. This attitude rings clearly throughout our whole school, and it has made a tremendous difference in the energy, effort, and success at RCA.

✳ 49 ✳

Increase teacher quality
instead of reducing class size.

I know the big trend for years in our country has been to reduce class size, and for kindergarten through second grade, I think that the argument is valid. For higher grades, however, reducing class size can be a waste of time because if you have a bad teacher educating thirty students, she's still going to be a bad teacher educating thirteen students. Reducing the number of students rarely affects the overall quality of instruction in the classroom; it only decreases the number of students who are affected by the lessons presented by that particular teacher.

The teachers at RCA put a great deal of effort into each of our lessons; in some ways they are more like performances or choreographed art than a regular lesson. It's an educational experience that requires a lot of effort. If I am going through that much effort, I'd much rather have thirty students in the classroom than twelve. In my mind, the more the merrier.

When schools do have teachers who aren't being successful with a larger class, professional development is needed to assist that teacher. Teachers need to see, feel, and experience great teaching themselves. They don't need to hear about it from a PowerPoint presentation or be told how to discipline or how to teach.

In most cases, workshop presenters will tell teachers that they should teach in exciting ways, but the workshop presenter is dry and beyond boring. At RCA, we invite teachers into our classrooms to see us teach firsthand and to see how we run our school. It's real and it's effective. If we are never learning from one another, then we are performing in a bubble and denying ourselves the opportunity for growth. All educators must be provided with the experience of watching one another in action. Every time I visit another teacher's class, I learn something. At times I will pick up strategies I want to use, and other times I will see behavior that I want to make sure I never repeat. Regardless, it causes me to compare my techniques to the ones I see and offers an opportunity for me to grow as a professional.

For educators who are unable to visit RCA, I strongly encourage you to develop a peer observation program at your school. The more you observe each other, the stronger you will grow as professionals and as a staff.

✴ 50 ✴

Set an electric tone on Day One.

I believe that if you are going to do something, you have to do it right and put all that you have into it. On the first day of school each year at RCA, we want it to be unlike any other opening day in the world. We want it to be a day the students will never forget and a moment that says, "This is going to be the best year of your life!"

The first year at RCA, we were able to arrange for a local high school's 110-member marching band and drum line to be playing full force as our parents dropped off their students. The entire RCA staff met each car as it pulled up, and we hugged and high-fived every child as he or she stepped out of the car. Many of our staff members picked kids up over their shoulders and ran with them through the RCA gates. It was an electric and mind-pumping moment!

The next year we had a local band playing hot tunes as the students were greeted with much fanfare, and the year after, the students arrived to see one hundred pairs of skates lined up along the road. We had closed off the streets and turned the roads into our own private roller rink! It was an incredible start to the day and the perfect way to kick off the entire year.

After the first hour's celebration, we head inside RCA and our first-day ceremony begins. Each staff member is introduced to great applause and thunderous cheers. They come flying out of the slide and running down the halls, and their energy sets the tone for the entire year. It is electric!

Mr. Kassa swept Onyx Simpson off her feet and ran with her all the way across the parking lot!

The next part of the ceremony involves the introduction of our new students.

While reading the Harry Potter series, my mind was running wild. I can't imagine there is any child in the world who can read the series and not have visions and dreams of attending Hogwarts, and I knew as we built RCA that we had to place a little bit of J. K. Rowling's influence within our walls.

One of the cornerstones of the brilliance of the books lies within the development of the four houses: Gryffindor, Hufflepuff, Slytherin, and Ravenclaw. Rowling did such a good job of developing the qualities of the students in each house that I found my heart beating wildly as the sorting hat was placed on Harry Potter's head.

Kim Bearden, RCA cofounder

Before the first day of school at RCA, we put a plan in place to build a similar foundation with four houses. We knew that the strength of the system would rely upon getting the students to truly have a connection to the characteristics and qualities of each house, and we wanted to make sure we devoted time to getting the students to have a sense of pride for their teams.

As you enter the Ron Clark Academy, there are six words over the gates. Each of the words is from a language on one of the six continents where our students travel:

Rêveur: Dreamer (French)
Amistad: Friendship (Spanish)
Altruismo: To Give (Portuguese)
Isibindi: Courage (Zulu)
Nukumori: Kindness (Japanese)
Pinal: Knowledge (Aboriginine)

We wanted the names of our four houses to have special meaning, and we decided to go with four words from the gate:

> *Rêveur, the blue house*
> *Altruismo, the black house*
> *Amistad, the red house*
> *Isibindi, the green house*

We found a company that designs coats of arms, and we got them to create crests for each house, placing elements and characteristics in each that would instill pride in the students. We then ordered customized ties for the students that would contain their house's crest.

Mehari Kassa, director of admissions

We were all set to explain the symbolism of each house to the students and to present them with their house's tie, but there was only one problem: we didn't have a sorting hat. We discussed several possible options for sorting the students, from marbles in a bag to rolling dice. Those options, however, didn't create the same magic as J. K. Rowling's sorting hat, and we finally came up with an idea that seemed perfect.

We called a friend and asked him if he could possibly build a wheel six feet in diameter that could be mounted to the wall. I wanted to be able to spin the wheel, and I wanted there to be four distinct sections, like pieces of a pie, that would be painted blue, green, red, and black and designed with the name of that house. We decided that the students would spin the wheel and then take Mr. Kassa's hand and run up the stairs as quickly as they could to the top of the electric blue slide.

Steven Moore is about to discover he will be in Isibindi!

Mr. Kassa rushes Elijah Colson up the coin stairs.

As the wheel would slow to stop on one of the four houses, the children would be told to slide for the very first time. As they would shoot out of the slide and slide across the lobby floor, we would all scream at the top of our lungs the name of their new house.

The idea worked beautifully, and in coming years, as allegiance and pride grew over the houses, the first-day ceremony became more and more intense. The upper classmen were anxious to get new students into their houses, and the lobby started to turn into a wild ride where students pleaded, cheered, and wished with all their might that each new RCA student would make it into their house, which in many ways developed the same spirit and unity that you find in fraternities and sororities.

Everyone in Rêveur was hoping that Adejah Parrish would land in their house. They weren't disappointed, but as you can see, I was stressed. My shirttail was even out. Crisis.

The students are so hopeful to add students to their houses because each year they compete with one another in various competitions, and with more students, they have the opportunity to acquire more points. The students can earn points for academics, athletics, good attendance, and great behavior and citizenship. At Hogwarts, they keep track of the points on magical cups in the lobby. We, obviously, couldn't build magical cups, but I was determined to come as close as possible.

I was giving a tour to a group of people from Panasonic, and I described the magical cups at Hogwarts. I told them it was my dream to have a flat-screen TV in the lobby that would show four cups, one for each house. I described that teachers would be able to walk over to their computer, type in for a child to receive, say, four points, and that a circle would appear in the cup, and inside you would see the child's face along with the number four. There would then be a total at the bottom of the cup that would show the overall total for that house. I then asked, "Do you think there is anyway someone could ever build something like that?"

They responded, "Well, our top software developers could make it if they wanted to."

I then asked, in my best naïve Southern accent, "Don't they want to?"

A few weeks later, the TV was up and operational. The cups were filled with faces of students who had earned points, and, as they walked by, students would check the cups to see which of their teammates had earned points for their house. They would then give them high-fives and thank them for the points they had earned.

The system works better than we ever expected it to, and the best part about it is that the houses really feel like families. From the first moment the fifth graders walk into our school and are placed in a house, they are loved, hugged, and told that they have a group of friends who care about them and want them to succeed.

Jordan Still lands in Altruismo, the black house that won the House Championship three years in a row and is presently undefeated. Their symbol is the snake, and when members of their house earn points they all hiss to show approval.

After the sorting ceremony, the students are instructed that from that moment on, there is to be no talking for three days. Students can speak only if an adult asks them a question, it is lunchtime, or if they raise their hands. Our purpose behind the strict beginning is that it is better to start off with strong discipline. You can always lighten up as the year goes along, but it is near impossible to start off lenient and then to try to become stricter later.

It's a brilliant way to start the new year. We have a vibrant celebration, a ceremony that instills a sense of family and unity in our school, and then a disciplined start to the academic beginning of our year.

From Andrew Chismar, Teacher

I immediately fell in love with the idea of having students in "houses" for behavior. I have a Broadway-themed classroom, so I have four "musical" behavior teams. On the first day of school, students draw their team names out of a jar and throughout the year, teams will earn marbles based on group activities or someone's individual contribution. My students *love* this and are always so proud when their team earns a marble. At the end of the year, I have a dinner with my students acknowledging their achievements.

—Andrew Chismar, first-grade teacher,
Benton Grade School, West Frankfort, Illinois

⁂ 51 ⁂

Don't constantly stress about test scores. We have to stop sending the message to our students that the purpose of learning is to take a test.

I am in support of end-of-grade testing, and I think it is important to hold schools, teachers, parents, and students accountable for their academic growth over the course of a given time. You can give me any group of students in the country, test them, and then give me one year to show marked growth in those scores. That's fair.

Where we go wrong in our efforts, however, is that most states place too great an emphasis on the final achievement level, rather than the amount of growth that takes place. If one teacher starts her year with gifted students and another starts her year with struggling learners, it's hardly fair to hold them both to the same final standard.

Because the system is flawed, it has sparked a revolution of "teaching to the test." Teachers are told to spend the entire day preparing students in math and reading and to tie in the other subjects whenever and however possible. Teachers, and entire school systems, are under investigation for tampering with students' score sheets in order to improve results. There are teachers who are telling students that if they don't do well, the students will cause them to lose their jobs. It's an embarrassment and a shame.

I was at a book signing with about fifty teachers in line when a lady approached from the side. She said, "Hey, come here." I was in the middle of signing another lady's book, and I never allow anyone to jump the line because I don't want to upset anyone. I tried to ignore her, but she kept on, "Hey, Mr. Clark, come here."

I finally said, "Excuse me one second," and I walked quickly over to the lady.

She said, "Lean closer," and as I did she whispered, "I got the secret. I got the secret to raising them test scores, and I'm gonna tell you so you can tell everybody." Well, she's about to get her wish, because here goes her secret:

"First, you got to get you one of them spray bottles. Any old kind will do, and then you got to get ya some water. Now, you can get that bottled water or whatnot, but I just get the tap water 'cause it does just fine and I ain't trying to spend no more money and teachers ain't got money to spend like that. Then, you put the water in the bottle and in the morning, first thing, you got to get the kids in a circle and you all pray over that water. The longer you pray, the more powerful the water becomes, and when you done, you got yourself da 'holy water.' Now, whenever the kids ain't paying attention or focused, I just spray them right in the face with it and I spray them in a good fashion, too. And sometimes I just start spraying the whole class, and sometimes they said they feelin' stupid and they ask me to spray da holy water, so I do. And I got some of the highest test scores in the school, so you need to tell everybody so they can do it, too."

I said to her, "Thank you for believing that all of your students can be successful," walked away, and sat back down at the book-signing table, dumbfounded.

Today, students in our country are sitting in that woman's classroom and getting sprayed with a water bottle. And if that story shocks you, I am sure there are hundreds more that are even more shocking. What are we doing in our educational system that would allow such behavior?

The first day I met with the staff at RCA, before the school ever opened, I stated that we, as a staff, would never, ever mention that the students were learning in order to take an end-of-grade test. Discussing that we are learning to take a test and to raise test scores has been outlawed at our school, and no one even mentions it. We want our students to realize that they are learning because learning is fun and acquiring knowledge is one of the world's greatest joys. Saying that the students are preparing for a test takes the entire heart and soul out of the school. It cheapens our system and belittles our teachers and students.

How do we handle testing? During the last week of school at RCA, we tell our students that they will take some tests. We tell them it's more like a celebration of learning so that they can show all they have learned throughout the year. The students are relaxed but focused, and we ask them to try their best. Each year our students' test scores have made tremendous improvement when compared to national scores. On the Stanford 10, our students' scores generally equal double-digit growth in each subject area.

Don't get me wrong: the results don't come just from not mentioning end-of-grade testing; the results come because we taught our butts off. But more important, we show our students the joy and excitement that comes with learning. Once they catch that magic, our jobs become much easier, and the results are much, much better.

If you happen to be in a school that has strict guidelines about teaching to the test, you need to follow your system's expectations. You can, however, be upbeat and positive about the testing process. Show your students that you aren't stressed and that they shouldn't be either. Do all you can to prepare the students to the best of your ability. If you are a teacher who *wants* to be innovative and creative and have autonomy in your classroom, the best way to earn that freedom is to have outstanding test scores to validate your teaching methods.

52

Open up your home to your students.

I remember trick-or-treating when I was in the fifth grade. My mom took me to my teacher's home, and I can still remember being shocked when Mrs. Edwards actually opened the door. I think it was in that moment that the realization hit me that teachers actually have homes and are real people. Now when my students see me at the grocery store and exclaim,

"Mr. Clark, what are you doing here?" I just smile and explain to them that I actually eat on occasion.

I can see Mrs. Edwards standing in her doorway so clearly. My eyes were darting everywhere—the carpet, the paintings on the walls, the wooden table with pictures that I struggled to see. I was so curious. I wanted to know everything about Mrs. Edwards. I spent forty hours a week with this woman but knew nothing of her outside of the curriculum she taught each day. As a teacher, I remember the curiosity I felt as a child, and I use that to help make connections with my students.

During our first year, our budget was really tight, and we tried to think of a creative way to provide something special for our students who were working hard. In our sixth-grade class, about half of them were doing all we asked while the other half wasn't. We decided to take the half who were working hard to my home for dinner and have the entire staff cook them spaghetti and dessert. I recall a staff member commenting that the students really wouldn't see that as much of a reward, but we decided to give it a shot.

On Friday at the end-of-day school-wide meeting, I announced the reward of the home-cooked dinner, and all of the students erupted into applause. As we called out the names of the students who would be participating because of their hard work and effort, they ran up and gave us huge hugs, and some of them even cried. The reaction was even better than we expected.

When we were finished calling out the names, I noticed the faces of the students whose names hadn't been called. They looked none too pleased. I wasn't sure how this would affect the complexion of the class, but I hold fast to my belief that not every child needs to be rewarded all the time, and it is completely fine to reward those who deserve it while others go unrecognized. One of the most annoying parts of that, however, and one of the most unfortunate aspects of picking only the students who deserve the reward is that students, and their parents, will complain about not being picked.

Imagine Little League teams when some children don't get as much playing time. Parents complain. It's the same situation at RCA at times, when only the students who are displaying the most effort, respect, and discipline are selected for rewards. At times, parents have said we pick favorites for rewards. Well, I guess that is true, if by "favorites" they mean the students who have worked hard enough to be recognized. And those picked aren't selected just because they are doing well academically or are well-behaved. Any child who is striving to improve is picked, whether they are struggling with grades or behavior. It's the effort to improve that is rewarded.

In class the following Monday, I saw that the students who were invited to dinner were sitting upright and focused, as normal. The rest of the class, surprisingly, was sitting focused and intent as well. The reward had worked to not only inspire the students who were invited, but it had also lit a fire under the rest of the class. They didn't want to be left out of the reward the next time.

And the dinner at my house was so much fun. The staff served spaghetti to the students, and we played music and games and laughed for three straight hours. I showed the students around my apartment, pointing out pictures of my family and friends and showing them where I sit when I grade their papers; they loved that! It bonded me with the students, but it also bonded them to the staff and with one another. It made us all closer and gave us wonderful memories.

For teachers who are going to attempt this, I think it's a good idea to make it a group effort among faculty members. You never want to invite students to your house when you are the only staff member represented, and you want to have approval from your administration first.

✳ 53 ✳

Stay connected; have parents on speed dial.

As an administrator, I want my faculty members to contact our students' parents as often as possible, when the news is good as well as bad. I want their relationships to be strong, and I know they are far more likely to reach out and make a phone call if the numbers are easily accessible. Therefore, as soon as we obtain the information on our new students, we program our phones with each parent's name and phone number. It is one small act that makes my life so much easier. Every time I need to contact a parent, I only have to perform a quick search on my phone and dial away.

For parents, consider yourself lucky if your child has teachers who give out their cell numbers. Unfortunately, that seems to be the exception rather than the norm. If they do give the numbers, then please make every effort to add them to your speed dial and use them when appropriate.

I always give my number at the beginning of the year. I provide it to the parents at our open house, I tell them to feel free to call me during the home visits, and I give it to my students on the first day of class. Still, I will have parents tell me that they had an issue but they didn't want to bother me. Parents, if a teacher gives you their number, please use it. I would much rather have parents call me to get clarification than to misunderstand instructions or to have an unclear assumption about anything dealing with my classroom.

Also, I will have parents tell me they didn't know how to get in touch with me. This is frustrating because if I am going out of my way to tell you to contact me with any issue at all, I would hope you would make keeping my number a top priority. If you are concerned with being bothersome, ask the teacher for clarification about acceptable times to call and for examples of when you should reach out to contact them. When we provide you with our number, we are letting you know we want to hear from you, so don't hesitate to reach out. You have the green light!

✴ 54 ✴

Give children a chance to respond and don't give up so quickly.

When visiting teachers come to RCA and observe me teach a math lesson, one of the techniques they comment on the most is how I wait for students to give answers. For example, I will call on a child to tell me how to find the cube root of twenty-seven, and if the child just stares at me, I wait. Every student in the class knows the rules, and no students will wave their hands in the air. No one will fidget and look longingly at me as if to say, "I know the answer! Select me!"

With a classroom full of superintendents, principals, and teachers watching me, it would be very easy for me to turn to one of my brightest students to save the day. I could easily say, "Osei, can you help Sarah out with this answer?" But in my class, that bailout isn't coming. I want every child in that classroom to know that he or she is responsible for performing at the same academic level, and I am not going to glide past anyone who doesn't know it in order to get the answer from someone else. If we continue to do that in all of our classes, the students learn that all they have to do is sit there, zone out, and say that they don't know the answer in order to make their lives easier. Kids learn they can just vanish in class, and while we have a lot of Hogwarts themes at RCA, there are definitely no invisibility cloaks and we "see" every child.

And, in my class, we wait. If the child asks me questions that will lead him or her to the answer, I will provide the information they require. If they say they don't know, I will tell them to try to figure it out. If they sit there and stare, we all sit there and stare.

The process, however, doesn't last long. After about eight seconds of silence, something special happens. A student will say, "Come on, Sarah, you can do it," and the entire class will start clapping.

That behavior doesn't necessarily come from the altruistic nature of our students at RCA. Some visitors will say, "Wow, when I saw those students encouraging one another, I realized you are teaching a different species of human than I am. My students would never think to do that."

In all honesty, when they first come to RCA, our students wouldn't have thought of it either. We have actually told them to do that. I tell them during the first week of school that if a child has been called on and we are waiting for an answer that I don't want to see hands waving in the air and students sitting on the edges of their seats waiting to steal the thunder and give the answer.

I tell them that behavior is perfectly fine if I ask a question in general, but if I have called on a student, it becomes that student's opportunity and that student's moment. All others must sit quietly and listen. I do tell them, however, that if they are about to burst and they feel like they just have to raise their hand, they should channel that energy by saying, "Come on, [insert name], you can do it!" Then I tell the rest of the class to join in clapping. I tell them by doing that, we will lift up that person, clear the air of any tension or nervousness the child may feel, and give the student the best opportunity to come up with the answer.

It is the darnedest thing. Every time they clap and cheer, I can see the student's face relax. It's almost as if the cheering is buying them five seconds of clarity. About 75 percent of the time, as soon as the claps cease, the child will give the correct answer. It blows me away, and it makes me so thankful that I didn't just skip over the child to go to someone more likely to know the answer. It also shows me that our students know more than we give them credit for, and sometimes all they need is the time to clear their heads, focus, and process their answers.

What about the 25 percent of the time when the answer is not there or it is not correct? In those cases, I will begin to guide the student through the answer. I may say, "Okay, let's all look up here at the problem." By telling the entire class to look up at the board, it takes the pressure off the one student. Everyone in the class knows it is still her question to answer, but when we all begin looking at it together, it lightens the atmosphere.

I may draw the problem on the board and ask Sarah to tell me step 1, or I may even show what step 1 is and then ask Sarah if she can tell me why I did step 1. Depending on the situation and the student, I may make the process easier or I may keep it complex. Eventually, however, I will get the student to a point where she gives the answer. It comes from her words, and it is her success. There are no gimmes in my class. And when she does provide the answer, the students cheer, everyone claps, the drums go off, and the child looks elated and feels proud and confident of her success.

The reason this system works is because it has been explained to the students and they all know that eventually they are going to have success. The reason it transforms my classroom so successfully is that after a few days of using this method, I see more alertness and effort in the eyes of my students. They all want to be prepared because they know that they are all being held accountable for all of the information provided, and they know if I come to them, they will have to be on point.

If we pass over those students too quickly and give up on them because they didn't give the correct answer immediately, we are sending the wrong message to the entire class. And we are giving those students an opportunity to coast through our classrooms and to expect less of themselves as well.

From Lynn Lindsey, Teacher

The best thing that I did after returning from the conference at RCA was getting the students to encourage one another. We talked about how important it was to support our peers. We practiced clapping when someone did a good job even on a small task. I was so proud of my students for waiting patiently when one of the students was trying really hard to get an answer. As I was prompting him and waiting for him, I realized that all the students were on the edges of their seats, and as soon as he answered, I was going to make a big deal about it, but then the class erupted in cheers and clapping! The student was not embarrassed, but was very proud that he worked hard to get the answer.

—Lynn Lindsey, fifth- and sixth-grade Behavior Disorder Class,
Willard Intermediate, Willard, Missouri

From Les Nicholas, Teacher

I attended the Ron Clark Academy as part of the Great American Teacher Awards in 2009 and was privileged to witness Ron teach a math class. During the class, Ron asked a girl a challenging question to which she didn't know the answer. The student didn't say, "I don't know the answer," and Ron didn't move on to another student. In fact, he didn't say a word. I began to feel sorry for the student during the long, uncomfortable silence that ensued, and then the most surprising thing happened. The other students shouted encouragement to the student who was working to solve the problem.

Ron later explained that this approach is taught to his students and the silence allows the student time to think. He said, "Moving on to another student would be an abandonment of the first student." He felt it would send the subliminal message that that student's input didn't matter. It was interesting that what I assumed to be stressful was not perceived that way at all by the students. I soon realized that the real pressure occurred in my classroom when other students would raise their hands if a student didn't know the answer immediately.

—Les Nicholas, Middle School Language Arts,
Wyoming Valley West Middle School, Kingston, Pennsylvania

☀ 55 ☀

Realize that kids need to move!
Bring education to life with kinesthetic learning.

For years, Norway has had what is regarded as one of the world's best
education systems. Their test scores are consistently at the top, and their
students often outscore the world on standardized assessments. What are
they doing differently than we are? For one thing, they recognize the importance of getting children moving! For each hour, from their youngest
students to the oldest, they have forty-five minutes of classroom instruction and then fifteen minutes of physical education. They claim that they
don't have an obesity problem in their country, that their kids are healthy
physically, enabling them to be healthy mentally. They claim that their
kids are getting blood and oxygen to their brains and that their endor-
phins are up, causing them to be happier and better able to focus in class.
They also state that the forty-five minutes of instruction is maximized because the students are at a point where they are ready and able to learn.

In our country, we expect children to sit for hours, staring at a board,
and then, in many cases, eat an unhealthy lunch, only to go back to staring for three more hours. It's torture, it's unfair, and it's not smart.

At RCA we do all we can to make sure our kids are moving and learning all at the same time. Kim is constantly transforming her classroom
into a world of kinesthetic learning, where the students are actually learning by participating in hands-on activities. One of my favorites is her
transformation of her class into an operating room. She puts white sheets
over groups of two desks and uses coat racks to hang ziplock plastic bags
filled with water dyed with red food coloring. She has the outline of a
body on the desks and before the students enter, she welcomes them as
"Dr. James," and "Dr. Merrick," et cetera. She gives them surgical gloves
to wear and tells them that their assistance is needed in the operating
room. She tells them that a group of grammarians have lost their parts of

speech and that they must operate immediately! The students rush into the room, where Kim has the sound of a beating heart playing over the sound system. The students have to look at different places of the body where the incorrect grammar has been written, and they have to cut out pieces of words and glue them on top of the sentences (conducting transplants) to make them correct. If a "doctor" makes a mistake, she runs over, uses her stethoscope to check the heart rate, and then screams that the patient is in critical condition. Code Blue! The students absolutely love the activity because they are up and doing something instead of sitting and staring.

The picture is good, but imagine the sound of a beating heart playing in the background. Mrs. Bearden runs from operating table to operating table giving instructions as if she is the chief of staff. It's great fun!

One activity I do that is much simpler and takes less preparation involves having the students act out the lesson. For example, I may teach a lesson on Greek mythology, and then tell the students to break into groups of five and to take ten minutes to figure out a way to act out the story. I have a huge closet full of props, things I have collected over the years—from wigs to baskets to candlesticks—and the students are allowed to collect any items they'd like. With just ten minutes, they have to work quickly, and the first time I do this, it is always a crisis. Soon, however, they get the picture and jump into the preparations for the activity.

After the ten minutes are up, they take turns presenting their reenactment of the story. It is a great way for them to remember the events that took place, but it also sends a powerful message for future lessons. As I am teaching about wars and historic events, I can see the students really paying close attention. They will often ask if they are going to have to act out the events, and I just say, "You never know." Actually, we have "act out" days only about once a month, but that's enough to keep the kids on their toes. The activity also goes a long way to help the students get over their fear of presenting in front of people, because I don't give them time to think about it; they just have to jump in and do it!

✱ 56 ✱

Use chants to create a supportive, encouraging, exciting environment!

One of the main ways we get our students at RCA moving and engaged involves chants that we do during each class, usually to the chorus of popular songs. For example, we may use the song "Ain't No Mountain High Enough," during a math class. If the problem is tricky, we may all stand up and sing with passion, "Ain't no problem hard enough / Ain't no challenge that's too tough / Ain't no sweat we've got this stuff / We're gonna get the answer; it's true!"

Changing the words and singing the chorus of a popular song will take only about twenty seconds of class time, but it gets the blood flowing and adds much needed excitement to the lesson.

We have also found that using chants to get students to uplift one another is an incredible incentive for getting students to work harder. Having your classmates cheer for you is a powerful experience. For example, when a student does something well, I may ask, "Is Ahjanae on?"

The entire class will turn to her and shout, "Wipe her down!" while we also wipe our hands in a downward motion in her direction.

Another simple one that we do only involves me praising a student by saying, "To James!"

The class will point to him and say, "Get, get, get *it!*"

It's quick, easy, and much more powerful than me saying, "Good job, James."

In another situation I may ask, "This question is hard. Have ya'll got this?" And they will respond:

Yeah!
We're doing fine
We're gonna shine
Now throw your hands up in the sky!
We're gonna keep trying
Adding those lines
Now throw your hands up in the sky!
[Solo: We're learning geometry, mama, I'ma, I'ma keep it down!]
Hey! Hey! Heyyyyy! Yul!

That goes to a popular Kanye West song, "Good Life." I apologize to those who haven't heard it. First, because you probably didn't understand how that rhyme went. And second, because that song was mad popular, and if it passed you by, then you may not be in touch with what kids are listening to these days. Make sure you are constantly checking out what's new!

Doing the chants gets the students up and moving, their blood gets pumping, and they get a burst of energy! I can count on them to focus with me for a good five to seven minutes more before I will throw in another quick ten-second chant to keep the energy up.

Gina Coss, science and social studies teacher at RCA.

From Jennifer Breedlove, Teacher

Since visiting RCA I have implemented numerous chants and "attention getters" in my classroom. I do a chant that goes like this: I say, "Wow—you guys are on fire," and they say, "Somebody call Mr. Steck [our principal], we kids are really burning up this math class, whoa! We've got to use our brains to try and get an A in this math class, whoa!" One of my students made it up to the tune of "Fire Burning" by Sean Kingston, and they all love it.

Once you set the tone and expectations for how they are to chant/sing/dance, they get into it and get back to work quickly. I found that since they know I will do it often, they are more likely to follow the procedure. A few times, there would be another teacher who would tell them they were on fire and they would instinctively start up with the chant. It was great!

I also had my students singing songs; they did a synonyms song to Miley Cyrus's "Party in the U.S.A." We also sang a punctuation song to "Poker Face" and a song for antonyms. I did not realize how much of an impact learning through music had on children until I did this. They were singing them all the time. In fact, when I see them in the hallways, they still know all of the words.

The most important part is that I would see the students singing the songs to themselves while they were completing their assignments, so I knew that not only did I give them lyrics they could use, but they were really putting them to work. Something else I am also proud of is the fact that many of my students scored very high on the Ohio Achievement Assessment (OAA). I attribute their success to implementing the rules and song ideas. Thank you, RCA, for helping me have a very successful first year!

—Jennifer Breedlove, kindergarten teacher,
Williard K–8, Warren, Ohio

Get on the desk!

The curriculum allows for "organized chaos," says Clark.

Anyone who has visited RCA has seen me teach on top of the desks. Instead of just standing at the front of the room, I love to jump on the desks to place as much passion into the classroom as I can and to bring the lesson to life! Our students comment all the time about how much they love it when we teachers get on our desks, and it has become a bit of an RCA trademark.

When I first started teaching, I would occasionally hop on top of a stool, but never the desks. Then, one day I was teaching a lesson on the Incan civilization, and I could tell the kids were starting to zone out on me. I will do absolutely whatever it takes to keep the kids from zoning out, and when I started to describe how the Incans built their cities high in the Andes Mountains, I jumped up on a student's desk and stared upward, as if I were looking at the mountaintops in the distance. When I looked down, I saw that every single face was staring directly at me. They were alert, focused, and speechless.

Honestly, they may have been waiting to see me fall. Regardless, they were "with me," and I continued with the story of the arrival of the conquistadors and Francisco Pizarro. As I told of his journey, I walked from desk to desk, stirring up the energy of the room and adding to the drama. They followed me wherever I went, and they seemed to be sitting up straighter and trying harder to take good notes.

And I realized I liked the view. I could see everything! And I think the reason that the students were trying so hard in class is because they realized I could see them, their notes, and everything else on their desks. But more important than the functional reasons for being on the desks, it was *fun*! It was different, bold, and exciting. I was having a blast, and, as I learned years ago, if you are having fun when you're working with kids, then they are going to enjoy it, too. And, boy oh boy, I could see in their eyes that they loved it!

On the first day of school at RCA, I jumped right on Willie's desk to start the lesson, and he later said, "When Mr. Clark first jumped up on the desk, I was like, whoa! I mean, I'm not even allowed to jump on my bed when I'm home."

I started jumping on the desks on a regular basis, and I found that the more I did it, the more the students loved it. One day we were singing a chant, and I could tell in Jordan Brown's eyes that he was itching to get up on the desk. He could barely contain himself, and so I just motioned to him and said, "Come on then," and in one leap, he was right beside me. That was all it took, and before I knew it, the entire class was on the desks, singing and having a blast. My initial thought was, *Someone is going to die here,* but when the chant was over, the students stepped down and no harm was done. Luckily, at RCA, we have sturdy desks, and unless the students were really careless, there was really no way for them to fall off.

Disclaimer: Do not go to school and tell your students to get on their desks. It works at RCA because our desks are sturdy and our environment is so strict that even when students are celebrating, there is decorum, respect, and restraint. If your administration allows it, perhaps they can stand on their seats if they are flat and stable. Get permission first!

At RCA, however, we will continue to allow them to hop up and express themselves whenever they like. It's absolutely wonderful. Kids get on their desks to state their opinions, to make speeches, to sing educational songs, and to cheer for their classmates. It's a freedom that they love and appreciate. We do have rules:

1. Don't jump from floor to desk or desk to floor; use the chair.
2. Don't bump into anyone when you are on the desk.
3. Don't fall.

For the most part, however, we trust them to go for it and to use common sense.

Do This:

A man at one of my recent speeches asked me what he should do if his students' desks aren't sturdy enough to hold him. I first told him, "Don't stand on them," and then I followed with some other suggestions he could try:

- Purchase a small exercise trampoline that you can place in the middle of your classroom. Run to the middle and jump on it from time to time to stir up the energy and provide a different spark to the class.
- Find a two-foot-high table that you can stand on to provide a different perspective.
- Teach one day wearing skates. They make you three inches taller, and the students would find it way cool. Their eyes would also follow you wherever you went in hopes of seeing you fall.
- Stand on chairs instead of desks.

From Kim Easterling, Teacher

After leaving my visit to RCA, my mind was buzzing as I boarded the bus back to Barrow County. I came home, and my husband heard for hours all the great things I was going to do when I returned to my students. The next school day, I walked into my classroom, and I jumped on the table, and I yelled, "Are you ready to learn geometry?" I had a rowdy bunch of students, and for the first time all year they sat silent with their mouths open. I said, "Well, if you are ready, get up and dance!" I turned on the music and we danced for a few minutes before jumping into the lesson. It was fun and the students paid better attention that hour than they had all year!

Before the school year ends, I always ask my students to tell me things that they enjoyed about the year and ways they think I could improve. Every student said the best part of the year was when I jumped on the table for the first time.

—Kim Easterling, fifth-grade teacher,
Auburn Elementary School, Auburn, Georgia

From Nikki Clotfelter, Teacher

I was fortunate to be able to visit your school in the first few months of opening. It was a delight to meet you, as well as your students. I had been an educator before having children (1997–1999), but stayed home with them until they were in school. I really had no intention of going back to work. The inspiration I found in the two days I spent with you is something I will never be able to replace. When I left your school, I once again had the desire to be in a classroom. I contacted the principal of my old school the minute I got home from the Ron Clark Academy and sent her an updated résumé. I'm proud to let you know I am now teaching kindergarten again.

What I learned from your school is what I believe, too: that kids need love and motivation, whether it comes from teaching from your heart or from the passion of teaching on a desktop! They need teachers who really care about them! Because of you, I am working hard each day to be one of those teachers. From the bottom of my heart, thank you.

—Nikki Clotfelter, kindergarten teacher,
Hickory Hills Arts Academy, Marietta, Georgia

✳ 58 ✳

Resolve to find your own Red Button.

If you aren't keen to jump up on desks, rap a lesson, or dress up in a costume to inspire children, then I encourage you to find your own "Red Button." By that, I mean that you need to find your own clever way to add a spark of energy, fun, and surprise to your classroom.

I always had a dream of having a big red button in my classroom that I could press when kids did well. Upon pressing it, the room would instantly go completely dark, a hundred strobe lights would fill the room, and music would explode from wall to wall for about twenty seconds before the room suddenly returned back to normal. When I was teaching in Harlem, I tried my best to create the effect. I had my boom box at the front of the room, and when students did well I would press play and we would dance for twenty seconds. Once in a while I would flip the light switches on and off over and over again to create the feeling of a disco. It was definitely fun, but after a few years at RCA, I was determined to make my makeshift light show something even more special.

Weeks of planning, ordering strobe lights, and finding electricians later, it was complete! The entire process took tons of rewiring and attaching of small strobe lights to the ceiling, but after short-circuiting the entire second floor we finally realized how to make it all work. Now, on my wall you will see a big red button that, when pressed, creates magic! I was very excited to try it out on my students and give them the surprise of their lives.

On the first day of school that year during the middle of my lesson, I stopped and told the students, "Listen, if you don't all pay attention and focus, I am not going to press the red button." They all just looked at me as if to say they weren't sure if they wanted me to press the button or not. Soon, however, curiosity got the best of them, and they were trying so hard to do as I asked so that I would press the mysterious button. Finally, it was earned, and when I pressed it, we were transformed to a different world! Instantly, the students jumped out of their seats and began to sing and dance like crazy. When the twenty seconds were up, they were still laughing and talking about what had happened. I immediately had to implement a rule about how to "pull back" quickly so that we could get back to work, and the students accepted the restriction without any problem at all.

In order to teach the "pull back," I asked all of the students to scream over and over again and to stop instantly when they heard me say, "All right." They started screaming like crazy, and when I said all right they stopped screaming, but it wasn't crisp. I told them that they had to stop instantly and that my students in Harlem could actually stop instantly in less than seven tenths of a second. Well, I could see on their faces they weren't going to be outdone. Again, they screamed and when I said all right, it became completely silent. I simply said, "Better," but not quite. We practiced over and over until it was crisp and perfect. I then asked the students to stand up and dance and scream. When I said all right, they had to get in their seats instantly with no talking at all. We practiced over and over until it was down to perfection. After letting the students know my expectations, it made "pulling them back" actually quite easy. Now, the entire school can be eating lunch, and I will say in my normal voice, "all right" and every voice will be instantly silent. It's all about expectations and giving students boundaries.

Celebrate the beauty of their ancestries.

We have hundreds of students apply to RCA each year, and 99 percent of them are African American. We have made efforts to reach out to other ethnicities because we would like to have more diversity, but it has been a challenge. Once a school is almost all of one race, other races seem to shy away, unfortunately. We see this with all-white private schools as well; African American students can often be hesitant to attend.

One thing that concerns me, academically, about teaching African Americans in our country is that we give a great deal of attention to slavery. I think that is imperative, but I also think it can be a mistake if we don't also take the time to teach our children about the great kingdoms and people of Africa prior to the slave trade. We want our young children to feel proud of their history, but when we tell them over and over that they come from slaves and we don't show them the richness of their heritage, we are doing them a disservice.

At RCA, we offer our students the option to be DNA tested through AfricanAncestry.com. It allows them to trace their history back hundreds of years to the country of their origin. We then have a ceremony where we call up each child individually and tell them all of the wonderful characteristics of their land of origin. They hear of the great kings of the Sudan, the artists of Sierra Leone, and the great warriors of Cameroon. The children and their parents rejoice as they hear about the past of their people, and the families cry as well because the history of their child is their history, too.

One year we had two young boys who didn't particularly get along. I called them both up at the same time and told them about the power of their people. I then said, "What is wonderful is that you both come from the tiniest region, where your ancestors focused on family above all else. They loved and supported one another and defended one another from any threat. The love of family was what made them powerful."

The boys looked at each other and said, "Ah, we're brothers," and they hugged. It was beautiful.

I encourage everyone, both teachers and parents, to learn about your history and the history of our children. If you don't know a great deal about the history of Africa or Asia or other cultures, it's because we all came through the same education system, which just doesn't place enough emphasis on those areas. It's up to us, therefore, to make a point to do the research ourselves and to learn more so that we can teach our students and give them more of their histories and, therefore, a sense of pride for the ancestors who came before them.

Show them examples of excellence.

During preplanning for our school year, I took the entire staff to see the musical *Wicked*. We sat there in awe at the flawless effort with which the actors danced, performed, and interacted with one another. It was clever and surprising, with twists that weren't expected and shocks at every turn. The ensemble sang their individual parts brilliantly, but when they joined together to sing powerful notes in unison, it made chills go down our spines. It was sharp, on point, and impressive.

We left the show and immediately went to debrief over coffee. I asked everyone's opinion of the show, specifically of the cast. They went on and on about how all of the actors onstage, no matter what the role, put their whole hearts and souls into the performance. They loved that the entire cast looked as though they were enjoying themselves and that the show was uplifting, energetic, and inspiring.

I told our staff that we needed to be that strong an ensemble throughout the school year. We needed to perform our individual roles beautifully, but as a team we were going to have to be unstoppable. At many staff meetings that year, individuals would bring up *Wicked* and how various members of a team had performed at the highest caliber. It gave us a great standard to shoot for, even though the musical had nothing to do with education.

Do This:

A great way to do this for children is to take them to see individuals who are performing at the highest levels. It might be a ballet dancer, an author at a book signing, an artist working in his studio, or a professional athlete. Talk with kids about the work that is required to achieve that level of excellence.

Teachers should ask similar individuals to make classroom presentations. Invite an oncologist, an archeologist, an architect, or a web designer to your school. The more occupations our children are exposed to the more excited they will become about working hard in school so that they can join that profession.

Set the bar high for parents, too!

When people know better, they do better. That's why we do all we can at RCA to let our parents know what we expect of them and how they can help us. We actually spell it all out in a contract that they are given at the beginning of the year.

The contract basically states that they will support our discipline efforts at RCA, that they will attend school functions and parent meetings, that they will make sure their child is at school on time and every day, and that they will contribute forty hours of community service at RCA throughout the school year.

The community service hours include attending study nights, serving lunch, working in the library, and an array of other ways to volunteer. We make sure that we provide opportunities during the day and night.

This is our fourth year of implementing the forty-hours expectation, and we haven't had a parent come short of hours yet. In fact, last year our parents contributed more than 6,500 hours of support. Why do they abide by the contract? I honestly think it is because we are simply letting them know our expectations. We tell them, specifically, what we'd like them to do, and I have never worked with parents who weren't willing to help me when I told them exactly what I needed from them. Also, they see how hard we work at RCA, and out of respect for the impact we are having on their children, they want to make sure they are showing us their appreciation through their contributions to the school. Some of you may be reading this and thinking that your students' parents would never be willing to volunteer forty hours in the school each year, but you never know until you ask. Once you have let people know your expectations, they will often rise to the occasion.

62

Use an Amazing Race to bring learning to life!

One of the highlights of the year at RCA is the Amazing Race! We set it up much like the TV show, and it can be done in any city or town. Basically, we place our students in groups of three with one adult chaperone. At eight in the morning, the team is given a test on information about the city we are in; this is usually content that we have been integrating in class for weeks.

Each team works together, and has ten minutes to answer approximately fifty questions. It is a fast-paced and exhilarating time! When the tests are finished, I grade them quickly while the teams huddle together to decide a team name, talk about team strategies, and pump one another up for the big race.

I then announce the name of the team that scored the highest on the test. They are given an envelope and they go rushing out the door! Every two minutes I announce the team with the next highest score, and they rush out of the door with their envelope as well.

The envelope contains everything they will need for the day: money, all necessary entry tickets, and their first clue. The money is usually $50 and it is all they can have for the entire day; adults can't use credit cards or other forms of payment. If they do, they are disqualified.

The first clue may read something like this:

> Make your way to the top of the rock. Find a lady with purple shoes.
> Recite every president in order to her, and she will give you the next clue.

The "top of the rock" refers to going to the top of the observation deck at Rockefeller Center in New York City. One year, every group figured that out immediately, except for one. They went to Central Park and climbed on the rocks there and searched all over for a lady with purple shoes before realizing, "Something's not right here!"

Once they figured out their mistake and completed their task with the lady with purple shoes, they were given a code word, "Flags," and asked to text it to me. Upon receipt of the text, I let them know they had to go to the flags outside of Rockefeller Center and text me the name of the flag that is to the left of the Brazilian flag. Well, there are two hundred flags surrounding the ice rink, and it is a daunting task to find the correct one, especially if you have no idea what the Brazilian flag looks like. To make matters worse, it had rained the night before and all the flags were hanging down and impossible to read. Love it.

The beauty of the competition is that it is completely student driven. The chaperones are there only for safety reasons, and we encourage the students to take the lead, to pay for taxis, to figure out the subway, to decipher clues, and to make all of the crucial decisions. Figuring out how to problem solve and work together are all part of the game, and the Amazing Race teaches those lessons in a way that is exciting and thrilling.

The race also gives me the opportunity to show the students dozens of important features of the city all in one day. I have had them search old war ships, find artifacts in museums, navigate complicated maps, and use trains, cars, and buses to get to particular destinations. I have also thrown in challenges along the way where they have had to get their faces painted, scale a rock-climbing wall, complete an archery challenge, bungee jump, and ride a mechanical bucking bronco for ten seconds before receiving the next clue. It's an exhilarating day and the students never know what to expect next.

One year, I asked a local deli to participate, and they were thrilled to help. I had them make ten special sandwiches, one for each group, and I had them place a small piece of paper inside each containing the next clue. On the day of the race, the prior clue instructed the students to go to the deli and ask for "the world's best sandwich!" The deli workers would then hand the group one of the sandwiches and the team would be on their way. Each group, realizing the sandwich was more than a "sandwich," ripped through it to get the next clue.

One group, however, wasn't so lucky. Kim's group got their sandwich, and they were grateful that "Mr. Clark knew we would be hungry and got us something to eat."

Kim sent me a text and said, "We have the sandwich, what's next?"

I just wrote back, "Nothing; you're good."

Her response: "WHAT? WE HAVE THE SANDWICH!!! WHAT NEXT!!!????" Kim, like the other adults, is a tad competitive, and she hates multiple exclamation points, so I knew she was freaking out.

I simply asked, "Are you sure you have the right sandwich?"

Her response, "YES, WE ARE EATING IT RIGHT NOW."

Okay, so now I freaked, and I was about to text that the clue was in the sandwich, but Kim beat me to it. In the middle of her frantic texting, she said she looked up to see the kids scarfing down the sandwich and briefly saw a piece of paper sticking out of Richard's mouth. *"Stop eating!"* she screamed.

What a mess.

They eventually got back on track and won the race. In fact, her team has won four years in a row.

All of the students—except for the ones who end up in her group—and especially all of the adults want to beat her team. It is competition in the most fun way, and everyone in the entire school looks forward to it.

The best part is that the Amazing Race can be completed in any city.

You can even do it with friends and family. The keys, however, are to make sure that most of the stops the students make are educational and to really stress that it is the students' time to shine. Allow them to make the mistakes, to solve the problems, and to navigate their own ways. In the end, when they complete the race, they will feel a sense of accomplishment like no other. They will feel that they have "conquered" the city, and they will have stories to share for a lifetime.

☀ 63 ☀

Love your eighth graders.

I adore them as fifth graders. I bond with them as sixth graders. I tolerate them as seventh graders. And I wonder, "Who are these children?" as eighth graders. The eighth grader is a different beast, and I honestly wonder if I am looking at the same child I knew in years past. There is good news for us all, however. I have taught long enough to see those wonderful personalities come back around after they get through those challenging teenage years. It isn't easy, and I know as parents that you will want to strangle your child at times, but this is where our patience is really tested and we come to acknowledge that we have to give our young adults a special kind of love.

At RCA, we do our best to look past the negative and lackadaisical attitudes that you can get from eighth graders and realize that even though they are projecting one thing, they still want the same things all children want: to be loved, to be accepted, and to have your attention. In addition, they also want a taste of independence, which can be hard because their behavior is often not deserving of such freedom.

We try to provide opportunities for our kids, therefore, where they feel special and realize how much we love them. The first step is that we have Midnight School for them the week before school starts. We usually have it on a Friday night, and only the staff members and eighth graders are invited. We send out invitations that school will last from 9:00 p.m. to midnight, and we instruct the students to wear all black. No other details are given, and, unfortunately, since Midnight School is a surprise, I can't really tell you what happens. I think it's better that way, though, because this can encourage you to come up with your own ideas for your school's Midnight School!

I will tell you that one year, as part of the night, we played laser tag in the school. It was staff against students, and every light in the school was turned off. It was wild fun, and we all loved it! We played for forty-five minutes, and when we had to stop, everyone was devastated; I think we could have played all night long.

The heart of the night, however, is that we let each and every child know the potential that we see in him or her. We make a point to highlight each child, to honor his or her gifts, and to give each encouragement and challenges for their eighth-grade year. It is a very emotional and powerful night, and the best way to start the year off on the right foot and set the tone for our entire school.

A second event that we have involves having a Girls Night Out for the eighth-grade girls. The summer before eighth grade, RCA's female staff holds a special event celebrating the path to womanhood that the eighth-grade girls are set to embark upon.

The Ladies-in-Waiting wear black and white to symbolize this new beginning and are later adorned with corsages and gifts in a signature color selected especially in their honor.

The Ladies of RCA present the Ladies-in-Waiting with their signature colors, words of encouragement, and sage advice before ending the evening with a memorable outing to punctuate an unforgettable bonding experience.

You have to make them feel special and loved. Just because eighth graders seem as if they don't care or want anything to do with you, they still want your attention and your love, and to know that you see them as special and wonderful.

One of our eighth graders, Mysty, developed a habit of rolling her eyes whenever we asked her to do anything. She had been a simply lovely child for years, and then suddenly something changed. I found myself giving her silent lunches and detentions, but nothing was working. I finally sat down with her in my office and asked what was wrong.

"Nothing," she replied.

I asked if anyone had bothered her or if she was worried about anything.

"No."

I then asked one of my favorite questions: "On a scale of one to one hundred, how happy are you? A one means you want to go crawl in a hole and never come out, and a hundred means you honestly could not be happier."

Her answer, "I don't know. Low."

It was obvious she was extremely unhappy, but I couldn't get her to open up no matter what I did. I finally asked, "What makes you happy?"

"Going to the movies with my friends," seemed to crawl out of her mouth as if the energy to talk was just too much to bear.

Kim walked in at this time, and I explained to her our conversation, and Kim quickly said, "Oh, Mysty, I would love to take you and your friends to the movies tomorrow night, and you can pick who gets to go with us."

Mysty's voice was barely audible. "Really?"

Kim reassured her that she was serious, and I added that I would love to pay for the girls to get manicures, as long as they didn't get snakes on their fingers (the Altruismo mascot).

Mysty cracked a smile and said, "Thank you."

Kim sent me a text message that night that said, "We're having the time of our lives! I am about to pass out from exhaustion, but Mysty and the eighth-grade girls are so happy."

Mysty gave me a big hug that Monday morning. She smiled and didn't roll her eyes at me for the rest of the year. She just needed a little love, to know that Kim and I still adored her, and to know that we were willing to do whatever it took to encourage her to stay on the right path.

It's important for me to remind myself that just because eighth graders are the oldest doesn't mean they aren't still children.

✳ 64 ✳

Don't give children second chances on tests and projects.

This is simple. If you give a test and students don't perform well, you can't allow them to retake the test. If you do, you are sending a message that you don't really need to study that hard the first time because you'll have another chance later. It's just not a realistic expectation to have for school or for the real world.

If a child fails a test, he learns that he had better study harder for the next test because he is going to have only one chance. School systems all over the country are working to bail out students and give them multiple chances, but in return we're actually just dumbing down education and setting our expectations too low.

At RCA, we work really hard to encourage our students to perform at their highest level the first time. In order to support them, we offer study sessions, practice tests, one-on-one tutoring, and study guides. When the test is over, we then do all we can to uplift the students who do well. Mr. Townsel has a crown that the top-performing student is given to wear. Mr. Dovico uses a wrestling belt the students wear when they are the champion, and I give out buttons that say, "Ask me how I did on Mr. Clark's global studies exam." I then tell everyone on staff to go crazy with praise when they see a student wearing the button.

I usually have only a handful of students make an A on each test because my tests can be a bit of a nightmare. I generally have 250 to 400 questions on my global studies exams that deal with political issues, economies around the world, and global relations. I have so many questions that the students realize, "Crap, I have to study everything because that test is going to cover it all." If you have a twenty-question test, kids will realize, "Well, hopefully I'll get lucky and he'll put stuff on the test that I had time to study." I want my students to know it all and to realize that my expectation is that they will master every topic we have learned.

When those students who made an A walk down the hall, the staff members ask them about their grade, and then they go crazy! They pick up the kids, twirl them around, high-five them, and tell them they are so proud! The students beam with pride, and the students without buttons look devastated. Internally they're saying, *I'm going to get one of those buttons next time.*

The more you allow kids to retake tests, the more you are watering down your expectations. Teach them to be prepared the first time and to strive for excellence.

Now, I am sure some of you are wondering about the students who have learning disabilities and need to be evaluated in different ways. People always ask, "How do you modify things for students who have learning issues?" Well, first of all, we feel that the world doesn't modify itself for those individuals, and so we try to avoid modifications when at all possible. In extreme cases with students who just can't handle looking at a 250-question test, I give them one page at a time so that they don't have an overwhelming amount in front of them at once. As they finish one page, I will collect it and hand them the next page. For students who have severe challenges and struggle with extensive essays, I have allowed them to explain their answers to me orally. At times, I have had the test read to certain students in order to help them finish the test more quickly, but at RCA in almost every situation for every test, each and every child is held to the same high level of expectations and by the end of the year the growth and progress they make is tremendous.

⋆ 65 ⋆

Encourage children to cheer for one another.

It never fails. We always have a meet-and-greet for our newest students, the upcoming fifth graders, and as they sit over to the side watching our upperclassmen sing songs of welcome and make presentations for them, they are listless with their heads down and their posture poor. They barely clap, and someone is always chewing gum.

It is at that part of the program that I stop everything and point out to the three hundred people in attendance that the attitude and behavior of the new fifth graders is pitiful. I tell them that we are doing all we can to welcome and excite them and yet they look like they don't even want to be here. I explain to them that if they want the faculty, staff, and students to welcome and uplift them, they should be doing their part to sit up straight, smile, and clap appropriately for their fellow RCA students.

The current RCA parents and students always clap and cheer after my minor fuss-out, but the new students and their parents look a little shocked. It's good, though, because they get a good introduction to the way we roll at RCA.

On the first day of school, I project a photo from that day of the students sitting lifelessly on the Activboard (like the one on page 228). We talk about body language and how the way they were sitting would have been perceived by the students who were doing the presentations for them. We then talk a lot about the energy we expect them to bring to RCA and the importance of contributing to the positive environment at our school and not detracting from it. One person's negative attitude can affect everyone, and we always say, "Negativity breeds negativity."

We then move the conversation to our classroom environment and how we should support and uplift one another. I tell them that I visit classrooms all over the country and that I see teachers praising students, but I hardly ever see students praising one another. I tell them that we have an opportunity to be the most supportive class in the world if we will work together to clap, cheer, and inspire one another. We then run through drills where I give a student a compliment and all of the students start to clap. Some will clap halfheartedly, and I will tell them that the way they are clapping is actually pulling down the energy of the class rather than lifting it up. I then tell the class to clap for that person to show him how it feels when the applause comes with passion. I then tell them to clap for one another often, with veracity and sincerity. I explain that if you lift up your classmates, you are actually lifting yourself up as well, but if you are putting people around you down, you are just pulling yourself down.

Check out our new RCA kids on the left! They are just blah and not motivated by the amazing performance right in front of them. This is a great snapshot of the passion and confidence students show before and after at RCA!

As the day progresses, I will compliment a student and no one will clap. I will remind them that it would have been a great time to clap, but some will say, "Mr. Clark, but I didn't know if he had given the right answer or not." My voice, I explain, gives you the clue. If I say, "That was a good answer," in a mild voice, it might not be something worthy of clapping for. If I say, "*Yes!* Wow, that is it!" then you might want to jump in with claps and cheers. I then add a couple of other rules, explaining that we don't want to clap more than three to five seconds or so, and if one person claps, we all should clap.

It doesn't happen overnight, but eventually the students start to get the hang of it, and soon the class is really rockin' it. The change happens when the students finally realize, "Hey, if I clap for others, then they will clap for me when I do well."

One of the biggest keys to the success of getting kids to uplift one another is that we as adults have to set the tone. We have to be cheering and showing support. We have to show that we are thrilled at the success of others, and we have to involve our kids in the celebration. When that happens, you can create an environment where bullying, fights, and name-calling are less common, and uplifting others becomes the norm.

From Dira Harris, Teacher

The most memorable experience of visiting your school was when I was able to see your students use the "cheer on" strategy to set the tone for a supportive and safe learning environment. I subsequently returned to my school and implemented this strategy in my classroom in the form of multiple classroom cheers with great success. My principal has even used my classroom as an example for staff development.

This year, my fifth-grade students took a trip to Stone Mountain Park in an attempt to climb to the top of the mountain. None of us had completed or even attempted the feat before, and when we were midway to the top of the mountain, a few students were ready to turn back. A couple of students and I realized that we have an overwhelming fear of heights, and even my parent chaperone was ready to throw in the towel. One of the little girls on the trip began crying that she wanted to just stop and wait for us to return from the top of the mountain. Then suddenly, and to my surprise, without being prompted, a male student (a troublemaker, who I was hesitant about taking on the trip) began cheering loudly, "You can, you can, do it—do it, do it!" It was the very same words that we had used in many classroom chants before. Two other male students lifted the little girl up and began literally carrying her to the top of the mountain. If we had been in our classroom, I would have expected it, because it would have been the norm. Yet, once one student had begun the chant, all the others chimed in. I felt more proud than I had ever felt before. I was elated that my usual troublemaker was encouraging another classmate that usually he would be flicking boogers at. He was able to take what was taught in a classroom setting and apply it to a real-world circumstance.

The cheer strategy is excellent, and I feel privileged that I was able to visit RCA, learn this method of student encouragement, and make it my own in our classroom. So, on behalf of eighteen students, one parent, and myself, we would like to say thank you, RCA, for helping us to make it to the top of the mountain.

—Dira Harris, lead teacher,
fifth-grade social studies and science,
Lee Street Elementary School, Jonesboro, Georgia

✶ 66 ✶

Paint the walls with positive memories.
(If their faces are on the walls,
they are less likely to pee on them!)

Students love our school from the instant they see themselves on the walls.

When I was a little boy growing up in Chocowinity, North Carolina, I used to love the living room. It felt cozy, warm, and safe. During the winter, my dad would put bricks in the fireplace to heat them, then wrap them in towels and place them in my bed so I would stay warm at night. I felt so loved.

All around the fireplace in the living room were pictures of our family, young and old, new and tattered. Even though I had seen the pictures a thousand times, I used to stare at them, just soaking them in and thinking about the images and people that they represented. Even though we weren't always together in that room physically, those pictures pulled us all together and it made me feel safe and secure. It solidified our family for me.

When we started building the Ron Clark Academy, I wanted to find a way to create that same feeling within the walls of the school. At our first orientation with our new fifth and sixth graders, we took head shots of each child, used Photoshop software to blend them into one huge picture, and had the final, 3 feet by 36 feet image installed in the school's foyer. As the students first entered our school, many had definite hesitations, and some were quite honest in telling us that they didn't want to come to RCA and leave their friends at their previous schools.

I remember one young man who walked in with his fists clenched. He looked up, saw his picture on the wall, and said, "What's my face doing up there?"

I replied, "This is your school and your home, and you belong here." His face suddenly softened, and he began to look around as if to see where else his face might be.

When students graduate RCA, their pictures and their memories grace these walls. We call this area of our school the "Hall of Memories."

Over the years at RCA, we have taken pictures of our students traveling around the world, winning awards, celebrating successes, and participating in all of our traditional RCA activities. We have framed those pictures, blown some of them up to life size, made some into wallpaper, and displayed them all over our school. You can't look anywhere without seeing images of happy children who are enthralled with the magic of learning. It has made our school warm and inviting, and the memories that line our walls, like the photos around the fireplace in my childhood home, bring a sense of family that enables our students to relax, feel comfortable, and focus on what is most important: getting the best education possible.

67

Never read a speech.

I have had the honor of attending several graduations, and one of my biggest pet peeves is when the valedictorian reads his or her speech. If you are at the top of the class, shouldn't you be able to remember the words of advice you have for your classmates? I would honestly rather hear a two-minute speech that comes from the heart and is delivered making direct eye contact with the audience than hear someone read to me for ten minutes. It seems so impersonal and routine, and it doesn't have anywhere near the impact it should. There is no life or energy, creativity or spark. Why stand behind a podium and read words off a page? Move in front of the podium, look your audience in the eyes, and truly tell them what you want them to know. Make a connection and bring it to life.

At RCA, when students are making speeches or announcements in front of a group, they are never allowed to read anything from paper. The only time it's allowed is if they are reading a long list of names or items; otherwise, they're expected to do it from memory.

At the beginning of fifth grade, speaking without notes can be a bit of a train wreck. Students are nervous, and they make a lot of mistakes. One way to set the tone so that they don't get discouraged is to tell them that it's okay to do poorly on your first attempt. Let them know that you realize every one of them will find it difficult and struggle a bit but that you are there to support them and that every one of them should work hard to uplift their classmates in the process.

With that said, another one of the keys to getting them to improve is that you simply can't tell them that they did a good job if they didn't. You have to let them know if their presentation wasn't on point, and you have to tell them and show them ways that they could have done a better job. Be gentle at first, but don't praise their technique if it wasn't good. You can praise the effort, but make sure they realize the areas where they need to improve.

One of the ways we build confidence in our students is by having them conduct school-wide tours. During our first year of operation, a big event was being held at RCA, and we expected more than fifty alumni of East Carolina University (Pirates . . . Argh!) to attend the nighttime gathering. I asked forty of our students to stay that night to give tours to the individuals, but in all honestly, only about ten of them were ready at that point to give a tour with confidence.

I kept the students upstairs in my classroom, and as people started to arrive, I would send down a couple of students at a time to begin the tours. I sent down only the ones I knew would feel comfortable with giving a tour, and I kept the others upstairs to give them some final tips about how to explain the design and programs at RCA.

Suddenly, Jordan Brown came running into the room. With a look of urgency he said, "Mr. Clark, Mrs. Bearden told me to tell you that over a hundred people are in the lobby and that you need to get everyone down there right now!"

One hundred people. Are you kidding me? What in the world!?

I turned to face my students and with one look at their faces I knew they were petrified. I reminded them of our school's motto—"We have no time for fear"—and I told them to smile above all else. "A smile will erase any error," I told them, as I sent them out to welcome the guests to our home and to begin their tours.

As they walked out, I stopped two very young fifth graders, Kennedy and Merrick. Merrick was really shy, and Kennedy's bellowing was quite a force. I told them to give the tour as a team, and I told Merrick that I wanted him to do 50 percent of the talking and not to let Kennedy take over. I told Kennedy not to be so dominating and to share the tour with Merrick. Above all else, I told them to stick together, hoping their weaknesses would offset each other.

As the tours began, things were going extremely well. I was standing in the loft upstairs talking with a few ECU graduates when I heard a really loud, overpowering voice downstairs shouting, "And this is when our school used to be da factory." The horror must have been evident on my face as I asked the couple I was speaking with to excuse me. I looked over the edge of the balcony to see Kennedy. She was standing before more than fifty adults who had all joined her tour. The student tour guides who had been leading those adults were standing behind them with their heads down, looking pitiful. Kennedy had found a way not only to overpower Merrick, but she had also collected all of the other tours along the way.

I panicked.

I suddenly saw Jordan Brown walking by me to head downstairs. I quickly pulled him over to the side. I said, "Jordan, you have *got* to go downstairs and take that tour over from Kennedy. I don't care what you have to do, you have *got* to take over that tour! Understand, buddy?"

He said, "Yes, sir," and took off.

I turned back to the couple I was speaking with and tried to force a smile. Suddenly, not one minute later, I heard a song bellowing up from the lobby:

So don't forget the party that we're throwing

The warm fires of the fireplace will be glowing

It's been a long long time

Still can't figure out why you crossed my mind

I guess it's just to say

Gee whiz, it's Christmas.

Complete panic! I looked over the balcony to see Jordan singing and dancing in front of Kennedy. She had her arms crossed and looked like she was ready to kill him, but he just kept on singing and dancing with all his heart, and the visitors clapped and shouted and loved it. They couldn't get enough of his Christmas song.

It was March.

As soon as he finished his song, he said, "Hello, everyone, my name is Jordan Brown, and I'll be finishing this tour for you tonight. If you will please come right this way . . ." The people did as he asked, and he proceeded to give one of his charming and delightful tours.

Kennedy looked as pitiful as the other students had looked when she took over their tours. I asked Jordan later why in the world he decided to sing that song, and he said, "Mr. Clark, you told me I had to stop Kennedy's tour no matter what, and that was the only thing I could think of to get everyone's attention."

To give him credit, it did work. And over time the students became much, much better at giving their tours. The best part was that in practicing the tours over time, Kennedy learned how to be more reserved and engaging, and Merrick learned how to be more assertive and entertaining. Those characteristics carried over into class presentations, school speeches, and other areas. By building the confidence of the students with the tours, they learned how to present in front of a group with ease and in an appropriate manner. It worked out better that I could have ever imagined. Kennedy actually turned into our best tour guide, and she eventually turned into the student leader of her house, Altruismo. She now is a confident, composed, and eloquent speaker. Without the practice and lessons she learned along the way, I doubt she would be so polished at such a young age.

Do This:

Instead of having your students give a tour of the entire school, perhaps have them give a tour of your classroom to their parents at open house. Walk them through the process, showing them what details to point out and how to explain certain stations with flair and enthusiasm. Encourage them to stand on a chair in order to add a special spark to their presentations, and work with them on techniques such as maintaining eye contact, keeping a smile on their face, and how to answer potential questions from their parents.

Another way we improve the confidence of our students is by having them occasionally teach five-minute lessons. It happens at random, and I may ask a student to take over a math lesson or lead a discussion in global studies. As they walk to the front of the room, the class chants, "It's Brian . . . It's Bri—an!" Brian then teaches for a few minutes, and we'll all applaud his effort. I then join him at the front of the room as his classmates offer their critiques. The areas of focus are also key points that we follow as teachers at RCA (described in the following five tips).

✴ 68 ✴

Make eye contact with
your classroom or audience.

I tell the students all the time that when you are in front of a group of people, you want to make a connection with them and pull them into what you are saying. It doesn't matter how long you're in front of the room, because you can successfully make eye contact with thirty people in thirty seconds. If you don't make a point to look them in the eyes, they will tend to drift off and daydream. You want to hold them accountable and let them know that you are expecting to see in their eyes that they are "with you."

I also point out that it is especially important to catch the eyes of the students in the back of the room and in the corners. They are the most likely to wander off, and if you don't let them know you see them, that lack of attention can lead them to shut down.

After the student teaches a five-minute lesson, I ask the students to raise their hands if the student-teacher was able to make eye contact with them during the lesson. When the students raise their hands, you can almost always count on the students in the front and middle to raise their hands. The students on the sides or at the back, the ones most likely to feel left out, rarely receive eye contact.

I often suggest that teachers should ask their classes at the end of a lesson if they felt like they received individual attention. For the next lesson, the teacher should make a mental note to look every child in the eyes at least once and then ask again, "Who in this class feels you received individual attention from me during that lesson?" It is a simple thing to do, but it comes with great results. If the students feel as though you "see" them, they will be more likely to focus, try harder, and earn your praise.

Move around the room throughout the lesson and never remain in the same place.

I always encourage my students, and teachers, to move around the room throughout the lesson. It stirs up the energy of the room and cuts through potential boredom. At RCA, we have our students track the focus of the room. For example, if I am speaking, all students' eyes are on me. If I call on a student to give a response, all eyes move to that student. It takes a bit of practice, but after a week or so, the students begin to track without even thinking about it; it becomes natural. With all the students tracking, if the teacher moves, the students move as well. It helps them maintain focus.

After students teach a short lesson and we ask the students for their critiques, they always say, "I wish he had moved more," or "I didn't like how she stood in the same place the whole time." Students want us to move and to show energy, and when we stand in one place, we are pulling down the energy of the room.

Teach the students, not the board.

Of every ten classrooms I observe, nine teachers will turn their backs to the classroom at some point during the lesson. Why? One reason is because it's hard to write with your hand turned back toward the board so that you can face the class. It's hard, but it's not impossible, and once you master it, you never have to look away from the students. Another reason is because it's easier and less intimidating not to look directly at the class, but it is a major mistake. If you look away, the connection is broken and you are lending yourself to mischief behind your back.

Exhibit the same energy you expect from your audience.

Do you teach dead people? If the answer is yes, then use your own passion and spirit to resuscitate them! I tell my students all the time that if you want your audience to be engaged, excited, and encouraging, then you need to exude those characteristics as well. A typical comment from my students after their classmate has taught is that they wished the "teacher" had shown more passion and energy. It never fails: they always comment that they want the teacher to look more excited. Children like adults who are dynamic and full of life; they want to be around someone who makes them laugh and who shows a passion in all that they do. (Don't we all?) Teachers and parents need to work to show those characteristics. Once we do, we can expect the same from the children in our lives.

72

Smile.

One of the easiest and most effective ways to handle students is to smile—to show them I am happy, content, and enjoying myself, no matter how much misery teenagers may try to dump on the world. I stay positive and happy, and I have noticed that in most cases, the good energy I am showing rubs off on the kids, and they become more pleasant.

For students in the sixth grade and younger, a smile from the adult in the room can light up the entire class. Once you go older, it can be like trying to chop an oak tree with a feather, but overall it does help and can at times have surprising results. When the students I allow to teach in my room get their feedback, the other kids are quick to point out those who smiled during the lesson. They say, "You looked happy, and that made me feel good," and "You looked like you were enjoying yourself, and that caused me to pay attention and enjoy the lesson as well."

From Aliyah's Mom

The first time I saw Aliyah teach math in Mr. Clark's class, it was as though I was seeing her for the very first time. I remember thinking, *Is that my child up there?* She exuded a confidence and a presence that I always knew was in there but had yet to be discovered or seen. She commanded the attention of the audience and was beyond comfortable in front of a classroom of students and parents.

Aliyah has always been strong academically. However, she was in a shell, her comfort zone, that did not allow you to see who she truly is. The irony of it all is that she went from having breakdowns— I am talking major tears about how hard the algebra was and how she couldn't do it—to teaching it on many occasions for many educators. The missing piece of the puzzle all along was confidence. As a result of her finding this confidence, she is now a very dynamic twelve-year-old. She is assertive, direct, and outspoken in every facet of her life. I am so thankful that she has become a little powerhouse at such a young age. RCA recognized right away that she was not at her full potential and assured me that they would pull it out of her. I am so thankful that they saw the untapped potential in Aliyah and that they helped her become the phenomenal young lady she is today.

—Ms. Cofer, parent, Class of 2012

Never allow students to begin a statement with "Umm," "Well," or "Me and."

This is a rule across the board at RCA. When students first come to us as fifth graders, these things are commonplace. The first thing they say before they give an answer is "Umm" or "Well," and it drives us crazy.

We explain that by starting your statement directly, you will deliver it with more power and it will be taken more seriously. One of our teachers,

Mrs. Coss, encourages the students to say her name before giving their answer instead of resorting to "umm" or "well." For example, "Mrs. Coss, I feel that the issues between North and South Korea have many angles." It helps them to know what their first words will always be so that they never resort to pause tactics.

Also, another pet peeve of ours at RCA is when students say, "Me and James were at the store." We teach them why it's incorrect grammar, and we repeat over and over again how you aren't supposed to start a sentence with the word "me." We even considered giving punishments to the kids if they didn't stop, but we decided it would be better to ask the students to help us help them correct the problem. They said that instead of giving a punishment, when they use "umm," "well," or "me and," we should ask them to stop speaking instantly and move on to the next person. We work so hard to get our students to speak up and to express themselves that it may seem counterintuitive to have them sit down during a speech or to stop speaking during discussions because of grammatical errors. But the whole student body agreed that we should try it, and so we did, with much success.

Since the issue was addressed with the entire school, and since we agreed we were all going to work on it together, none of the students seem embarrassed or offended when they are asked to stop speaking. It got to a point where they would even catch themselves before the other students or I did, and they would just say they were sorry and stop speaking.

The good news is, those students would raise their hands a few minutes later for another chance, and they would be focused on speaking clearly and with correct grammar.

Educators visiting RCA always comment on the articulation and poise of our students. They say our students have better grammar than some of the teachers at their schools. A major part of that is because Mrs. Bearden and Mrs. Barnes are phenomenal language arts teachers, but I know a large portion of it is also due in part to our school-wide effort to stop typical errors that happen often. Once those initial errors were handled, we moved on to others, like saying "mine" instead of "mines" and learning proper pronoun usage.

When students teach at the front of my classroom, they soon learn that not only are they being judged on the content that comes out of their mouths, but they are also being held accountable for its delivery.

☆ 74 ☆

Fake it to make it.

I am telling you, I run myself from the moment I wake up until the moment I go to bed, and when my head finally hits the pillow, I am out in seconds. I have to find other times of the day to say my prayers, because they sure aren't happening at nighttime.

Also, I am a night person, and staying up until three in the morning grading papers comes naturally for me, so when I do finally hit the bed I average only four to five hours of sleep a night. When the alarm goes off in the morning, it can be like death. I honestly feel as if the weight of the world is pushing down on me, and those warm sheets feel so good. I purposely keep my bedroom chilly so I have to submerge myself deep in the blankets. I sleep so well at night, but the thought of getting up to the cold is horrible.

Also, to be honest with you, there are some mornings when I just don't feel like teaching. It is the hardest day's work there is, and I just am not up to it. Parents can be difficult, students can be ungrateful and lazy, and trying to handle all of the issues with running a school can be like playing Wack-a-Mole—as soon as you hit one issue, another arises. It can be overwhelming.

I just open my eyes really wide and say, "Fake it." I get up and bounce into the shower. Remember those commercials for Zest when the guy would smell the soap? Yeah, I do that. It works, too, and if you haven't tried it, you should. I get dressed and head off to school. I am still in "Ick-Mode" a lot of the time, but I push myself on. I head into my class, get ready for the kids to arrive, and when they walk in, I fake it. I give a big smile to the students, and say, "Good morning, ya'll! Let's get started!" I jump into the lesson full force! I am laughing, excited, and filled with anticipation for all we are going to learn and experience.

Now, the kids will oftentimes look as though they are starting the day in "Ick-Mode," too, but soon they start to feed off my energy, and the best part is that within ten minutes, I am feeding off their energy. I see the smiles on their faces, I hear the energy in their voices, and it inspires me to truly be happy and excited. My day really begins at that moment.

Sometimes when my nephew Austin asks me to play a game with him, I will be too busy or not in the mood. But, just like in my classroom, I will fake it and say, "Okay, buddy, let's do it," and I find that after a few minutes I am always enjoying myself. Sometimes it may not be what we feel on the inside that matters; sometimes it's what we are able to project on the outside that counts. Once you exude a certain feeling, it will oftentimes transfer itself to how you feel on the inside as well.

I tell my students when they walk up in front of class to exude joy, confidence, and passion. Even if you don't feel those things in that moment, put it out there, and you'll be surprised how quickly you start to have those feelings.

75

Use a djembe drum.
Every classroom in the world needs one.

During our first year at RCA, there was a young man who couldn't keep his hands to himself. He was always fidgeting, tapping his pencil, and annoying other students. I sat him right in front of me, dead center, but I found that he was making so much noise tapping that he was annoying me more than he had been annoying his classmates. Ugh! I had to do something to keep that boy's hands occupied.

An after-school drum class had met in my room the day before, and I walked over, grabbed one of the djembe drums, and put it under the boy's desk. I told him that I needed his help: whenever the entire class clapped, I wanted him to let it rip on the drum. I told him that if we start to sing a chant, he should play along, and if I made a joke, he could even add a "ba-dum dum." He looked thrilled.

The entire lesson his hands held the drum, and he sat quietly and intently listening to every word of the lesson. When we clapped, I watched him hit the drum, and I realized, he wasn't only hitting the drum, he was releasing something. He was letting all of his built-up energy and nervous tendencies out on that drum. He grinned from ear from ear.

I was so focused on the impact it had on him that I didn't immediately realize the impact it had on the entire class. With the added boost from the drum, the clapping of the students sounded like thunderous applause. It raised the intensity and energy level of the room tremendously, and the kids loved it!

I asked myself, "How is it that every classroom in America does not have a drum?"

Soon, other kids wanted to take a turn at the drum. Some would try it and realize that it wasn't for them, while others loved it. We ended up placing drums all over our school, and whenever kids wanted one, they would just pick it up and carry it with them to the next class.

The students all know our rule: if anyone ever complains about not getting a drum, that someone took "their" drum, that they haven't had a turn on the drum, or any other comment about the drums, the student who brought it up is no longer allowed to have a drum. We told the kids that they must share and work together, and that we don't want to have to deal with problems. In four years, I have never had to deal with any drama regarding the drums. The kids love them so much, and they share them willingly. What it has added to our class atmosphere is priceless.

Visiting educators to RCA will say, "Wow, I wish I could have a sound system in my classroom like that, but we could never afford it." I

246 THE END OF MOLASSES CLASSES

explain to them that it wasn't a sound system; it was simply a child beating a drum that is placed under his desk. Their next comment will be, "Well, I don't think my students could drum like that." Some people will make every excuse in the world to avoid trying something new, even if it could bring them success and happiness. I tell those teachers to give it a shot and that I am sure they will be surprised with the outcome.

Teachers all over the world who have been to RCA have written to us about how they have obtained small drums, how the students love them, and how this has uplifted their classrooms. The only negative comment they make is that they have a hard time picking which students should get the drum because they all want it. This is where teachers need to remind themselves that they are the bosses of the classroom. They are in charge! A simple remedy is just to pick the best drummer and tell the class that he will be the only drummer from now on. Done. If teachers are concerned that they are going to hurt the feelings of the other students, they should focus more on the best interests of the class as a whole rather than as individuals, and the tremendous impact the drum will have on the class far outweighs hurting a child's feelings because he isn't allowed to play the drum.

☀ 76 ☀

Don't put the blame on students unfairly.

When my colleagues in the education profession tell me that they have had a horrible day with their students and that the students weren't focused and were causing discipline problems, the first questions are always, "How many detentions and silent lunches did you have to give?" or "How many parents did you call?" Suddenly, I see the recognition on their faces when they realize that, as the leader of the room, they didn't take the necessary steps to bring order to the class.

If you allow students to be rambunctious, they will be rambunctious.

If you let them know your expectations and hold them to it, your life will be much easier and the entire class will learn much more. In the past, I have witnessed teachers whose discipline wasn't at the same level as the rest of the staff's, and that always leads to a great deal of problems. If one teacher allows students to have the freedom to talk and goof off, then they will be much harder to discipline and bring to focus in the other classes.

Two of the most dreaded places for teachers to be with students are in the cafeteria and on the school bus. It's in those two areas where students tend to lose all good sense. It doesn't have to be that way, however. A teacher recently told me that she wanted to pull her hair out on the bus during a field trip from Georgia to Orlando, Florida. She said the back of the bus was crazy and that the students were practically screaming. I asked her why any adults didn't go to sit at the back of the bus, and she said they didn't want to be in the middle of the chaos and that they all sat at the front. I am sure the teachers were also enjoying each other's company.

If you set no boundaries for students, then you'll always be disappointed with the results. A simple way to handle problems on the school bus is to have one faculty member at the back, one in the middle, and one in the front. If students are talking too loudly, just separate them. Have one sit beside you and the other sit beside another staff member. If that doesn't work, then tell the students who are being too loud that they can't talk for an hour. Teachers and parents who are on field trips shouldn't be stressed. If the students aren't behaving, then they have lost any right to talk.

The same goes for the lunchroom. If a table is being too rowdy, just separate them. I told that to a first-year teacher, and she said, "Yeah, but I want them to be able to sit with their friends. I don't want to be a meany." What she didn't realize is that by letting the students know your expectations for an appropriate volume you are making your life easier, making the cafeteria a more enjoyable place, and then allowing them to sit back with their friends once they have learned the boundaries.

If you allow students to be crazy, they will be crazy. If you let them

know your expectation and hold them to it, your life will be much easier
and your stress level greatly reduced.

Lift up your teachers. No, really, lift them up.

Good teachers are actors. They have the ability to capture the attention
of their students, to bring calculus to life, to infuse the spirit of Shakespeare in their students' hearts, and to make children feel as if they are on
the front lines of the Revolutionary War. In order to create that magic, it
helps considerably if you have an extroverted personality that will enable
you to command the attention of your classroom. If you don't quite have
that type of personality, we have a strategy at RCA that can help.

In several of our classrooms, we built stages for our teachers. The
stages are about 10 inches high and generally 10 feet long by 5 feet wide,
and they fit directly at the front of the classroom. When you stand on the
stage, however, it completely changes the way you feel and your outlook
on the classroom. And it changes the way the students view you, too.
If you are a five-foot-two teacher, you are barely visible to the students
when you stand at the front of the classroom. Making eye contact with
them and having a commanding presence is hard to do, unless you are
quite the firecracker. When you have the stage, however, you instantly become six-foot tall, strong, powerful, engaging, and commanding. You can
see the entire room clearly and make eye contact with ease. If you are trying to add an emphasis to your lesson, you can stomp your feet and add a
thunderous sound. When you walk across the front of the room, you are
a strong presence that the students can't help but follow. The stage lifts
you up in more ways than one.

✻ 78 ✻

Have fun.

Sometimes it's important not to take ourselves too seriously and just have some silly fun. One day I was teaching algebra to the sixth graders, and they looked as though their brains were about to explode. I was hopping around, excited, and very into the lesson, but for some reason it just wasn't transferring to the students that day. I have no idea where it came from, but all of a sudden I just jumped into my best country accent (okay, so I just talked in my normal voice) and I said, "All right, ya'll, this here farm isn't going to tend to itself. We've got these problems to solve, and I need help from all of you—the chickens, the horses, the ducks, the pigs, and the cows. So come on, ya'll, let's get to work!"

Garth Brooks is one of many famous individuals who have been slide certified!

The kids looked at me as if I had lost my mind. I asked Aliyah a question, and when she answered in her normal voice, I freaked out. I said,

"Ducks don't sound like that! If you all want to get these problems correct or if you want to ask Farmer Clark a question, you better use your
animal voice!"

The kids soon caught on quickly and started responding to me in different farm animal voices. We laughed so much that it was hard at times
to focus on the math. I had to hold it together and keep the class focused
or it would have turned into the crazy farm pretty quickly. I had to tell
a few of them that they were going to be up for slaughter if they didn't
focus, and when Tajee wasn't paying attention, I told him he was about to
be bacon. I started having so much fun with it! When Imani gave me an
incorrect answer, I told her she had laid a rotten egg. When "cow" Nadia
made a great point, I told her she had just jumped over the moon. We
had a blast, and as the students walked out of the classroom, they were
saying how much they loved the class. And it had a great academic outcome; I noticed that every kid in the class was focused and had a hand in
the air. They all wanted to participate so they could use their farm animal
voices, and they were all sitting rapt on the edges of their seats. In the
midst of the silliness, we got a ton covered in that lesson, almost assuredly
more than we would have covered during the regular class period.

I remember that one day it started to snow in Atlanta and school was
let out early, at one o'clock. About ten parents were stuck in traffic, and
our staff remained at the school to wait with the kids. We were all sitting
in the lobby talking and chatting when Dasia, a seventh grader, jokingly
said, "Let's play hide and seek in the school!"

Everyone laughed, but Kim and I looked at each other and said, "Let's
do it!" After putting up our dukes, Jordan started to count, and we all ran
to hide. I somehow managed to crawl to the top of the lockers and slide
all the way over to the wall so that anyone walking down the hall could
not see me. I had an outside view through a classroom window, and I
could see the snow coming down much heavier than before. As Jordan
found several kids and adults, I could hear laughter ring throughout the
building. I just watched the snow and decided to say a prayer for how
wonderful and peaceful that moment felt, me lying on a row of lockers,
watching the snow, and listening to the happiness within the school.

At RCA, we try never to take ourselves seriously to the point where there is no fun and joy in our day. No one wants to work or learn in a dull, dry environment, and we realize that, as adults, if we are laughing and having fun, the students tend to want to be around us and are drawn to us. My nephew and his friend, Devin, will often go off on their own to hang out in Austin's room, but as soon as they hear the adults laughing, they will come over and ask, "What's so funny?" People just want to be around people who are happy, laughing, and enjoying themselves.

On a visit to a local museum our eighth graders were divided into two groups, each with its own tour guide. The tour guide of the group I was in was laughing and joking with us. She made everything fun and brought it to life. I recall that the other group's guide seemed dull and lifeless, and the students in that group stared at our group longingly. I know they were miserable, and so I doubt they paid attention or learned much that day.

I can't stress enough how important it is for us adults to show our kids the fun side of life. We need to laugh with them and show them that we find humor in the world. Laughter can help us all through any problem, and it can make any task seem manageable, and we need to teach our kids at a young age the importance that laughter should have in our lives.

Robyn Johnson, educator training coordinator at RCA.

Sarah Hildebrand, social studies and reading teacher at RCA.

PART IV

Reaching Out Beyond the Classroom

The following are ways in which all of us—teachers, parents, and community members—can make our children our first priority and guide them in their quest for success. A portion of this section is dedicated to how we raised the initial funds for RCA and how we continue to maintain the support.

✳ 79 ✳

Teach parents the correct way
to tutor their children.

When a teacher tells a parent that her child isn't doing well in her class, the natural response from the parent is, "What can I do to help my child?" The most common response from the teacher is usually that the parent needs to find a tutor. While that response can work in some cases, it can be a disaster in others. Many parents don't even know how to go about finding the best tutor for their child, and sometimes they'll just get Uncle Leroy to be the tutor, and Uncle Leroy needs a tutor, too. Good grief.

I tell the parents of my students that they need to be the tutor, and instead of just telling them, "Your child isn't doing well," or "Your child is in danger of failing," or "Your child's work needs to improve," I actually show them what they can do to help their child's grades improve.

At RCA, we are specific with our students about our expectations, but we are also specific with our parents about what they can do to help their children. The most successful way we do this is by having parent nights. I invite the parents to come to my classroom, usually on a Wednesday night from six to seven-thirty, to learn from me the exact same information I am teaching their children. I always have food and drinks out for the parents and their children.

I have done this for years, and I recall my principal in New York City asking me, "Do you know why they all show up for your parent nights but they won't come to my parent meetings? It's because you bribe them with food."

I just responded, "Well, getting them in the door is all I want, no matter what it takes. Once they're in there, great things can happen!"

And once they are in the room, great things do happen. I have the parents sit with their children, and as I go through the math problems on the board, I call on the students as if it were a normal lesson so that the parents can see how their kids respond. I am very aware of not putting a parent on the spot or embarrassing them, and I also don't call on any parents unless they raise their hands. If you embarrass a parent once, she will never return!

The parent nights are great for all subjects, but I really love math sessions because I can show the parents exactly how I want the problems to be solved. I can also show them common mistakes most kids make so that they can look for those errors in their own child's work. Parents who seem apprehensive and have math anxiety at the beginning of the night start to relax and show confidence by the end. I usually include some sort of a game in each session, and by the end, when I ask parents to volunteer to play, there are normally dozens of hands in the air. I usually get a local gas station to donate gas cards for prizes, and the parents are thrilled with the unexpected surprise.

The most important part of the night, however, is that I give the parents "paper gold"—in other words, practice tests. The tests look very similar to the actual test that will be given the following week. I usually make them about ten pages in length, and I suggest that the parents take the test home and have the child work on it at his or her own pace. I tell them that they could do one page a night or try to knock it all out in one sitting. I then hand the parents the answer key so that they will be able to check their child's work, and many of them look at me as if I just handed them a million dollars. What's more important, however, is that underneath each problem I show them how I found the answer. Even if they don't understand why their child missed a problem, they can show them what I did, step-by-step, and how I obtained the answer. It enables the parents to have the power and knowledge to become their child's tutor, even if they aren't good at math or whatever other subject that is being tested.

Currently at RCA, more than half of our school is scoring over the 90th percentile in math, and I can say, with full confidence, that it is largely due to the role the parents are playing in the preparation for the tests throughout the year. While some teachers simply tell parents to work with their child on a subject, we show them specifically what to do, and that has made all the difference.

For those teachers who say that they are getting paid to teach the children and not the parents, we say phooey. If you take the time to educate the parents, then you are making your job much easier, and you are creating an army of tutors who will bring you success in the form of outstanding student achievement and test scores.

From Jordan's Mom

Having the opportunity to see firsthand the learning style my child was experiencing each day was priceless. By seeing Mr. Clark's methods and expectations, I was able to adjust the way I was working with my child at home.

The way Mr. Clark taught the parent nights was always fun as well, and I never felt stressed or uncomfortable. We even played a game at the end, and I have never seen my son so proud as he was when I actually won. For a brief moment, he really believed I was cool. Being invited into my child's learning environment provided me the insight I needed to support him, and I will always be grateful for that.

—Ms. Burney, parent, graduating Class of 2010

80

Build strong bonds with parents.

At our field day, we have a competition between parents and staff members. It's just musical chairs, and sometimes we have to have four or five rounds in order to make sure everyone participates, but it is worth it. The kids think it's a hoot, and it gives the adults a time to bond, laugh, and see one another as individuals separate from the classroom.

It seems like such a simple thing, but it gives me a positive and happy memory of those parents frantically searching to find a seat, laughing as they try to squeeze on the same seat as another parent, and walking around the seats nervously as they wonder when the music will stop.

At the end of field day, we have a water balloon war. The parents prepare about five hundred water balloons that they bring in coolers and set at the side of the field. At 2:45 p.m., they become fair game, and if you don't want to participate, you need to stand on the concrete. If you step on the grass, it's on. Parents are invited to participate, and for about ten minutes all you see are parents, staff members, and kids running, laughing, and dodging a barrage of balloons. Water is flying everywhere, the sounds of dozens of *splats!* are in the air, and people are running for their lives. It's wonderful fun, and we look forward to it all year long.

I wonder how many schools incorporate their parents into days such as field day. Every school should. Parents need to be as much a part of the school as the students and staff members. They need to feel loved, respected, and a part of the education of their children.

In order to build that unity, we visit the home of all of our incoming fifth graders during the summer. I know that this isn't realistic for most teachers and that the school's administration might not even be willing to allow it, but we know that the home visits we make do more to bond us to our parents and students than anything else we do the entire year.

The visits are relatively quick, usually no longer than twenty minutes. We compliment something in the home, sit down, and accept any food or drink offered. We then talk about our goals for the year and answer any questions the parents or students may have.

If you aren't able to visit every home, we at least encourage you to visit the home of any child who is giving you disciplinary issues or who isn't performing well academically. It sends a powerful message and can turn around a problematic issue. During the visit, you want to make sure that you remain positive and avoid any negativity. I don't care if the child tried to set your leg on fire, you should go in that home and say, "You know what, he brings a certain spark to the classroom." You have to build up the relationship first, and just going into the home and talking about all of the bad things he has done will only make matters worse. Show the parent you care first, and then take it from there.

After the home visit, we have the parents come to RCA for an orientation meeting. When they arrive, we have every staff member lined up on either side of the door, and, as they enter, we cheer for them as if they were rock stars. The parents often tell us that they felt as if previous schools didn't even want them involved, but at RCA they are cheered as they enter. They say it is definitely unusual, and definitely wonderful.

A couple of months into the school year, we have a Thanksgiving feast where we invite all family members to come and eat with their children. We set our desks up with tablecloths and turn it into a true sit-down dinner. We play classical music in the background and show streaming pictures on the Activboards of great moments so far that year.

After the dinner, the parents go to the "house" of their child, and they all have to work together to come up with a song and skit to perform before the entire school, with the parents as the focus. I am telling you, it is one of the funniest and most memorable moments, and the parents talk about it the rest of year. We give them the chance to "shine," just as we do our students, and they relish the moment and go for the opportunity to show their RCA pride. It's brilliant.

The key is to open the doors of your school to the parents, to invite them in, and to make them feel like a part of their children's education. Once you have done that, it becomes so much easier to work with them on issues that are standing in the way of their child's success, and it makes dealing with any parent issues so much easier to handle.

⁎ 81 ⁎

Ask the hard questions—
"What do you want this school to be?"

One of the truly pivotal moments of our school year happens when Kim
and I meet with our staff. We ask them to reflect upon the previous years
and to determine what they want our school to be. We want them to describe the perfect scenario and give us examples of what needs to change
in order to get it there.

I think that this is such a valuable moment because sometimes school
staff members can feel powerless as individuals. By asking the team to
describe their "dream school," it enables us all to get on the same page in
terms of what we want to create. Asking the parents will have the same
effect. If the parents all tell you that they want a school that is challenging, then that gives you the perfect opportunity to remind them not to
complain if their students' grades drop due to the higher standard of performance they are asking for. It also gives you the chance to remind them
that the added difficulty will probably require more effort on their part
working with their children.

If parents say that they want the school to be a safe environment, you
should remind them that in order to make the school safe, it will need to
be strict. They would need to be supportive, therefore, of a code of conduct and discipline plan that has a no-tolerance policy.

If the parents say they want a school that is focused on giving the best
education possible, ask them to help in your efforts by never talking negatively about the teacher or the school in the home. Ask them never to
show up at their child's classroom door unannounced, because it will be
interrupting instruction. And let them know that they need to make sure
their child is on time and at school every day in order to assist the school
in its efforts. The conversation gives you a great opportunity to discuss

with the parents exactly how they can support the school, regardless of what they say they hope the school will provide for their child.

As a follow-up to our initial staff meeting at RCA, I asked our team, "Who runs this school? Is it the parents, the students, or do we?" The staff all agreed that we are in charge, and I then reminded them that if we are in charge, then we can't blame anything that happens at this school on the students or their parents. I said, "If we are in charge, then we control this school and we can turn it into whatever we need it to be for our students."

I then asked the staff what they wanted the school to be, and they all agreed they wanted it to be a family. I explained that if they want the school to be a family, we had to exemplify that. We had to handle issues one-on-one and not talk behind one another's backs. I said that Mr. Bruner would need to pick me up and hug me in the hall and that Mr. Kassa would need to run forty feet in order to give me a high five. Ms. Mosley would need to get up out of her chair at the front desk to hug Kim when she walked in every morning, and that we all would need to treat one another with respect and love in order to set the tone for the environment we want our students to experience.

The staff heard me loud and clear, and soon our school became a love-fest. It was great and not fake. The staff truly did love it because they knew that through loving one another they would really be helping the children.

When the kids first come to our school, they see nothing but a team of individuals who want to be at RCA and who love one another. They seem to relax and behave more kindly toward one another and to give us love in return. We have never had a fight at our school, our students' test scores soar, and they carry themselves with dignity and respect. There are many things we do to contribute to that success, but of them all, I know the most influential is that we as a staff model the type of environment we expect in our school. That's why the students follow our lead.

The next part of our meeting involves discussing what we want our school to be in terms of discipline and consistency. No characteristic of a

discipline plan is more important than making sure that every staff member is on the same page and in agreement on how to handle the consequence for broken rules. I may ask the staff, "What would you do if you saw Martha put gum in Mae's hair?" The responses will range from "I would give her a detention and call her mom" to "I would take the girls to the bathroom and ask Martha to get the gum out of Mae's hair." Some will say it wouldn't deserve a detention; others will say a detention is necessary. And one or two will claim that it is physical abuse and that the child should be suspended. We then discuss the situation as a team and decide what the appropriate punishment is, and even though we don't all agree with how it will be handled, we all decide to follow the school's policy for that particular instance.

We end up discussing about fifty different scenarios, and, while we don't cover every bit of mischief our wonderful children can wander into, we get a better understanding of how we think as individuals and how we are going to operate as a staff in terms of how we handle discipline. It puts us all on the same page, and it adds consistency, unity, and clarity to the way we handle issues with behavior.

The initial meeting goes a long way toward building a team that is committed to responding to and delivering consequences for inappropriate behavior in a way that works. The result is a school full of children who are happy, content, and performing at high academic levels regardless of any issues they may have faced before arriving at RCA.

I remember Rakim walking in on the first day of school with his fists clenched. He told us that he didn't want to be at our school, and his face was full of anger and tears. Within minutes, Ms. Mosley was giving him a big hug and Mrs. Lokey was talking about how handsome he looked. Mr. Kassa put his arm around Rakim and said, "Come on, buddy, I need you to help me get this party started!" Mr. Kassa, with Rakim at his side, ran outside of the building and started cheering "R—C—A!" All of the staff members followed suit instantly, living with no fear and going for it. The kids jumped in behind us, and soon the entire school was cheering at the top of our lungs.

Mr. Kassa would not let Rakim out of his sight. And soon Rakim

was smiling, laughing, and beaming with joy. That boy's smile lit up our school many days over the years, and it started because a dedicated and loving staff reached out to him and set the right tone. I am afraid that at many schools, that love wouldn't have been so obvious and that Rakim and others like him in that situation would have gone down a very different path.

Looking at the joy our students feel and the success they achieve, regardless of their prior experiences, demonstrates clearly that every child can be successful in the right environment.

From Morgan's Mom

There isn't just one thing that I like most about the school. But the one thing that is the foundation of the school, in my eyes, would be the warmth expressed by everyone. There has not been a day since my daughter was accepted as a student that I came in contact with either a staff member or another parent where I wasn't greeted with a hug and words of encouragement. The genuine display of togetherness puts me at ease knowing that my daughter is with family when she is at school.

It is also comforting to know that the concerns of the students expand far outside of the realms of the school building. It is the show of love displayed by the staff that has not only helped my daughter to blossom, but has strengthened us spiritually as well.

—Adryan Fambro, parent, Class of 2011

✴ 82 ✴

Join parents, teachers, and community members together to create "theme days" for the school.

Each year we have one "beyond belief" theme day at RCA where the parents and teachers work together to completely transform our school. This takes a tremendous amount of work, but the outcome is always worth it.

The process begins about a month before the date of the theme day when we meet as a staff to determine the year's theme. In the past, we have decided to turn the entire school into a pirate ship that was in search of treasure in the Bermuda Triangle, a carnival from the 1930s, an Egyptian pyramid, and a town in the Wild West. Our first objective is to determine a theme and to make sure we can figure out a way to decorate the entire school with that theme inexpensively. Occasionally we will call around to various businesses and prop companies to see what they have available and what they would be willing to donate. From there, we will determine a theme that fits what we have to work with.

The next step is to meet with the parents and to get them on board with decorating the school. We tell them that they will have only from three o'clock the day before until eight the next morning to have the entire school transformed. The biggest key to the transformation is always pipe and drape. By hanging the drapes in the hallways and lobby, you can completely cover every inch of the school. You then need to find props, such as bales of hay and ropes, to treasure chests and wagon wheels. It all depends on your theme and what you have at your disposal.

The final step is to determine the "story" that will unfold throughout the day. That is the hardest part of the process, but it is the most important.

When we were a pirate ship, we sent the students home the day before with an invitation to go on a cruise through the Caribbean. The invitation was for the next day, and we made the invite look as realistic as possible. As the students entered the lobby, they were shocked to see that it had been completely transformed! There were red drapes covering every inch of the school, and decorations that made the lobby look like the deck of a cruise ship. Mr. Adkins was dressed as the ship's captain, and Mrs. Lokey was dressed as the ship's hostess. They welcomed the students on board and invited them to sample the punch and cookies before the ship left the port. As soon as all of the students arrived, ocean sounds began playing over the sound system, and the journey had begun! The windows were completely covered with drapes, so if you used your imagination, you could convince yourself you were actually sailing on the high seas.

Suddenly, the rest of the staff jumped out dressed as evil pirates, and we stormed out from all over the ship! Mrs. Bearden actually threw a rope over the balcony and slid down in the midst of the madness. The students freaked out and didn't know what was going on. We told them, in our best evil pirate voices, that we were taking over the ship and sailing directly to the heart of the Bermuda Triangle to find our lost treasure. We told them that they were our prisoners and that we were going to force them to be part of our crew and to help us. The students were then split up into groups and sent to various parts of the ship "classrooms" where they had to help with various tasks. In science class, the students had to learn about magnetism and how it could affect our experience in the area. Another group had to learn about latitude and longitude so that they could help us read the map. My group had to decipher a treasure map filled with riddles to determine exactly where the treasure was located. During lunchtime, the students learned about the dangers of scurvy and rickets. Everyone was in character the entire day, and the students played their parts to the hilt as well.

At the end of the day, we heard the sounds of storms playing over the sound system. We told the students that we were in the middle of the Bermuda Triangle and that we had to get to the bottom of the ship (the lobby) for safety. As we ran down the hall, I saw students swaying back and forth as if the waves were rocking the ship. I realized in that moment that we had really transported those students to somewhere special.

Once everyone was in the lobby, we explained that we had found the treasure, but that the treasure was actually knowledge, and that they displayed an enormous amount of intelligence that day. We told them that knowledge is the best kind of treasure, because once you have it, no one can ever take it away from you. It's yours forever. I know, I know: it was corny, but the kids ate it up, and the staff thought it was so much fun playing as pirates all day. It was great, and the students got to see the results of their teachers and parents coming together to do something truly special for them.

The next year we were a carnival from 1934 that was auditioning for new acts. The students went from room to room trying out for different stations of the carnival. For example, I was running "The World's Biggest Brain" exhibit, and I needed to find the smartest child. I began to quiz the kids, and when I asked them to name the Democrat who was currently president, most of them yelled, "Obama," but Arsene, remembering that we told him it was 1934, shouted, "FDR!" In every class throughout the entire day, the staff pretended it was 1934, and we were able to teach the students a great deal about the Great Depression, politics, and the popular culture and issues of that time.

If you are a teacher in a school where you don't envision ever getting the support of the entire staff, you can easily transform your own room. I was doing a unit on Rome with my students, and they were fascinated with the Coliseum. I decided to turn my room into the Coliseum by getting tan drapes from Home Depot and covering all of the walls. I then placed the desks in a circle around the edges of the room and put all of the chairs in the closet. I placed sheets over the desks and then used a fog machine and a few strobe lights to bring the room to life. I borrowed Mrs. Bearden's flaming lamps, placed some large peacock feathers around the room, and as a last touch, I put two large columns by the entrance. I asked the students to bring sheets to school that day, and before they entered the room, we made togas for them to wear over their clothes.

The students entered the room to a recording of thunderous applause and powerful music. I explained to them, in my best Roman accent (one that unfortunately sounds more like a British accent), that they would be gladiators in the Roman Coliseum that day. Throughout the class, individuals were selected to battle each other, and they met in the center of the room where they were given academic challenges. The students cheered one another on, and I encouraged them to "be" gladiators and to "feel" their surroundings. The students loved it.

I honestly don't do days like that often. If we did that all the time, we'd kill ourselves because it's just so much work. By doing it once in a while, however, it gives the students a magical moment that they will love and remember forever. When people ask them ten years from now to name a memory from their childhood in school, it won't be a lesson on Roman history; it will be the day the room was transformed into the Coliseum. That is powerful and something that can ignite children's love for learning as well as their desire to be in school.

✳ 83 ✳

Accept the fact that if kids like you all the time, then you're doing something wrong.

Sometimes, as parents and teachers, we have to be the bad guy, and we can't feel bad about it either. I think that one of the biggest mistakes teachers make, especially those new to our profession, is that they are afraid that the students won't like them. They want the students' approval so much that they won't discipline them or be as strict academically as they should. This is a huge mistake, because in the end, you're reaping easy instant gratification rather than hard-won long-term respect.

Hanging in my home is a framed note a child handed me during my first year of teaching. It is one of my most prized possessions and serves as a symbol of how I feel we should raise and discipline our children. The note was given to me by Theo Lee after I had given him a detention for slack work. He had completed the assignment, but it just wasn't up to my standards. In a rage, he handed me the note and stormed out with his lips poked out and hands on his hips. The note read:

> Mr. Clark you are not my friend no moore.
>
> love, theo

Even though he was upset with me, he still made sure to write "love." When we hold kids accountable and show them we expect the best from them, they love us for it. Children want us to be strict, they want us to set boundaries, and they want us to be consistent. When we are able to pull all of that together, we earn respect in their eyes.

Years later, I attended Theo's wedding. At the reception I asked him if he remembered the note, and he said he remembered it like it was yesterday. He said he was so furious that day. I said, "Yeah, I could tell you were mad with me the way you stormed out of the room."

He replied, "I wasn't mad with you, Mr. Clark. I was mad with myself because I had let you down. I just didn't know how to express it. To me, there was nothing worse in the world than letting you down."

Set your expectations high, hold kids accountable, and show them that you won't take less than their best. They want and need that from the adults in their lives.

⁎ 84 ⁎

Recognize that the heart of the school is the teacher. Hire the best and never settle.

People often ask what I consider the key to improving our education system. That is a loaded question, and if there were an easy answer, someone would have provided the solution. If I had to give one quick answer, however, I would suggest that the key lies with increasing teacher pay. The problem with paying teachers more is that we have a broken system where teachers can receive tenure after a few years of basic service where they manage not to strangle a random student.

I always say that the average teacher salary needs to be $100,000 a year. That range would entice the best college prospects to give our profession strong consideration. Currently, we are, on average, seeing only the bottom third of college graduates choose education as a career, and the best countries, educationally, have the best and brightest teachers. If we insist on allowing inadequate educators to stay in our profession by protecting them with tenure, our lawmakers will never agree to give such high salaries. It's just too hard to fire a bad teacher.

As I have traveled across the country, I will often ask administrators what percentage of their staff they would replace if given the choice. I tell them there would be no hard feelings, lawsuits, or drama; I'm just curious. The typical answer is about 70 percent.

It breaks my heart to hear stories of principals who have fired teachers only to have those teachers file lawsuits. Often there is public outcry from parents against the administrator, because they may like the teacher as an individual but have no idea how poor of a teacher he is.

Imagine if the Coca-Cola Corporation decided to give everyone job security after three years' employment. Then—and this is laughable—what if they told all their employees that they were going to pay them all the same amount, regardless of their job performance, depending on the number of years they have worked at Coca-Cola. Therefore, a person who has worked there for ten years will make the same amount as all of his ten-year colleagues, regardless of his effort, job performance, accomplishments, or value to the corporation. Any employer who does that is completely removing his employees' incentive to perform to the best of their ability. They are telling their employees, "We don't expect you to work harder. Just remain employed here and you'll get paid the same amount, regardless." That is what we are telling our teachers, and it has caused a lackadaisical, status quo mentality that has permeated the entire educational system.

At RCA, we realize that the key to excellence and having a successful school is having a successful teaching unit. To achieve that, we take months and months to complete the hiring process. Our first step is to ask teachers to complete an application and to submit a teaching video. In the video, we ask them to show creativity and what makes them unique during a classroom lesson. We receive hundreds of videos a year, and some of them are good; most of them, however, are not. Some of them, and I hate to say it, are even scary.

I remember one video where the man stopped teaching in the middle of the lesson and yelled at his students, "Would you shut up?! Do you know how important this video is for me?" I have no idea if he meant to edit that part out or leave it in, but, either way, it was just bad.

We have seen teachers wearing tank tops that revealed their belly buttons, and we have seen videos of teachers who were instructing an entire class of students who had their heads on their desks. As we always say at RCA, the best indication of the success of a teacher's lesson is the students' body language and attentiveness. When students are wide-eyed and sitting straight up, or leaning toward the teacher, you can tell instantly that something good is happening with that lesson.

After we find videos depicting teachers who show sparks of creativity and involved and excited students, we then usually have a phone or Skype videoconference with them. If teachers tell us that they can't use Skype because they have never done online conferencing and that they would feel more comfortable on the phone, we usually scratch them off the list. If you aren't able to research and figure out how to conference online, then you're not the type of teacher we're interested in having at RCA. On the other hand, if teachers say they have never heard of Skype but that they'll figure it out and would be thrilled to have an online conference, they receive props.

If the conference goes well, we then ask them to visit RCA and to teach a thirty-minute lesson to our students. I can't tell you how many administrators have complained to me that the person they interviewed is not the teacher they thought they were. Before you purchase a car, you test-drive it. Before we hire a teacher, we want to see him or her in action . . .

✷ 85 ✷

Always observe a teacher applicant teaching a lesson before offering him or her a job.

One teacher, whom I initially loved in her interview, taught a demonstration lesson to our seventh graders about Henry VIII. She put a shawl around her shoulders and ran back and forth across the front of the classroom acting out a scene where she was Henry VIII's wife and she was afraid she was going to have her head chopped off. She kept saying, "I know he is going to chop it off! I know he is going to chop it off!" She must have said that fifty times. Suddenly she stopped right in the middle of her demonstration and said, "I'm pretending to be one of his wives, and I am afraid he is going to cut off my head." And then she went back to, "He's going to chop my head off!" As the seventh graders walked out of the classroom, Jordan looked at me with big eyes and asked, "What was that?"

The biggest fear I had after watching that lesson is that I was about to hire her to teach at our school. She would have become one of the most important individuals in the lives of those children, and she would have, potentially, had more influence on them than any other adult in their lives.

Administrators, don't settle for just an interview. Take your time and make sure you hire the right individuals. Even if it makes your interview process much longer, it will save you the time it would take to deal with an inadequate teacher and the heartache you would experience knowing that your students are in a classroom with someone who is doing more harm than good.

In the end, the most important quality that we look for in hiring at the Academy is a dedication to making a difference in the lives of children. There are a lot of teachers who are passionate about their curriculum, and there are some who like the idea of teaching more than they actually enjoy teaching children. Their classroom is very neat and their lesson plan is crisp, but they act as if the kids are ruining the scene by having the gall to simply be there. It's apparent they are focused on the lesson they are teaching instead of placing their attention on the students.

When teachers visit RCA, we try our best to see who connects with the children. I remember when we interviewed Mrs. Goff. During her visit, she was watching me teach my math class, and instead of just watching, she actually leaned over and started to work with a student who was struggling. When the students jumped up to sing a math song, she jumped up and went for it with them. Despite everything she said in her interview, those moments with the kids made the biggest impact on our decision to hire her.

We interviewed another individual that year who was probably one of the smartest individuals I have ever met. He was on point during the interview, he had his doctorate degree in educational philosophy, and he came with glowing recommendations. He spent almost an entire day at RCA, and after the students left, we sat down to talk with him. We asked him what he thought of the students, and he said they were wonderful. I asked him if any child in particular made an impact on him, and he said, "I'm not sure of his name, but the little one seems really sharp." In the course of the interview, he never mentioned the names of any of our kids, and he kept directing the interview back to his content knowledge. It just didn't feel right, and we didn't hire him.

Sometimes you just have to go with your gut, and if you know it isn't the right fit, then listen to yourself and don't hire that person. On the other hand, sometimes your gut can lead you, surprisingly, in the right direction.

I was at the Nike store purchasing sneakers for my basketball team. At RCA, we have a basketball league where six or seven students are on a team with one adult from the school. We play in our own recreational league after school on Thursdays, and it's great fun.

I was having trouble finding shoes for the team, and a very tall gentleman stepped in and asked if he could help. I had noticed he was really busy helping multiple customers and operating the register as well. I figured it would be forever before he could assist me, but there he was, managing to juggle everything. And somehow he had every customer satisfied. He was joking, being respectful, and truly meeting everyone's needs.

I explained to him that the shoes were for my school's basketball team, and he jumped to it, knowing exactly what I needed. Before I knew it, I had my two bags of shoes in hand. I turned to leave, but he stopped me. He said he would help me carry the bags to the car. I refused, but he insisted. He said that his wife is a teacher and that he always goes out of his way to help educators because he knows how hard we work.

When we got to the car, he placed the bags in my trunk, told me good-bye, and turned to head back to work. I called out to him and asked him his name. He told me, and I then invited him to come to RCA to see the great work we were doing there in person. He said he'd be honored. As I left I said, "It was really nice to meet you, Mr. Bruner."

During his visit to RCA, he made a point to talk with every child, to make sure he remembered their names, and to inquire into the details of each student's strengths and weaknesses. It was obvious he had the "eyes of a father," and he seemed to connect with the students immediately. I told him that afternoon that I would love to have him volunteer at RCA, and he said he'd be thrilled to help out in any way possible.

After a week of observing Mr. Bruner volunteer every day, I talked with Kim and we decided to follow our hearts and offer him a job. I sat down to tell him, but before I could, he had something to tell me as well. He had turned in his two-weeks' notice at Niketown. I was shocked and asked, "Why'd you do that?" He responded that he had an intrinsic assurance and faith that God had clearly appointed him to work at the Ron Clark Academy.

If you live your life by faith, it is for certain that you will attract others who are similar, because in order to bring a vision to fruition, it takes others who have that same faith to help make it a reality.

Mr. Bruner, forever uplifting and inspiring!

Mr. Bruner continues to be a role model, a mentor, and a father to our children. We are blessed to have him as part of our team, and I know he has done more to uplift our students and our school than the gentleman with the doctorate could have ever done.

If you don't have what it takes in your heart, what's in your mind is useless.

✴ 86 ✴

Teach children the history and symbolism
of their home and school.

A few years ago I received the most precious Christmas gift from my mom. She made a book filled with photos of every ornament that hangs on our Christmas tree each year. Beside it, she described in detail the year we first obtained the ornament and why it is sentimental and means a lot to our family. She said that when she passes on, I will have the ornaments for my family's tree and that I can use the book to pass on the stories to future generations. By giving me that gift, she was really giving me our family's past so that I could carry it forward to the future. It was powerful and beautiful, and I treasure that book.

Prior to learning the history of each ornament, I honestly just thought our Christmas tree was beautiful. I never truly understood the meaning of all that hung on the tree.

I knew that I wanted to create that same type of awareness and feeling my mother provided for me at RCA, so we spend a lot of time talking with our students about the pictures that hang on the walls, the symbolism of the items we display in our school, and the overall background of the hundred-year-old factory that houses our school.

For example, the grand staircase in our school contains more than three hundred pounds of coins, and there is at least one coin from every country in the world. That staircase is a symbol of our school's emphasis on a global curriculum and our efforts to get our students to be global citizens. Each year, we make sure our students understand the purpose behind the stairs, along with all of the other areas of symbolism throughout our school.

Last year, we forgot to explain the history of the stairs during orientation. Weeks went by before we realized it.

Then, as part of our fifth graders' introduction to RCA, they have to give a tour of our school to their parents. As I was walking throughout the school with the fifth graders and demonstrating the information they would need to share, I stood on the steps of the stairs and began to explain how if you look in the stairs, you would clearly see more than three hundred pounds of coins, with at least one coin coming from every country in the world. The fifth graders gasped, "Ohh."

I asked them, "You all knew that, right?" and they let me know that they had never heard that. One student even said he just thought it was a bunch of fake money.

I let the students get on their hands and knees to look throughout the stairs and to see what coins they could find from different countries. They became so excited and were shouting out different locations and commenting on the cool designs. For weeks after that day, I would notice them looking down intently as we walked up the stairs, trying to get another glimpse of a cool coin.

If I had never taken the time to explain to the students about the meaning and symbolism of the stairs, they would have continued to think it was just a bunch of fake money. Now that they know the true meaning of the stairs, they see them differently, and when the students know the ins and outs of RCA completely, their bond and their love for RCA increases.

> **Do This:**
>
> Involve your students in a research project where you discover the meaning behind the name of your school. What other names were considered? And if your school is named after an individual, what was the meaning behind that selection? Does the individual have family members in the area who have never visited the school? You could set up a tour for them and have them stay for lunch and talk with your students about the history of their family member.
>
> You can also encourage your students to figure out the symbolism of the mascot and the year the school was constructed. You can even take the project a step further and have them research street names, the name of the town, and the founding fathers of the area.

⁂ 87 ⁂

Remember that children are literal thinkers and, as adults, we really have to spell out what we mean.

One of my best friends, Jeff Anderson, told me about a time when he took his five-year-old son to the doctor. His son, Austin, was instructed to pee in a cup. Afterward, he went back and sat beside his father, holding the cup in his right hand and looking really worried. Mr. Anderson asked his son, "Austin, what's wrong, buddy?"

Austin replied, "Dad, when do I have to drink it?"

As adults we often assume that children understand our expectations and that we are clear when we express ourselves. A parent at RCA told me that she was really upset with her son one day and she told him, "Get in

the shower right now!" She said she walked in the bathroom a few minutes later to see her son standing under the water with all of his clothes on. She freaked out and asked him what he was thinking, and he just replied, "You were mad and said I had to get in the shower right then, so I did."

We took a group of our fifth graders to Washington, DC, and it was the first time staying in a hotel for many of them. We explained that one student in each room would keep the hotel key and that he or she had to keep it safe. When we returned to the hotel after a day of sightseeing, one group of girls was locked out of their room. I asked them who was in charge of keeping the key safe, and Daryl Ann raised her hand. I asked her what happened to the key and if she had forgotten to take it with her. She said no, that she had just left it in the room. I asked why she would do such a thing, and she said, in a matter-of-fact tone, "I left it there because you told us to keep it safe, and I couldn't think of a safer place."

Wow.

When we took our students out of the country for the first time, we landed in London and boarded the bus to our hotel. After driving a few miles, one of our students, Syndei, kept staring out the window at the passing cars. Finally, she turned to me and said, "Hey, Mr. Clark, look! In this country they make the passengers drive."

For those who aren't aware, in England the steering wheel is located on the right-hand side instead of the left. I had taught the entire history of the British monarchy, but somehow such a small detail escaped me.

As parents and teachers, we should never assume what students know or that students understand clearly where we are coming from. One of my favorite lines to use with students is, "Can you tell me why you think I'm upset with you?" It's brilliant, and honestly, 90 percent of the time the children will not truly understand why I am upset. Most of the time they will think they have done nothing wrong, or if they will admit they did something wrong, they will not understand exactly why it bothered me.

I remember one time I was passing back a major math exam that I had graded. When I handed Trevor his exam, a 79, I gave him a look that

said, "This isn't your best." Trevor easily had the ability to be a straight-A student, but it was hard to get him to put forth the effort. As soon as he received his exam, he balled it up and threw it under his desk. I quickly told him to put his name on the board, because that type of behavior isn't acceptable at RCA.

When Trevor walked to the board, he mumbled something under his breath. Normally, my eagle ears can make it out, but I couldn't quite catch that one. Regardless, I told him to give himself a check, because, another rule at RCA is that when you put your name on the board, you will do it calmly and without making faces, smacking your lips, or mumbling. He gave his name the check, meaning he would have to sit at silent lunch that day. I could see he was about to start huffing and puffing, so I just stopped things right there by saying, "Trevor, we can talk about this after class."

After class I asked him, "Why do you think I wanted to talk with you after class?"

He responded, "Because you're mad at me."

I told him that I was not mad at him and rarely, if ever, did I get mad at any student. I explained that I would be disappointed or upset with their choices, but not mad. I then asked, "Why do you think I had you put your name on the board?"

He said, "Because I didn't do well on my test."

That shows how the mind of a child works. Rarely will they realize the true reason we are upset, and if we don't take the time to explain our feelings and the situation to them thoroughly, they will have misguided thoughts about the situation. For parents who have children who continue to misbehave by doing the same thing again, it may be because the parent has never fully explained the specific behavior that is causing the problem.

I told Trevor that I was disappointed with his test grade because I knew he could do better, but I had him put his name on the board because he threw the test under the desk. That is why his name was on the board, and the check came because of the mumbling. If I had let him walk out of the room that day, he would have served his silent lunch thinking that he was being punished for not doing well on his test. We should never assume we know what children are thinking. We have to ask them, find out, and then explain to them how and why we feel the way that we do.

Remember that the little things can make all the difference.

When dealing with people, you can never underestimate the impact of small gestures that show appreciation and thoughtfulness. At RCA, we try our best to do those small gestures in a clever and meaningful way. It is the RCA style.

A few years ago, we were honored to have Robin De Jesús from the Off-Broadway musical *In the Heights* stop by RCA for a brief visit. We knew we had only a short time to make an impression, and we quickly decided that the best way to greet him would be by performing a song from the musical. That, in and of itself, would be fine, but we had to push ourselves to make it more clever, more meaningful.

We pulled up a clip from the musical online and saw that the opening number contained dozens of singers and dancers performing on a city street full of life and energy. The scene started soft and slow, with the city waking up, but soon everyone was in action and on fire. We had to bring that feeling to RCA.

It took six hours of practice on a Saturday afternoon, but when Mr. De Jesús walked through our doors, he saw students sprawled all over the lobby, lining the stairs, leaning on the slide, and lying on the counter. They were frozen in time. Suddenly, one young man turned his head quickly to Mr. De Jesús and looked him directly in the eyes. The music started, and Tajee instantly began to sing:

Lights up on Washington Heights, up at the break of day
I wake up and I got this little guy I gotta chase away.

As he sang, the students started to wake up and come to life. As the tempo quickened, the students started to dance and join in with the song. They completely acted out the entire scene from *In the Heights,* jumping, singing, flipping, and twirling all over the entire lobby. It was as if you had walked right into a musical. The most powerful part was that the students looked Mr. De Jesús directly in the eyes; they sang with confidence and with joy, and he was blown away.

Before he left RCA, he told me that he had never experienced anything like that in his life. He invited our students to attend the musical in New York in the spring and he let me know that he and the entire cast would be honored to have us perform "In the Heights" for them. At the time, I didn't know whether he was serious or not, but four months later I found myself watching my students perform on a New York City stage as the entire cast watched in the audience. When the students finished their performance, everyone in the cast rose to their feet and burst into applause. It was unreal.

That moment came because we didn't just settle for welcoming him to RCA with a sign and a handshake. The students sang—no, they *performed*—for him in a way that was special and meaningful. It was that certain something that made the difference.

I received an email from a principal who had sent a number of her teachers to RCA for training. She wanted me to know that she would be sending another group soon and that she had great news to share. She told me that they had received the "Gold Award" for outstanding test scores. I almost shot her an email congratulating her, but then I saw it was only twelve noon, and I realized that we had a chance to get something sent to the school. I asked Ms. Mosley to look up the school online, find the address, and send a bouquet of gold flowers to the principal with a note that said, "Congratulations! Continue to Go for the Gold! Love, The Ron Clark Academy Family."

Ms. Mosley just looked at me, lowered her head so she could see me clearly over her glasses, and asked in her Ms. Mosley way, "Mr. Clark? Gold flowers? Where have you seen gold flowers?"

I just said, "Ms. Mosley, I have no doubt you can find gold flowers."

Ms. Mosley smiled, said "Uh-huh," and jumped on it immediately. The flowers were delivered by three that day.

That night I received this email:

Hi Ron,

All I can say is . . . NOTHING shocks me after being a principal because it is ALWAYS CRAZY every minute of EVERY day, but you completely shocked and surprised me today with the absolutely gorgeous "GOLD" flowers. I was speechless when I walked into my office. The office staff ran to get the camera and then we called my husband because for me to be speechless is literally impossible!!! I went to every grade level in the building and showed most of our 750 students and 106 staff members the flowers. I told them all that you sent them to celebrate their success. The kids were all cheering and were so happy in the classrooms and the hallways!!! I am even so nerdy that I walked up the hallway with them and told a hallway full of parents during dismissal all about your academy and how you sent them to us to celebrate . . . they were all so happy!!!

Thank you for the impact you have had on all of us.

—Cheryl Thomas, principal,
Quail Run Elementary School

Sometimes what takes us such a short amount of time can bring so much joy and inspiration to others.

I was at the grocery store one day when I received a text from Christopher, a fifth grader, who loves global studies. It said, "Mr. Clark, where can I get books on the 1970s?" We were learning about Watergate, the life of Elvis, and the Iran hostages crisis in class, and he wanted to learn all he could about the time period. I sent back a message letting him know that he could probably find a good book at Barnes & Noble or any other bookstore.

After I pressed "send," I stood there for a minute in the produce section looking at the tomatoes. I was exhausted and had a ton of things to do that night, but I went to the checkout, paid for my items, and then pulled out of the grocery store parking lot and headed to the Barnes & Noble up the street. I walked out ten minutes later with an incredible book for kids on the 1970s. I sent a text back to Christopher that said, "I'll be stopping by your house in ten minutes." I drove straight there, knocked on the door, and handed him the book. His mom looked shocked, and he looked sort of bewildered. I apologized to her for showing up unannounced, and she told me she was thrilled to see me and so appreciative.

I didn't know the impact that quick visit would have, but when Christopher came to class the following Monday, he ran up to me with an enormous smile. He said, "Mr. Clark, I read the whole book." I could tell from the look on his face that he had, indeed, read the whole book. I asked him what he thought of it, and he went on and on about all he had learned. Christopher was always a quiet child, but after that day he greeted me with a big "Hello, Mr. Clark" each morning. He looked at me with respect beyond description, and his level of effort in my class soared. It was just a book, but it was so much more. It was that "added something" that makes all the difference. It was taking the extra step, and at times, that small step can have an impact that will stretch for miles.

✴ 89 ✴

Provide lessons in life that will
become lessons for life.

When educators visit RCA, they will often ask, "Where did you get these kids?" Our students can at times seem drastically different from other teenagers; they are respectful, happy, and eager to learn. They uplift one another and have a certain positive energy that is rare. To answer the question, the response is easy: our students are the same as children everywhere. Every child has the potential to have all of those qualities mentioned. The only thing we do differently at RCA is to take the time to teach them what we expect and to show them the appropriate way for them to handle themselves in various situations.

A lot of what we teach the students comes from the first book I wrote *The Essential 55*, which outlines the fifty-five rules that I have for my students. In order to make sure that our expectations are clear, we begin school two days earlier for our fifth graders. During those two days, we place them into groups of five and have them go from staff member to staff member to get training from our entire team. Someone will teach the students how to organize their lockers, someone will show them the proper way to wash their hands and leave the bathroom clean, while someone else will teach them how to work the air-conditioning controls. We cover everything from how to check out a library book to a detailed explanation of the history of RCA. In my class, I always demonstrate the appropriate way to put your name on the board without making faces or complaining, along with how to cheer and uplift classmates. By the end of the two days, those students have learned every possible thing they need to know to be a successful RCA student. They come in on the first official day of school ready to go! They know what we expect, and we have shown them how to handle every situation.

People comment that our students give the best handshakes and that they wish their children would do the same. They wish their children would maintain eye contact. They wish their children clapped for others. All of those things and many, many more can happen. It only takes us, as adults, to guide the children and show them what we expect. Does doing this make children perfect? No, of course not, and they will make mistakes often. But the issues we have at RCA with our students and the issues I had with my former students in Harlem and North Carolina are minimal because of the foundation that was put in place.

Uplift the students who have the furthest to go.

When you are operating a school, there are many times when tough decisions have to be made, and I will be the first to admit that there have been times when I made the wrong decision. With everything I do, I try to consider what is in the best interest of our students, but at times there are no easy answers and sometimes what seems like the right move at the moment turns out to be a mistake.

When we first opened RCA, we visited with other private schools to get some insight. Even though almost half of our students come to us below grade level, they still receive scholarships to attend RCA, and we were told that when you are dealing with students on scholarship, that you must hold them accountable for their academics. Most schools told us that if a child's grades aren't acceptable, he is placed on probation and that if his grades don't improve during the next quarter, he loses the scholarship. That seemed pretty standard across the board, and we put that policy in place at RCA. By the end of the year, we had several students who lost their scholarships and did not return to our school.

It was heartbreaking, and I felt sick to my stomach, but we kept telling ourselves, "We are doing so much for these kids. If they aren't willing to work hard and meet us halfway, then revoking the scholarship is the right thing to do." I also figured that it would send a powerful message to the students who remained at RCA; it would show them that if they wanted to stay at RCA that they would need to work hard. I also rationalized it in my mind by saying, "This is what every other school does." In the end, however, it just felt wrong. They are kids. Yes, they need to learn to work hard and they have to apply themselves, but I never wanted to see another kid leave RCA. In public school, students can be sent to alternative schools or placed in classes for special education, but that can feel wrong to me, too. I just knew we had to make sure that we had done everything humanly possible to help these kids.

That year, we implemented a program called "Second Parent," where we identified the students who were of greatest concern at RCA. We then paired each student with one RCA staff member who would, in theory, become that child's "Second Parent." The individual would be in charge of tutoring, monitoring grades and behavior, making multiple contacts with the student each day, reading the same novels so that they could discuss the content, sitting in on occasional classes to monitor effort, and working with the child to develop an incentive program. We knew it would be a lot of work for our staff members, but we all agreed that the lowest students in our classes seemed to take the majority of our time and that we could push the whole class so much faster if those kids were holding their own. We hoped that by uplifting the students of concern that the entire school would be uplifted as well.

It didn't take long to see that we were right on target. After only a few weeks of implementation, the entire school seemed different. The low-performing students were walking around the school smiling and with more confidence. They were doing much better in our classes and seemed altogether happier. It was an amazing transformation, and, while I think the academic support helped, I believe the real reason for the transformation had more to do with the one-on-one personal contact. Just knowing that someone cares about you and wants you to do well is powerful, and when our staff showed their concern and offered their help, the students' response was overwhelmingly positive and effective.

At the end of the year, honestly, we did have one student who lost his scholarship, but we, as a staff, felt that we had not only helped him all we could as individual teachers, but that his "Second Parent" had also made sure that we went even above and beyond our normal efforts to help that child. It did hurt to lose that young man, but instead of focusing on losing him, I encouraged our staff to celebrate the outstanding success of the other students. They were all in danger of not returning to RCA, but with the love, attention, and support of their "Second Parent" they made incredible gains. Five of them even ended up on the honor roll, and twelve of them had a C as their lowest grade. With the academic rigor we have at RCA, that is quite an accomplishment.

Allow teachers the freedom to make their rooms reflect their personalities— allow them to use color!

When we were envisioning what RCA would be, we met with several architectural firms to see which group we wanted to work with. They all were very quick to say, "We have worked with dozens of schools, and here's our portfolio." I recall sitting there looking at picture after picture of the same building. It didn't take me long to realize that we wouldn't be using architects to help with the design of the school; we decided to do it ourselves.

We wanted a school that looked like kids designed it, not adults. We wanted a school that teenagers would be proud of and find "cool." It had to be different from any school in the world. I asked myself, "What would I have wanted in the school when I was a child?" I recalled that I was always fascinated by the moving bookcases on the Scooby-Doo cartoons. Shaggy and Scooby would be running from ghosts, and just when you thought they were finished for good, they would run into a bookcase that would slide open and transport them to another side. I knew right then that we had to have a magical bookcase in our school. I called in volunteers and friends to find a way to make it happen, and two weeks later, the entrance to my classroom was a magical corner, complete with fireplace, purple couch, fat-lady portrait, and sliding bookcase doors that would fly open when you turned the torch on the wall to the right.

Normally closed, the bookcase will open only by the turn of a torch, a magic word to the lady in the painting, or the press of a secret button.

Kim also had an amazing idea. There was graffiti covering buildings all over South Atlanta, and she had an ingenious thought to have one of the artists paint inside our school. At RCA we push ourselves to be different and never to squash an idea, no matter how outlandish it may be, so we decided to give it a shot. Kim looked online and found a Norwegian website that listed the aerosol art of one of the world's top artists. His name was Mister Totem, but he was known by all as the "Michelangelo of Aerosol Art." Kim said, "Ron, we must have this guy paint our school!" She decided to email the site in hopes of finding out that Mister Totem might tour the United States at some point in the near future. No response. She continued to look for a way to contact Mister Totem, and finally after hours of looking online, she found him.

The next day Kim called me on 10. (When Kim calls me and she is talking so quickly I can't understand her, I call that "Kim on 10.") Once I calmed her down, she told me that Mister Totem had called her and that he was willing to paint our school as his contribution to our efforts. I told her that was outstanding! I asked her how in the world was he going to get to RCA from Norway, and then she said, "Ron, that's the best part. He lives two miles up the street from our school."

Sometimes in life you just know that things were meant to be, and this was one of those times.

We met with Mister Totem and soon learned that he is a genius. He completely understood our vision for RCA, and as we described what we saw in our minds, he took our thoughts and transferred them to the walls of our school. Looking at his creations, I remember thinking to myself that there is no way a child can walk through this school and not be inspired and motivated by the colorful works of art before them.

After he painted several places in the school, Mister Totem asked me, "So, when you envision teaching in your room, what colors and images would make you the happiest in that space?" In that moment I realized that we had to allow every teacher to create his or her own space. We needed to give the teachers the freedom to make the rooms their own, filled with colors and images that would inspire them as well as the students.

From that day forward, when teachers come to work at RCA, we allow them to create their own spaces, and Mr. Totem helps transform the place for them. We had one teacher turn her history classroom into a time machine. We have a room that is a Moroccan village, and we have a room that was constructed to be an entire city, complete with Superman in a telephone booth, rows of desks labeled with street signs (such as Adverb Avenue), and a highway that runs right through the middle of the room. The best part about the rooms is that not only do they inspire our teachers, but they are also loved by our students. If you visit RCA and ask our students what they love about our school, you can bet that many of them will say the designs on the walls. I have heard different students describe their old schools as prisons. It is surprising how impactful a little color can be.

I know teachers in most schools aren't allowed to paint their walls. When I was in North Carolina, it was a major no-no. I actually painted my room and then apologized and promised to paint it back to beige before I left. I was lucky to have a principal who just shook her head and let me get away with it. Most teachers aren't so fortunate. The saddest part about it is that paint is cheap, but the impact it can have is huge. I beg school systems, "Please, don't be afraid of color! Bring your schools to life!"

To those who argue that they hate to paint a room a certain color for a teacher when she might leave at the end of the school year, I counter that if they took the time to allow that teacher to create her space, perhaps she wouldn't want to leave and she would be more likely to remain at the school.

To those who will say they just don't have the money in the budget for things like aerosol art, sliding doors, a big slide, and dinosaur heads, I ask you, "Why isn't it in your budget?" Never underestimate the value of creating the right environment and building the appropriate atmosphere that will inspire our children to learn.

Not every school has to be as radical as having an aerosol artist decorate its walls, but if your school isn't using color to bring the walls, the ceilings, the closets, and the doors to life, then you are missing a great opportunity to build an environment that your students will love and where they will be inspired.

After all, are we building these schools for adults or children?

✷ 92 ✷

Let the students shine.

Whether it's in athletic leagues, talent shows, debate teams, or other activities, we need to do all we can to provide our children with opportunities to shine. It not only builds confidence and self-esteem, but it also provides the students with an opportunity to become comfortable while in front of crowds. Stage fright is a common fear among adults, and it's best to help children face the fear at a young age before it becomes a real issue.

Every Friday at RCA we have our students go to their "houses," Altruismo, Rêveur, Isibini, and Amistad. They then have thirty minutes to come up with a musical skit to perform in front of the entire school. The house leaders usually have a song and some ideas in mind; generally they take a popular song and change the words to show pride for their house and their desire to win points.

When we first started the "house cheers," it was a crisis. The students looked scared and unsure of themselves. The cheers were lame and in no way creative. The staff members are just supposed to be in the room to provide discipline and not help with the cheers at all, so we really couldn't step in and take over for the kids. Instead, every Friday after the cheers, we would tell them how we were disappointed and how they had to get better.

We encouraged them to come with their songs and a plan several days in advance and to pass out the lyrics to their house members prior to Friday so that they could practice. We encouraged them to "wow" us. We continued to provide the criticism, but when they did well, we really showed it with standing ovations, cheers, and mad praise. Soon the students began to learn what "wow" meant, and their performances got sharper, cleverer, and more impressive.

By giving the students only thirty minutes to prepare, we didn't take much academic classroom time; we instead forced them to think quickly, to come together as a team, and to put themselves out there with no inhibitions or fears. We watched our students who were quiet and withdrawn become confident, proud, and comfortable being in front of others. That is a gift that will travel with them for the rest of their lives.

At the end of the school year, we have a musical that is completely written by our students. They write all of the scenes and musical numbers, and it basically turns into a two-hour show full of skits, songs, and dances by the kids. The students perform it over the course of a week, and it is always sold out.

The most amazing part of the entire process is that we really don't start putting the plans for the musical in motion until about two weeks before the show. Again, we challenge our students to think quickly, to figure out the most successful way to work together to be creative, clever, and entertaining to the point that people will be thrilled with the outcome.

Every year it is a bit maddening, but the students always find a way to pull it together. The biggest issue is that they will write tons of skits that just aren't that good, and we will veto them and tell them, "You can do better." It takes a lot of effort on all of our parts to finally get the scenes to where they need to be, but once it's set, the students rush to learn the dances, the lines, and the flow of the entire musical. At the end of opening night, when the crowd is on their feet, applauding for what seems like forever, the students beam. They are more proud than you can imagine because they did it all on their own. They wrote the scenes, they learned the lines, they created the dances, and they put on the show. It is theirs, and it is something they can be proud of forever.

If you ever go to one of the shows, you are certainly in for a treat. The best part to me is that you can always count on RCA's trademark eye contact. During their songs, we encourage the students to look into the eyes of the audience members and not to turn away until the audience members turn away. We teach them to maintain that intensity, show them the confidence they have, and exude pride through their eyes. It is shocking for everyone who sits in the first few rows, and it is definitely an experience like no other. The smiles, the joy, the pride, and the eye contact are all impressive.

What I love the most, however, is that I know that our students will take that spirit with them to boardrooms, business meetings, political rallies, and countless other places where they will be in charge of a group of people. They will work the room, and they will own it because as children they were taught not to be afraid and they were given the opportunity to shine.

From Osei's Mom

I find it amazing how RCA helps eliminate the "fear factor" in all of its students. I was absolutely shocked during the first RCA musical, as many parents were, when we saw our kids on stage feeling very comfortable in front of an audience while delivering a great performance. I kept wondering: *Is that my child up there?* Today he is very comfortable holding intelligent conversations with adults from all walks of life, and I know it is due to the opportunities RCA took to "push him" out there and to give him opportunities to conquer his fears. This kind of education is *priceless!*

—Mrs. Avril, parent, graduating Class of 2010

From Jill Lebiedzinski, Teacher

I went to the Ron Clark Academy in May 2010. It was a life-changing experience!

One idea I took from RCA into my own classroom is using house cheers. All of my students are divided into four separate houses: red, black, green, and, blue. Each house has five to six students in it, and these students were randomly selected from a spinner. Each week the students get chances to do house challenges and work individually to help their house earn points. They can earn points by following our class rules, being kind to others, and working hard. At the end of each week, I tally the house points on a clipboard I carry around with me and update them on our class house board. At the

end of each week, I give the students ten minutes to get with their houses and come up with a chant, cheer, or dance. The students are very creative and come up with amazing house cheers. The students break out into song and have even made up their own raps. I have even had a student break-dance and teach the other house members all the moves.

The best part about the house cheers is the presentations. The students beat on the desks as I call out the house color and their total points for the week.

After each house gets called, the members perform their cheer in front of the whole class. The last house called is always the winner and gets the most applause. The winners get not only the respect of winning but also a prize from the treasure box. The house cheers have made us closer as a class and have truly helped us become a class family. The students are always happy for the winners and even give pats on the backs to show their respect. They never boo or get upset when another house wins because they know that rule number three is to congratulate a classmate when he or she does well. These house cheers have made my class stand out at my school!

—Jill Lebiedzinski, technology integration specialist,
St. Alphonsus School, Maple Glen, Pennsylvania

93

Leave the jealousy at the door.

I beg of administrators, please, please recognize when you have a teacher who is dynamic, energetic, and trying to be innovative. If you stifle his or her creativity, and if you tie the hands of the ones who are trying so hard to uplift their students, then you are hurting your entire school in

the long run. Honestly, sometimes I have had teachers at RCA come to me with a vision for a program or a strategy we should use that I initially wasn't excited about, but, not wanting to ruin their energy and passion, I would support them; I gave them whatever resources they needed and let them know I was proud of their efforts. In the end, almost every project turns out to be extremely successful and the staff members feel pride, an overwhelming sense of accomplishment, and gratitude that their idea was respected. And I have realized, over and over, that just because I might not be able to envision the outcome a staff member has in mind doesn't mean that it won't turn out to be a great success.

As a profession, educators cannot continue to cater to the old, established way of teaching and thinking. We have to morph with the times, highlight ingenuity, and celebrate when a teacher is trying something new.

And for those teachers who are negative and so set in their ways that no methods are right except their own, I wish they would just hush. I'd like to say to them all:

If you aren't going to go ahead and leave the profession, can you please just remain quiet and refrain from spreading negativity? Remember that we are all here to uplift children, and if someone is working hard to do that, how about honoring that commitment instead of pulling them down with snide remarks about their efforts.

While I don't think tenure is bad per se, getting it too often and too easily usually means that person stays with a district for life. When people are unhappy, they don't leave nor can they easily be asked to go, as in most other fields, because they can't go to a new district and land on the same pay scale. So we end up with a number of calcified, ingrained, senior staff who believe they own the place and who so dislike their jobs that they put down anything or anyone who even looks as if they're thinking of doing anything new, different, or effective.

I am sorry to sound so negative, but I am tired of having first-year teachers walk up to me at events, send gut-wrenching emails, and show up at RCA in tears because they are so depressed having to work around staff members who are mean and not focused on doing what is best for children. The average amount of time those new teachers are staying in our profession is just under five years, and it is causing the pool of candidates for us to choose from to be less and less stellar. Also, the way new teachers are treated in our profession is common knowledge, and it is keeping bright college students from choosing education as a major.

Though the negativity in our schools may be seen as harmless, our profession is shooting itself in the foot as long as administrators and teacher leaders allow pessimistic attitudes to persist and negative teachers to remain in the classroom.

☀94☀

Realize that you never truly know all that is going on in the life of a child.

About a month into the school year, I was shocked to see a young man's grades drop out of nowhere. He was normally a very solid student, but he now appeared completely out of it. I told him that I was disappointed and that I expected more from him. I soon found out that he was hearing the same thing all over the entire school. I asked him to stay after class, and when I asked him what was going on with his grades, he just shrugged his shoulders. I asked if he was trying very hard, and he said, "Yes, sir." I asked if he felt he was trying his absolute best, and he promised me he was.

I was floored and about to send him on to class when I decided to ask one more thing: "Has anything changed in your home recently?"

He responded, "Well, just the lights."

I asked him what he meant, and he proceeded to tell me that the lights were off, but that it was okay because his father had an extension cord that ran to the neighbor's house and they were able to have lights sometimes. He then told me that when they don't have lights, he has to sit in the car to read by the car light and that it gets cold out there so he has to hurry sometimes.

This child was staring at me like everything was normal and that I shouldn't be shocked by what he was telling me. I patted him on the back and told him to continue to try his best. Then I immediately went to see our counselor, Ms. Scott, to determine the plan for how we were going to help that family.

It is easy as a teacher to look out at a sea of thirty faces and pretend that everything is wonderful when they are at home each night, but it's just not the case. Children learn very young how to mask problems and to appear that they are fine when they really aren't. In many cases, we will never know what they are experiencing, but what we can do is love them, make their time with us special, and do all we can to provide them with encouragement, pride, and self-esteem that will help them to cope with the struggles they are facing.

✳ 95 ✳

Raise our children to be global citizens.

If we want our children to be successful and leaders in their various professions, then they are going to have to have a global perspective. With each year, our world becomes smaller and more connected, and understanding how the world works and the nature of global relations are imperative to international relations.

At RCA, we made the commitment to take our students around the world as one of the initial foundations of our vision. Since we are in Atlanta, we thought getting the support of Delta Air Lines would be a natural fit. We called and submitted requests, but our efforts weren't successful. We knew, however, that they would have to be an integral piece if we were truly going to take our students around the world, and we continued with our requests to meet with them.

In the years before RCA opened, I spoke at every Rotary and Kiwanis club, business league, and civic organization I could find. I was making dozens of speeches each month to drum up support for the school, and during one speech I noticed the individual from Delta Air Lines that we had so desperately been trying to meet with, Mrs. Scarlet Pressley-Brown. I said to myself, "This is your one chance," and I jumped off the stage, walked through the tables, and jumped right up on the middle of the table at which the Delta contingent was eating. I made my entire speech that day standing between plates of salmon, butter dishes, sweet tea, and Mrs. Scarlet Pressley-Brown.

When I finished, I looked her directly in the face and gave her a big smile as I jumped off the table.

Afterward, when I was talking with the crowd and signing books, I felt someone tug at my arm. I turned to see Mrs. Pressley-Brown. She handed me her card and said, "Call me."

You couldn't tell me anything after that. I was happier than a hog in hot mud, and I called her later that day. We arranged lunch, and I explained to her that RCA was about showing everyone the importance of global travel. Our trips would not be only about providing our students with the opportunity, but would be about showing *everyone* how important it is to travel. Thousands of educators, donors, and community leaders would visit RCA each year, and we wanted to show them the impact that travel would have on our students. I also pointed out that our trips wouldn't only be about traveling; they were going to be educational experiences that integrated each area's history, culture, economy, and religion with its current community needs. These experiences abroad would raise students who were global minded and who would be leaders with the capacity to consider the cultures and issues of other nations and people. I told her that we needed Delta Air Lines to make our dream come true. We were sitting in a booth, and I realized at that point that I had somehow pulled both feet onto the bench and that I was squatting as if I was about to hop right over the table and out the door. I am a mess.

Mrs. Pressley-Brown just looked at me, took a sip of her sweet tea, and dabbed the edges of her mouth with her napkin. I have rarely seen a woman so stunning and elegant as she, and I was praying she wouldn't think I was completely crazy.

She said, "After careful consideration, the team at Delta has agreed to support your vision."

I said, *"Great!"* After a second I followed with, "So what exactly does that mean?"

She said, "Well, Delta Air Lines will be the official airline of the Ron Clark Academy."

"Wonderful," I said, nodding my head up and down. "So what *exactly* does that mean?"

And then she said, "It means that we are going to fly your children around the world, and you aren't going to have to pay for it."

I slid all the way off the bench, under the table, and onto the floor, right beside Mrs. Pressley-Brown's stunning Louis Vuitton shoes.

As we started to lay the foundation for our curriculum at RCA, we realized very quickly that if we were going to take our students around the world that we had to be knowledgeable as well. As parents and educators, you can only teach what you know, and we had to make sure we knew a lot. I personally read two books about the history of the world and began watching CNN daily. I watched foreign films and researched popular music and cultural figures around the world. I immersed myself into learning everything possible about every country that we would visit with our students, and I soon realized that I was more excited to travel than I had ever been in my life. The more you know, the more you enjoy any experience. Traveling to a country when you don't know every detail is like going to a music concert when you have never heard any of the songs. When you are prepared, it's like hearing your favorite artist while you sit in the front row. It just reaches your core. I knew that if I was getting that excited about researching the various locations that the students were going to be thrilled beyond words, and I was right. They began to learn at rapid rates, and with every experience, they threw themselves into the process of learning every aspect of the country. When the trips finally happened, they were life changing.

The best part about the trips is that it's gotten to a point where thousands of individuals travel with us each time, not in person, but on Facebook.com and twitter.com. We are now able to take pictures and videos every hour and then post them to our accounts instantly. Everyone—including you, your family, and your students—can follow us and experience each step of the journey. Our Twitter name is: @ronclarkacademy.

One of the most beautiful experiences occurred as we were heading back from Paris. We had to fill out customs cards, and Ms. Scott called me over to look at how the students had filled them out. On the space designated for the "number of family members traveling with you," many of the students had written "40"—the number of people in our group from RCA.

From Michaela's Grandmother

After watching the students at RCA travel and learn about the world with such curiosity and confidence, I was inspired to follow in their footsteps, abandon all fear, and set out on my own journey. Much to my own shock, I applied for a job with Abu Dhabi Education Council and moved to Dubai to begin my own journey. I miss Michaela more than words can say, but I would never in a million years have had the inclination to do such a thing before Michaela started at RCA. The opportunities afforded her there are beyond anything I ever dreamed, and my dreams are bigger now as well. I know that we make much of our own destinies, and I wanted to "dream big," as we say at RCA. We just have to step out in faith, and believe in miracles!

—Mrs. Jones, grandmother, Class of 2013

From Chris Williams, Teacher

Since reading your books, I decided that I, too, wanted to be a teacher who would expand the borders of the classroom. I have hence found a way to take my students to New York City, Atlanta, New Orleans, London, Paris, Rome, Germany, Switzerland, and Austria. I've also taken students to Baltimore Orioles games and Washington Redskins games. Each time we go, I love seeing the looks on the kids' faces. The sense of wonder is just one of those teacher moments that can't be explained—it can only be experienced.

Other teachers will often ask me how I am able to take so many trips, and I explain to them that with determination and a dream, anything is possible.

—Mr. Williams, social studies educator,
Gretna High School, Gretna, Virginia

96

Recognize the big cost of big dreams.

When we first opened the Academy, teachers used to ask me all the time, "How did you do it?" or "I want to start my own school. Can you tell me how I can accomplish this?"

In response to their questions, I used to think, *You practically have to build an altar and sacrifice yourself.* It has been six years since the process started, and Kim and I are still operating on no sleep. We initially told ourselves that for the first three years, we would have to sacrifice our personal lives to get the school off the ground, but we learned that whenever you are trying to achieve excellence at the level we were shooting for, fitting in a family, friends, hobbies, and other activities can be challenging.

I honestly know that if I had children of my own, I wouldn't be able to accomplish all that I do at RCA. I do know, however, that I would still be the same teacher in the classroom, full of energy and excitement and a belief that all of my students can achieve greatness. Regardless of the situation, that is something that we all can carry with us, no matter what our responsibilities outside of our classrooms.

Once we purchased the old factory, we had no money to do the renovations, and no one seemed too excited to give us donations either. We decided that if people wouldn't give money, then perhaps they would give in-kind donations, and I started speaking at breakfasts, lunches, and dinners all over the city to garner support. After one speech, I was signing books and I noticed that a man's shirt said, "W. S. Nielsen Skylight Company." We had hoped to put a huge skylight in the middle of RCA, and I promptly wrote in his book, "Thank you for donating the brand-new skylight to our school."

He came back a few minutes later and said, "Why did you write this in my book?"

With my Southern drawl and innocent eyes, I replied, "Wishful thinking."

That gentleman, Mike Nielsen, gave me his card, and after touring the empty factory, he agreed to donate a $25,000 skylight to go directly in the middle of our school. He continued to watch our school grow, and the more we accomplished, the prouder he became of our success. He eventually donated many more skylights and student scholarships before finally becoming one of our board members.

He, like others who may have donated a window or a TV, became attached on a small but important level and enjoyed watching our school grow.

Kim and I realized that even though individuals were willing to help on small levels, there was no way we could receive enough in donations to complete the entire school. We had to find a bank to give us a loan, and we soon learned that would be a daunting task. We had to write business plans and prepare stacks of documents throughout the loan process. Each bank we approached required several meetings, a tour of the school, lunches, and formal presentations. It took enormous amounts of time, and Kim and I really couldn't decide how to choose between the four banks we were considering.

After the month-long process was over, we learned that our choosing which bank to go with wouldn't be a problem, since none of them agreed to give us a loan. They said start-up schools are too risky, and that no one had ever built a school that offered a scholarship for every child. They said successful private schools operate on tuition.

One lady at a major bank in Atlanta sat across from us, looked me directly in the eyes, and said, "I hope you don't mind me being frank, but no bank will give you this loan, and there is no way you will start this school."

I can't tell you how many times Kim and I have talked about that moment. That woman's comments actually fueled us to work harder. After four months and ten bank proposals, however, every answer was the same.

It was so frustrating and demoralizing, and I began to wonder how in the world we would get the warehouse renovated.

Finally, in a meeting with Highland Commercial Bank, as we finished our presentation, I realized that I was almost in tears. I put my head down, and when I looked up, I noticed the loan officer had tears in his eyes, too. He said, "I'll be right back." When he returned, he said that the administrative team at the bank would like to tour the warehouse. The following week a team of seven showed up. There was broken glass, dirt, and trash all over the factory, but I stood atop a stack of old boards and painted a picture of the most beautiful school in the world, full of magic, smiling children, passionate teachers, and love. I went for it with all my heart, trying to will the vision for RCA into their souls.

The next week, we signed our loan. The journey truly began.

We soon started to meet with major foundations in the Atlanta area to garner support. I was giving a tour of the empty warehouse to one very established organization, and halfway through I mentioned that we'd be placing a big electric-blue slide in the middle of our school. They asked me why in the world I would want to do that. I explained the philosophy behind the slide, and they told me that it was a ridiculous idea and they promptly left without allowing me to finish the presentation. I felt as though I had been hit in the gut.

Soon after that, I was making a speech for Great American Financial Resources, and the team there, Tom Maxey and Mat Dutkiewicz, suggested I speak with the owners of the company, Carl and Craig Lindner. They explained that the elder Mr. Lindner was an extremely wealthy and generous man but that he was approaching ninety. They suggested I "tone down" my presentation and calmly explain my vision for the school to him and his son, Craig.

I walked in to have lunch with them at a big white, round table.

Mr. Lindner slowly started eating a bowl of tomato soup, and he barely looked up at me. I sat before a Cobb salad with a glass of sweetened tea and calmly started explaining my vision for RCA.

Well, I couldn't stand it. Before I had even touched my fork, I found myself standing up, and within minutes, I was doing my Texas Embassy Cantina dance. (For those of you who have seen one of my speeches in person, you understand exactly what that looked like.) I went on and on about the school and our vision, hopping around the table, flailing my arms everywhere, and describing the dream of RCA. When I sat down, Mr. Lindner finally looked up from his bowl of soup and smiled at me.

We received a donation of $500,000.

That definitely helped to kick-start the process, but it remained a constant struggle. It takes $3 million a year to train thousands of teachers and run our school, and as soon as a big donation comes in, it usually goes right back out. At times I feel as if we are running in a race with no end in sight, and it definitely keeps me up at night.

Of all of the things that Kim and I have had to sacrifice to start RCA—time with our families and friends, our health, our personal hobbies, time for simply watching TV, going to a movie, or plain old relaxing—the one thing we have had to sacrifice more than any other is peace of mind. We love our students at RCA as if they are our own, and the thought of anything happening to our school terrifies us. It causes us to work harder than imaginable—to push ourselves even when we feel we can't go on anymore and to place the school's needs before that of our own.

That is why the strength of our educator training program is so essential to our survival. When educators visit RCA for professional development or for one of our national conferences, the funds go directly toward student scholarships, which therefore support the school. We currently train three thousand teachers a year, but we are in the middle of a capital campaign that will increase the size of our campus and allow us to accommodate six thousand teachers a year. The revenue generated will help RCA become sustainable by relying less on the community for support.

It isn't realistic for us to replicate RCA, and that isn't our mission. Our purpose is to create new and innovative ways to educate children and to share our findings with others in a professional development setting. We want to replicate our ideas around the world but not necessarily our entire model.

☀ 97 ☀

Reach out to the community to build a powerful network.

When we reach out to our donors for help, the main reason we have so much success is because of the strong relationships we have formed. I learned a very valuable lesson during my first year of teaching. I went to a local bank in Aurora, North Carolina, because I heard they gave donations to schools. I asked for $75 to help my students with a project where they would make papier-mâché globes.

The banker told me that their allocated money for donations was completely gone for the year. It was March. I asked him if his calendar year started in January, and he said it did and that I should check back with him the following January.

I try to never walk away empty-handed, so I asked, "Could we at least get a donation of five dollars?"

He responded, "I could give you five dollars right out of my billfold," and I told him that I would really appreciate that. He gave me the money, and the next night I gave my students extra homework. I told them that they each had to write a thank-you letter to the banker for the wonderful donation he had given our class. I also asked the principal to write him a thank-you card, and when I told her it was for only five dollars, Mrs. Roberson told me I was crazy. I bargained with her that I would type out a thank-you card if she would sign it, and she agreed.

The following week after our papier-mâché globes were completed, I took one of them to the banker as a gift. He looked pale in the face as he said, "Mr. Clark, I am some kinda embarrassed. I only gave five dollars and you had the kids send me those wonderful cards and the principal sent a note. I told my wife I only gave five dollars, and she just about fussed me out. I am so sorry; I should have given a bigger donation."

I simply said with my Southern drawl and big smile, "Well, we're doing another project right now!"

The bank, and the banker personally, became great sponsors of my class, that year and for years to come.

I tell teachers and schools that want to receive donations that they must realize it's all about building relationships and having the patience to start small, show appreciation, and then take the proper steps to increase the donation. And instead of targeting just one donor, target many. At RCA, we take the "fishing hook" approach. If you throw one line into the water, you might catch a big fish. If you throw fifty lines in the water, you are almost guaranteed a big fish. We reach out far and wide to numerous individuals who we work hard to build small relationships with. In the end, many of them come up as an empty hook with missing bait. Several of them, however, will turn out to be the big catch.

✳ 98 ✳

Once you have donors, work hard to keep them!

At RCA, we work hard to make a personal connection with our donors. We invite them to a donor appreciation day, where they eat lunch with our students and hear firsthand from them what they are learning and how RCA is affecting their lives. We send postcards from our trips, we send samples of excellent writing, we send video clips of our students singing "Happy Birthday" to our donors, and we invite our community partners into our school to volunteer at RCA and become connected to the mission of our school on an emotional level, not just a financial one.

Each year, we also conduct an "Xtreme Bedroom Makeover" that works better than any of our other efforts to connect the community with our school. Basically, we ask students to write letters detailing why they would like to have their bedrooms completely transformed into the rooms of their dreams. We also ask each student to describe their dream bedroom and to be as creative and descriptive as possible.

We then reach out to our donors and businesses in the Atlanta community and ask if they would be interested in having their staff, friends, and family come together for forty-eight hours over a weekend to make over a child's bedroom. We tell them that the family will be staying at a hotel, thanks to InterContinental Hotels, and that the design teams will have the place to themselves while they create their magic. We let them know we will provide pictures of the room and complete measurements, and we add that it is going to be a competition, with the best room receiving the distinction of being the Xtreme Bedroom Makeover winner. Each year, we have about ten to fifteen teams jumping on board to participate.

We then have a committee read through all of the students' essays, picking ten to fifteen winners and matching each with a team. We provide the team with their child's letter and they're off to the races!

Our staff will go around to the homes, periodically checking on the teams, and I am always amazed to find ten to twenty adults crammed into a child's room, painting, laying carpet, hanging pictures, putting together furniture, laughing, and having the most amazing time. It shows me that not only is the team doing a great community service project, but that they are also truly bonding among themselves through the experience.

On Sunday afternoon, the families can't arrive home until one o'clock, and when each child first sees the new room, it is a moment he or she will never forget.

I recall Osei telling us that when his mom pulled up into the driveway, she barely turned off the car before she and his sisters jumped out and his sisters pushed him out of the way to get into the house. They were just as excited as he was. As he ran into the home behind them, he heard them scream in shock, one at a time, at the beauty of the room. As he entered the doorway, he didn't scream—he just stood there, unable to move, unable to speak. It was his dream room.

A week later when Osei called me to ask a homework question, I asked him whose voices were in the background. He said, "It's my whole family; they refuse to leave my room."

One young man's entire apartment had absolutely no furniture; there wasn't one chair. The team that completed his bedroom transformed not only his room into a magical place, but they also provided furniture for the living room. When the family walked into the apartment, the team told us that the boy's mouth flew open and that he was jumping up and down and running everywhere. The mother, however, fell to her knees in tears and began to praise God.

One young boy's bedroom had holes in the ceiling where squirrels would come through to get paper and other items to contribute to the nests they were building in the walls. He had used "The squirrels took my homework" on more than one occasion.

The team completely redid the ceilings, making it impossible for squirrels to enter again. Imagine how your peace of mind would change if you went from wondering if squirrels would bother you at night to rest-ing in complete comfort. Once you have made that type of an impact in a child's life, you are connected forever.

One team realized that there was a younger brother in the home, and they decided, as a surprise to all of us, to completely make over his room as well. They said that when the first brother saw his room, the entire family screamed. The team said they watched the face of the younger brother and that he looked so happy for his brother; he was genuinely fine with him receiving such a special gift, and he wasn't bitter or jealous at all.

Then the team said to the younger brother, "Jibril, go look in your room." When he entered to see that his room had received a complete makeover as well, he screamed! He just couldn't believe it. The entire family cried, and the team cried with them.

When Nadia and her mother walked into her room, they were so overcome that they just hugged each other and cried. They told the team they were so grateful, and in order to show their appreciation they asked if they could join them the next year as they did another child's room. The team was thrilled at the offer, and Nadia and her mother were there the following year, painting, nailing, and helping to transform Robin's room. Once Robin calmed down after seeing her room, she asked, "Can I help with a room next year?" What a wonderful example of how to pay it forward.

Many of the teams are extremely clever and pay close attention to detail, in true RCA style. For their child's room, Delta Air Lines made a desk out of a real plane's wing. The Mixson family found a picture Kamran took on one of his trips, and they created wallpaper out of it to cover the back wall of his room. Tiara wrote a wonderful poem as part of her essay, and the team from NAIOP (National Association of Industrial and Office Properties) had it stenciled on the wall over her bed. Trinity wanted a "room in the sky," and Nielsen Skylight Company built huge clouds to stretch across the ceiling. Promethean had their staff members pay money toward the renovation fund, and in return, the employees could wear jeans to work. The money they used turned Arsene's room into something directly out of Harry Potter! They even took the time to make lamps with books that you can find at Hogwarts. It was all handmade and incredibly realistic. Amazing!

Initially, the purpose behind the project was to give our students a wonderful place to live and work. We wanted the beauty and energy they feel at RCA to be transferred to the place where they sleep. In the end, however, the project turned into an outstanding way for us to bond and connect with our donors and to build relationships with them that would last for years. And with that connection comes more support for RCA, our mission, and our efforts to change the lives of our students.

Before

After

Before

After

⁎ 99 ⁎

Send thank-you letters that are hand-drawn, colorful, and grammatically correct.

I attended an event years ago by an African dance company in Atlanta. I was so moved that I filled out a donation card as I left, including my credit card information. A few weeks later, I received a card beautifully drawn by a fifteen-year-old dancer. She had drawn a picture of herself dancing on the cover, and on the inside she wrote a lovely letter about how much dancing meant to her and how grateful she was for my support. In part because it really, really touched me, I mailed in another donation.

Similarly, I attended the event of another organization in Atlanta that also works with children. I made a donation, and a few weeks later, I received a thank-you card. It contained a generic typed message along with a child's signature. I didn't send in another donation, and, now that I think about it, I haven't gone back to any of their other events.

Appreciation, and how you show it, is crucial, and the generic card just wasn't the same. Our donors receive, on average, a letter or postcard from our students each month, but we always strive to do more. Reaching out to our donors and connecting them to our students and our mission is imperative for our success. When you make the connection, the funding comes. Too many people ask for funding first, but we have realized that if you start small and make the relationship first, the donations will come. And once that happens, the donations will only grow in size over time with the amount of effort you place on increasing your relationship with a donor.

⚝ 100 ⚝

If you need advice, ask for money.
If you need money, ask for advice.

Throughout the process of fund-raising, we would meet with foundations, corporations, and individuals to tell them our story. We would then ask for financial support for our dream, and the results were seldom as we hoped. People didn't seem to believe we could make it happen, and apparently several individuals had tried to start schools before us with no success. Individuals had placed funds into past dreams that didn't materialize, and they were burned to the point where they would only support well-established institutions that had large endowments. Can I tell you how frustrating that is? If we were well established and had a large endowment, we wouldn't be in such dire need of funding! It's the new nonprofits that need the support and help the most.

I learned a very important lesson when I went to meet with one of our potential donors. I was holding a proposal for a $100,000 request in my hand, and during the meeting, he said, "You know what I hate? I hate when people come to me and ask for money. I like for people to ask for my advice, because that, to me, is much more valuable. If they show me they are wise enough to choose my advice over my money, then they have passed the test and have earned the right to have my financial support as well."

I quickly said, "Well, sir, I am here to ask you for some advice!"

I walked out of there with the proposal in hand. I never showed it to him, and the only thing I obtained at that meeting was some good advice. The advice included the names of some individuals he thought I should meet with, at his request, in order to seek funding for RCA. All told, the connections made from that meeting garnered RCA more than $300,000 in support. That man became a consistent donor as well, sending checks of $15,000 each year.

From that meeting on, our approach with everyone we met was to ask for advice. I would ask foundations, "What would you like to see from RCA in order to get your foundation to a point in the future where you might consider a gift for us?" It seemed instantly that the foundations were pleased that I wasn't there to ask for a gift that day, and they noticed that I took careful notes of the checkpoints they said we'd need to fulfill before they could consider a gift. When we were able to visit those same foundations again, I made sure to list the items they said they'd like to see, and I addressed those issues first. We were making a case for taking away any reason they could have to turn down our request for funding.

After our first meetings with potential donors, we always walk away with only advice, but in the end, the relationships we build and the connections we make serve us much better in the future when we eventually do ask for a major gift.

✳ 101 ✳

Make your good-byes mean something.

Our first class of kids at RCA was indescribably special to us. At the end of their eighth-grade year, we wanted to create a memorable moment for them—one that would tie in with tradition and have symbolic meaning—as we so often try to do.

The very first moment that we met our graduating eighth graders was during their initial interviews, years before, at city hall in downtown Atlanta. I can still remember them like it was yesterday, coming in for their interviews so nervous and unaware of how their lives were about to change.

We decided to have a final graduation dinner for our eighth graders. It was to be held the night before graduation, and it would be the last meal we shared together. It had to be special.

After brainstorming ideas and discussing every restaurant in Atlanta, we finally realized that the most perfect place wasn't a restaurant at all; we decided no place would be more fitting for our final dinner than city hall, where we first met and where the RCA journey for us all first began.

We kept the location for the dinner a surprise in true RCA fashion, and we stated on the eighth graders' invitations to dinner that they would receive a text message at 4:00 p.m. letting them know where they had to arrive for the 7:00 p.m. dinner. We asked them to dress with a flare of creativity and told them it would be our final night together. The students were dying to know the location and more details, but we never said a word.

At four on the dot, they received a text that said, "Your interview is scheduled for 7:00 p.m. tonight at city hall. Don't be late."

Streams of texts came back in response, "It's perfect," "I just burst into tears," "There is no place that would mean more." We were thrilled that they understood the symbolism of the location of the first moment where we all met.

We set up in city hall just like we had done for their initial interviews. Ms. Mosley greeted them, and then Mr. Kassa conducted their initial interview where he answered any questions they had about RCA, just as he had done years before. Mrs. Bearden and I were stationed in the interview room, waiting for each student to be brought in by Mr. Kassa, one by one, exactly as it had happened the first time.

Kim and I decided to pretend that we didn't know the kids. We wanted it to be as if we were really interviewing and meeting them for the first time. We planned to ask them the same questions we had years before to see how the responses would change.

When we first met Aujahuna, she had been suspended from her school for throwing okra at another girl and getting into a fight in the cafeteria. When I saw that on her records, of course, that was my first question for her. I wanted to know what she had against okra.

She cried in her initial interview, saying that she was so sorry for the fight and apologizing profusely as tears streamed down her face. As she walked around the corner, wearing a beautiful white dress, standing tall, confident, and stunning, tears were again streaming down her face. She sat down, looked at us, and said, "I love you."

Kim and I couldn't stay in character. We responded, "We love you, too," and I followed with, "So what do you have against okra?"

Osei Avril was the quietest child we interviewed that year. He kept his head down and had a weak handshake. He lacked confidence and was very unsure of himself.

As he walked around the corner, we saw a dashing young man, confident and strong, the first valedictorian at the Ron Clark Academy.

Kim and I didn't have to reach out to introduce ourselves; he beat us to it. He walked up, stared us directly in our eyes, and said, "Hello, my name is Osei Avril. It's a pleasure to meet you, and I appreciate the time you have taken to interview me today." Osei is so clever, and he jumped right into the role-play with ease, and I could tell he was enjoying it.

As he sat before us, he talked of world politics, economic issues, and his passion for figuring out his own math theorems. He didn't resemble the young boy we first interviewed at all, except for one thing. The tremendous potential within him was there on both occasions at city hall; this time obvious, the first time hidden. It is there within all of our children if we look hard enough.

During Jordan Brown's first interview, I told him that RCA was going to be an extremely tough school, and I asked him if he was up for the hard work. He looked me directly in the eyes, and said, "That's good; I like a challenge." I hoped with all my heart that he would live up to that confidence, and he didn't disappoint.

Over the past several years, he added a tremendous spark to our school. He was always in the front row, smiling, jumping around, and full of energy. He was always talking, running, trying his best to allow all of the passion he has inside of him to explode out of his pores. He was a ray of a light, and he was constantly uplifting us all. I told Kim one time that it was almost as if Jordan had the entire school on his back and that he was determined not to let any of us fail.

As he walked around the corner, he introduced himself and sat down. I looked at him and said, "Now, young man, this school is going to be challenging. Do you think you can handle it?" He looked me directly in the eyes and said, "That's good; I like a challenge." He then lowered his head and tears streamed down his face.

When we first met Chi Chi Ugwuh, she stuttered to the point where she had to place two fingers to her throat in order to sound out her words. Even though she struggled to speak, there was a determination and a fire in her eyes. As she rounded the corner to greet us, that fire and light was stronger than ever. She looked us directly in the eyes, introduced herself, and spoke with such eloquence and presence that no one would ever realize she had once stuttered. She was captivating and so sure of herself. As we finished with Chi Chi and she walked away, I turned to Kim and said, "Look at her. She is going to change the world."

Kim looked back at me, her makeup completely ruined at this point, and simply said, "They all are."

☀ WHAT'S NEXT? ☀

The New Dream

When you started this book, I showed you the picture of a rundown, one-hundred-year-old factory that we hoped to turn into a school that would affect the lives of children all over the world. If you take into account all of the superintendents, principals, and teachers who have now visited RCA, the number of students whose lives have been impacted soars to over 10 million.

The future.

Now, there is a new dream. The property above is adjacent to our school and has recently been obtained by RCA. The building was generously donated to us by BB&T, and we are grateful beyond words for their support and belief in our mission. By expanding our campus, we will increase the number of educators who can visit and be trained at our school each year from 3,000 to 6,000. We are currently raising funds for the RCA Educator Training Center and hope to find individuals, corporations, and foundations that will be willing to join our family and become a part of the new dream. If you are interested in joining us on the new adventure with any level of support, please visit www.ronclark academy.com.

Ron Clark with the founding leaders of the House of Rêveur (*left to right*): Morgan Fambro, Zharia White, Richard Douglas, and Jordan Brown.

Acknowledgments

Years ago the first volunteers and board members of the Ron Clark Academy had our first meeting in the old warehouse that we had recently purchased. It was November and the floor was so cold that we had to sit with our feet in our seats, but no one left. When we talked you could see the air coming out of our mouths, but we stayed there that night for three hours, planning, brainstorming, and freezing. In our wildest dreams, we never could have imagined how successful the school would be today.

Thank you all for being the first to believe. You are the pioneers of RCA, and the students who pass through our halls each year will forever be indebted to you for your initial belief in the impact our school would have on their lives.

A tremendous thank you to our current RCA board of trustees as well. You have all given countless hours in support of RCA, our students, and our mission to uplift educators. To our board president, Alonzo Llorens, you are the nicest and most giving individual I have ever met, and on behalf of all of the students and staff of RCA, we give a heartfelt thank you!

To our founding students: You were the life, the heart, and the spirit behind all that is RCA. You will forever be etched within our hearts, our memories, and the walls of the school you helped create.

To our new and future students: The charge is now yours. Carry on the great traditions set forth by those who walked these halls before you, but also remember to be bold, live with no fear, and leave your own of mark of excellence on the walls of RCA.

Ron Clark Academy Educator Training

For more information on RCA's Educator Training Program, please visit www.ronclarkacademy.com. Educators can choose to spend one or two days at RCA observing classes, attending workshops, and interacting with the RCA staff. Mr. Clark teaches every day, and observing him teach and attending his workshop are always a part of each teacher's visit. The professional development experience does cost, but all proceeds go to scholarships for students at RCA.

RCA's Great American Teachers' Club website, where you can download lessons, watch videos, and video chat with Ron Clark and the RCA team.
www.greatamericanteachersclub.com

In addition to the educator training days, RCA conducts an annual three-day national conference that also includes classroom observations, workshops, and a night that is devoted to helping teachers relieve stress! The theme for the evening is "tacky prom," and it provides the conference attendees the chance to shake off stress and celebrate after a long weekend of learning new strategies and methods they can use in their classrooms. Information can also be found at the RCA website.